Palgrave Studies in Discursive Psychology

Series Editors
Cristian Tileagă
Department of Social Sciences
Loughborough University
Loughborough, UK

Elizabeth Stokoe
Department of Social Sciences
Loughborough University
Loughborough, UK

Palgrave Studies in Discursive Psychology publishes current research and theory in this established field of study. Discursive Psychology has, for the past 30 years, established an original and often critical understanding of the role of discourse practice for the study of psychological, social, and cultural issues. This book series will provide both introductions to discursive psychology for scholars new to the field, as well as more advanced original research for those who wish to understand discursive psychology in more depth. It is committed to the systematic representation of discursive psychology's contemporary ethos into all things social – from everyday interactional encounters to institutional settings and the analysis of wider social issues and social problems. Palgrave Studies in Discursive Psychology will therefore publish ground-breaking contemporary contributions on the relevance of discursive psychology for key themes and debates across psychology and the social sciences: including communication, social influence, personal and social memory, emotions, prejudice, ideology, child development, health, gender, applied interventions, institutions. The series editors welcome contributions from ethnomethodology and conversation analysis, as well as contributions more closely aligned to post-structuralism, approaches to analysis combining attention to conversational detail with wider macro structures and cultural-historical contexts. We invite junior and senior scholars to submit proposals for monographs and edited volumes that address the significance of discursive psychology in psychology, communication, sociology, applied linguistics. Please contact the series editors (c.tileaga@lboro.ac.uk; e.h.stokoe@lboro.ac.uk) or the commissioning editor (grace.jackson@palgrave.com) for more information.

More information about this series at
http://www.palgrave.com/gp/series/15475

Mirko A. Demasi • Shani Burke
Cristian Tileagă
Editors

Political Communication

Discursive Perspectives

Editors
Mirko A. Demasi
Psychology Department
York St John University
York, UK

Shani Burke
Psychology Department
Teesside University
Middlesbrough, UK

Cristian Tileagă
Department of Social Sciences
Loughborough University
Loughborough, UK

Palgrave Studies in Discursive Psychology
ISBN 978-3-030-60222-2   ISBN 978-3-030-60223-9   (eBook)
https://doi.org/10.1007/978-3-030-60223-9

© The Editor(s) (if applicable) and The Author(s), under exclusive licence to Springer Nature Switzerland AG 2020
This work is subject to copyright. All rights are solely and exclusively licensed by the Publisher, whether the whole or part of the material is concerned, specifically the rights of translation, reprinting, reuse of illustrations, recitation, broadcasting, reproduction on microfilms or in any other physical way, and transmission or information storage and retrieval, electronic adaptation, computer software, or by similar or dissimilar methodology now known or hereafter developed.
The use of general descriptive names, registered names, trademarks, service marks, etc. in this publication does not imply, even in the absence of a specific statement, that such names are exempt from the relevant protective laws and regulations and therefore free for general use.
The publisher, the authors and the editors are safe to assume that the advice and information in this book are believed to be true and accurate at the date of publication. Neither the publisher nor the authors or the editors give a warranty, expressed or implied, with respect to the material contained herein or for any errors or omissions that may have been made. The publisher remains neutral with regard to jurisdictional claims in published maps and institutional affiliations.

Cover illustration: Panther Media GmbH / Alamy Stock Photo

This Palgrave Macmillan imprint is published by the registered company Springer Nature Switzerland AG.
The registered company address is: Gewerbestrasse 11, 6330 Cham, Switzerland

This book is dedicated to the inspiring work of Michael Billig. Many of us would not be where we are today if it was not for his scholarly input, willingness to meet eager students and persistent encouragement, especially to younger generations as they begin their academic careers.

Preface

This book offers new insights into discursive psychology's contribution to the study of political communication, as well as an expansion of the scope of both fields. The book addresses the theoretical, practical and methodological challenges that discursive psychology and political communication face today and considers where the fields might go next. The book is wide-ranging in four main ways. First, it expands the scope of political communication by describing the substantial academic contribution of discursive psychology to the field. It does so by expanding our understanding of political phenomena in general and political communication in particular. Second, the book is comprised of chapters that address a wide range of political issues, thereby highlighting the diversity of topics that discursive psychology can cover. Third, the chapters report research that is conducted across cultural and geographical locations, showing that discursive psychological work on political communication is restricted neither to particular academic and geographic niches nor to English-speaking academia. Fourth, and final, the book showcases the diversity of approaches within discursive psychology; there are multiple ways of making empirical sense of political communication *as a practice* and this book demonstrates a number of such approaches.

Political Communication: Discursive Perspectives is essential reading for academics, researchers and students who are interested in political communication or discursive psychology.

York, UK   Mirko A. Demasi
Middlesbrough, UK   Shani Burke
Loughborough, UK   Cristian Tileagă
August 2020

Acknowledgements

We would like to thank the contributors to this book for their interesting and engaging chapters, especially during what has been a challenging time for us all as we have dealt with the COVID-19 pandemic—both at work and in our personal lives.

We would also like to thank Joanna O'Neill at Palgrave for her support and patience with us.

Contents

1   The Discursive Psychology of Political Communication 1
Cristian Tileagă, Mirko A. Demasi, and Shani Burke

Part 1   Political Communication of Contentious Politics 33

2   Accusations and Denials of Racism in Dialogical Context 35
Stephen Gibson

3   Lay Rhetoric on Brexit 63
Eleni Andreouli

4   Extending the Boundaries of Political Communication: How Ideology Can Be Examined in Super-Rich Television Documentaries Using Discursive Psychology 89
Philippa Carr

5   A Multimodal Discourse Analysis of 'Brexit': Flagging the Nation in Political Cartoons 115
Henry W. Lennon and Laura Kilby

xi

xii Contents

Part 2 Political Communication, Discourse, and New Media 147

6 The Discourse of Social Movements: Online
   Mobilising Practices for Collective Action 149
   Petra Sneijder, Baukje Stinesen, Maartje Harmelink,
   and Annette Klarenbeek

7 Analysing Multimodal Communication and
   Persuasion in Populist Radical Right Political Blogs 175
   Katarina Pettersson and Inari Sakki

8 "This Country Will Be Big Racist One Day": Extreme
   Prejudice as Reasoned Discourse in Face-to-Face
   Interactions 205
   Shani Burke and Mirko A. Demasi

**Part 3 Discursive Psychology, Discourse, and
          Social Problems** 231

9 Presenting Support for Refugees as Naivety:
   Responses to Positive Media Reports About Refugees 233
   Lise Marie Børlie and Simon Goodman

10 Consensual Politics and Pragmatism in Parliamentary
    Discourse on the 'Refugee Issue' 259
    Lia Figgou and Dimitra Anagnostopoulou

11 The Unsaid as Expressive and Repressive Political
    Communication: Examining Slippery Talk About Paid
    Domestic Labour in Post-apartheid South Africa 283
    Amy Jo Murray

Index 303

Notes on Contributors

Dimitra Anagnostopoulou has recently completed her postgraduate studies in 'Social Psychology and Psychosocial Interventions' at the School of Psychology, Aristotle University of Thessaloniki. Her research interests lie in the field of political discourse analysis and migration studies.

Eleni Andreouli is senior lecturer in the School of Psychology and Counselling at The Open University, UK. Her research is broadly situated in the social psychology of citizenship, focusing on the study of everyday and 'ordinary' enactments of citizenship particularly in changing political contexts (e.g. Brexit and COVID-19). Previous research includes work on identity dynamics, identity in border-crossing practices (e.g. processes of naturalisation and European immigration) and intercultural encounters (e.g. in education).

Lise Marie Børlie is training to become a psychological wellbeing practitioner, with a previous working background in mental health. She holds an undergraduate degree in Psychology (BSc) from Coventry University and a postgraduate degree in Psychological Wellbeing and Mental Health (MSc) from Nottingham Trent University. Her academic work reflects her interest in prejudicial language and anti-refugee discourse, largely revolving around ethnic minority groups in both the UK and her native country Norway.

xiv   Notes on Contributors

Shani Burke is Senior Lecturer in Psychology at Teesside University. She holds a PhD from Loughborough University (2017), which discursively analysed far-right discourse on Facebook. Her research interests are applying discursive psychology to Islamophobic and far-right/extremist discourse. Specifically, her interest is in how potentially prejudicial arguments are presented as 'reasonable'. Her work has been published in a range of journals, such as *Discourse & Society* and the *Journal of Community and Applied Social Psychology*.

Philippa Carr is Lecturer on Social Psychology and Qualitative Research Methods modules at University of the West of England UWE Bristol. Her research explores how wealth inequality is legitimised in the media using discursive psychology. Philippa's research is focused on how the super-rich are presented in television broadcasts and account for practices such as inheritance that impede social mobility.

Mirko A. Demasi is Lecturer in Psychology at York St John University. His research interest is in the study of political debates on the European Union in the context of Brexit, constructions of truth and factuality as rhetorical and moral concerns, contested political discourse and the study of racist discourse in Finland and beyond.

Lia Figgou is Associate Professor of Social Psychology at the School of Psychology, Aristotle University of Thessaloniki. Her research interests lie in the study of intergroup relations and social exclusion. She is particularly interested in the way in which these topics are discursively constructed and negotiated.

Stephen Gibson is Bicentennial Chair in Research Methods in the School of Social Sciences at Heriot-Watt University, UK. He is a social psychologist with research interests in areas including obedience, identity and citizenship, and representations of peace and conflict, all of which he explores through approaches informed by discursive and rhetorical psychology. His most recent book is *Arguing, Obeying and Defying: A Rhetorical Perspective on Stanley Milgram's Obedience Experiments* (2019), and he is editor of *Discourse, Peace and Conflict: Discursive Psychology Perspectives* (2018), *Representations of Peace and Conflict* (with Simon Mollan; Palgrave Macmillan, 2012) and *Doing Your Qualitative Psychology*

Project (with Cath Sullivan and Sarah Riley; 2012). Together with Laura G. E. Smith, he is editor-in-chief of the *British Journal of Social Psychology*.

Simon Goodman is Senior Lecturer in Psychology at De Montfort University. He uses discursive and rhetorical psychology to address a number of issues including the discursive construction of asylum seekers and refugees, including the ways in which potentially prejudicial arguments against asylum seekers are presented as reasonable and non-prejudicial. He is a committee member of the British Psychological Society's Qualitative Methods in Psychology and Social Psychology Sections and co-author of *The Language of Asylum* (2015) published by Palgrave.

Maartje Harmelink worked as a communication researcher at the research group Behaviour and Conversation in Digital Transition at the University of Applied Sciences Utrecht from 2014 until January 2020, where she contributed to research projects foregrounding the role of interaction in societal issues. She has a background in communication science. She is working as a programme officer at the Taskforce for Applied Research.

Laura Kilby is Reader in Social Psychology at Sheffield Hallam University. Her research examines relationships between power, discourse and the construction of marginalised identities and marginalised groups. Much of her research focuses on identity construction in the context of terrorism talk and in debates about citizenship and immigration. Her work draws on a range of analytic methods that variously cohere with a discursive psychology approach in order to examine differing forms of textual and visual discourse.

Annette Klarenbeek completed her PhD thesis in 2006 at Wageningen University, titled 'Crisis Ahead: An Interactional Perspective on Crisis Communication'. Since September 2017 Annette has been working as a Professor of Communication at the University of Applied Sciences Utrecht, leading the research group Behaviour and Conversation in Digital Transition at the University of Applied Sciences Utrecht. She is specifically interested in the way people discuss societal issues and transitions in their everyday lives and its implications for policy and communication practice.

xvi   Notes on Contributors

Henry W. Lennon is Lecturer in Criminal Psychology at the University of Derby. Drawing on social, community and critical psychology, his research is concerned with the construction of identity in relation to citizenship, immigration and belonging using a broadly discursive psychology approach. The context of this social construction and contestation has revolved around television media, interview narratives and political cartoons, being concerned with the implications such discourse has for conceptualising the way we see ourselves and others around us.

Amy Jo Murray is a researcher based at the University of KwaZulu-Natal. She is exploring creative ways of understanding injustice and inequality through qualitative research. She is studying how social processes, such as the unsaid, naturalise and maintain the status quo within racialised relationships, specifically within the context of paid domestic labour.

Katarina Pettersson (PhD in Social Psychology, University of Helsinki) is University Lecturer in Social Psychology at the Swedish School of Social Science, University of Helsinki. Her research interests include nationalist and radical right political rhetoric, political hate speech and political communication and persuasion in the online sphere. Methodologically, her expertise lies in critical discursive and rhetorical approaches, as well as visual rhetorical approaches. Her work has been published, for instance, in the *European Journal of Social Psychology*, *Discourse & Society*, the *Journal of Community and Applied Social Psychology* and *Qualitative Research in Psychology*.

Inari Sakki (PhD in Social Psychology, University of Helsinki) is Associate Professor in Social Psychology at the University of Eastern Finland. Her research interests include nationalism, populism, political rhetoric, collective memory and (multimodal) discourse analysis.

Petra Sneijder completed her PhD thesis in 2006 at Wageningen University, titled 'Food for Talk: Discursive Identities, Food Choice and Eating Practices'. Since September 2015 she has been working as a senior researcher at the research group Behaviour and Conversation in Digital Transition at the University of Applied Sciences Utrecht, where she analyses societal issues using a discursive psychological perspective. She is specifically interested in identity work in interaction, varying from medical interaction to social media discussions on societal issues.

Baukje Stinesen has been working as a researcher at the research group Behaviour and Conversation in Digital Transition at the University of Applied Sciences Utrecht since 2012. She has a background in applied communication science, and her main interest is in the analysis of interaction. She is working on her PhD research on patient-practitioner interaction in chronic pain rehabilitation in collaboration with the Department of Rehabilitation Medicine at Maastricht University. Insights from her research are used to stimulate practitioners to reflect on and further develop their communication practices.

Cristian Tileagă is Reader in Social Psychology in the School of Social Sciences and Humanities at Loughborough University. He has written extensively on discursive psychology, prejudice and discrimination, collective memory and interdisciplinarity. He is the author of a number of books, including *Discursive Psychology: Classic and Contemporary Issues* (2015, with Elizabeth Stokoe); *The Nature of Prejudice: Society, Discrimination and Moral Exclusion* (2016); and *Political Psychology: Critical Perspectives* (2013).

1

The Discursive Psychology of Political Communication

Cristian Tileagă, Mirko A. Demasi, and Shani Burke

The first 20 years of the second millennium have been full of charged events that have changed society: 9/11, the second Iraq War, the 2008 economic depression, the Syrian refugee crisis, Brexit, Donald Trump's controversial presidency of the USA, the COVID-19 global pandemic and the handling of racial tensions (particularly, but not exclusively) in the USA. These events share a particular type of political relevance—they all constitute sources of public political discourse.

What Blumler and Kavanagh (1999) have called the third age of political communication, an age characterised by "media abundance", has

---

C. Tileagă
Department of Social Sciences, Loughborough University
Loughborough, UK

M. A. Demasi
Psychology Department, York St John University, York, UK

S. Burke (✉)
Psychology Department, Teesside University, Middlesbrough, UK
e-mail: s.burke@tees.ac.uk

© The Author(s), under exclusive license to Springer Nature Switzerland AG 2020
M. A. Demasi et al. (eds.), *Political Communication*, Palgrave Studies in Discursive
Psychology, https://doi.org/10.1007/978-3-030-60223-9_1

signalled important and long-lasting changes in how people make sense of politics. This book is concerned with the question of how people engage with complex public political events and mediated communications in communicative practices. It is about what researchers across disciplinary boundaries call "political communication".

The book draws together a specific set of contributions to political communication: discursive studies that consider the various forms of political communication. The chapters illustrate ways of doing discursive psychological analysis in a wide range of settings and with a wide range of data sources. Contexts range from naturalistic encounters in public spaces and debates on social media to television programmes, parliamentary debates, political blogs and political cartoons.

In this chapter, we begin by defining our terms and explaining what we mean by "political communication". We then discuss the relationship between communication and mediated practices in the age of information. This is followed by a discussion of how political communication can be conceived as a social accomplishment rather than means of mass communication, an outcome of, as well as influence on, complex forms and networks of social practices. We close our introduction by drawing out some general themes and concerns related to the advent of discursive psychology of political communication and its new and distinct contribution. In the last section of the chapter, we outline the structure of the rest of the book.

What Is Political Communication?

Academic writing on political communication now spans a range of disciplines, including, most notably, political science, social and political psychology, communication and media studies and critical discourse studies. When one engages even in a very cursory review of the meanings of "political communication", one immediately notices that the term means different things to different people. Depending on one's home discipline, the term may carry different connotations. For instance, on the one hand, the term is used to refer to the science and conditions of effective communication in the service of progressive social goals. The

1 The Discursive Psychology of Political Communication 3

focus here is on the link between communication and the organisation of collective action or political mobilisation (e.g. Bennett et al. 2008; Klandermans 2003). On the other hand, political communication is about reforming communications in the service of politics, engaging with, monitoring and keeping in check new technologies (e.g. Kreiss and McGregor 2018). The two senses of political communication coexist, though not without tensions, and have relatively permeable boundaries that are able to accommodate other conceptions and perspectives. Contemporary scholars continually extend the scope of political communication scholarship either in response to social events (e.g. terrorism, mass migration) or driven by more mundane, but no less important, funder priorities.

It is beyond the scope of this chapter to offer an exhaustive review of the political communication literature. This literature is increasingly diverse, overlapping and eclectic (for reviews, see, *inter alia*, Semetko 2009; Valentino and Nardis 2013). Despite the diversity of approaches adopted in different disciplines, it is nonetheless possible to distinguish traditions of theory and research on political communication.[1]

One influential tradition of work in political communication originates in the psychology of political communication. Political psychologists are interested in the conditions under which political communications take place, are constructed and are generally effective: psychological antecedents and consequents (Crigler 1996), on the one hand, or both subtle and consequential effects based on understanding and analysing various forms and features of information environments (cf. Valentino and Nardis 2013), on the other hand. The turn to cognition in psychology (Anderson 1983; Fiske and Taylor 1984; Tversky and Kahneman 1981)

---

[1] There are several types of authors who write on the subject of political communication. There are those authors that adopt established paradigms and perspectives from their home disciplines. We include in this category researchers working within information processing and neural traditions in social/political psychology and political science (for overviews, see Nisbet and Feldman 2010). Empirical research takes the form of illustration or confirmation of foundational principles in political science, cognitive science and neurosciences. There are also those who write on the subject of political communication and often adopt a critical perspective in relation to their academic discipline of origin (e.g. Billig 1987; Tileagă 2013). There are also those who engage with political communication by drawing on interdisciplinary incursions (Byford 2011) or those authors that focus specifically on one of its aspects (see the example of "political rhetoric", Condor et al. 2013).

has oriented the study of political communication towards an information processing psychology of politics (e.g. Suedfeld et al. 2001; Taber 2003; Tetlock 1984, 2005) and fertile programmes of research around *framing, agenda-setting* and *priming* (Scheufele and Tewksbury 2007). Concerns with emotion and political choice (Mutz 2009), selective exposure (Mutz 2001), heuristics in political decision making (Lau and Redlawsk 2001) and political impression formation and management (McGraw 2003) are adding numerous insights to a now established psychology of political communication.[2]

Other influential tradition of work originates in political science. It is primarily concerned with how information spreads and influences mass political behaviour (Converse 1964). According to Kinder (2003), mass communication influences three key aspects: *attention, persuasion* and *action*. Mass communication organises "the command and control of public attention" (p. 358), whereas persuasion is about "the supply of arguments and evidence through which people are induced to change their minds on some aspect of politics" (p. 367). The latter aspect—action—has to do with participation in politics, from voter turnout to mobilisation in social movements. This tripartite approach equates political communication with mass communication and the influence of the media. Early approaches to electoral campaigns and mobilisation (Blumler and Fox 1983) and relationship between social movements and media (Gamson and Wolfsfeld 1993) are now being refined and extended by the study of political communication and new technologies. A new era of insights, it is argued, is destined to replace more traditional media effects especially related to citizen engagement in politics and mobilisation in social movements (Bennett and Iyengar 2008). Contiguous, and no less influential, strands within the modern political science literature examine persuasion and political communication networks (Huckfeldt 2009), mass beliefs and citizen politics (Dalton 2008) and Internet politics (Margolis and Resnick 2000).

Sociologically inspired media and communications studies represent another influential tradition of work in political communication. This body of work focuses on the ways in which social and political actors and

---

[2] For reviews and critiques of the cognition-inspired psychological literature, see also Tileagă (2013).

1 The Discursive Psychology of Political Communication   5

organisations make use of the media (e.g. McNair 2011; Negrine and Stanyer 2007). The rise of "self-expressive politics" (Stanyer 2007), the increased "personalisation" of politics (Castells 2011) and the "professionalisation" of political communication (Negrine 2008) shifted the balance of scholarship towards more detailed analyses of communication advances and affordances. Facebook, Twitter and, more generally, the Internet held the promise of influencing politics for good, although not everyone shared the collective enthusiasm and expectations (see, e.g., Deacon and Wring 2011, on the unfulfilled promise of the Internet as campaign tool in the 2010 British General Election). Influential lines of inquiry are being carved out in comparative political communication research (Downey and Mihelj 2012; Downey and Stanyer 2010) and civic health and misinformation in political information sharing (Chadwick and Vaccari 2019). Sociology itself, as a discipline, plays a relatively minor part in the study of political communication. However, original and promising programmes of work are being developed—see, for instance, Benson (2004, 2013) on the sociology of news or Richards (2004) on a sociology of emotions in political communication. Schudson (2004) was certainly right when he argued that "scholars educated as sociologists have pushed at the borders of the field of political communication rather than focusing on its core emphasis on electoral politics" (p. 272).[3]

Last, but by no means least, in what is known as critical discourse studies (CDS), the study of political communication has been equated with the study of political language. As Chilton and Schäffner have noted, "it is probably the case that the use of language in the constitution of social groups leads to what we call 'politics' in a broad sense" (1997, p. 206). CDS have marked a shift from earlier largely quantitative accounts of political language[4] to qualitative analyses of political language. CDS's essential purpose is "to make explicit the whole range of linguistic devices used to code ... beliefs and ideologies as well as the related practices" (Reisigl and Wodak 2001, p. 266). Research on political discourse

---

[3] See Volume 21 (Issue 3) of the journal *Political Communication* for a special issue on the role of sociology in the study of political communication.

[4] See, for instance, Lasswell and Leites (1949) investigations into quantitative semantics or Osgood's (1978) approach to semantics of international politics.

6   C. Tileagă et al.

(Wilson 1990; Chilton and Schäffner 1997; Wodak 1989, 2002) and media discourse (Fowler et al. 1979; Fowler 1991; van Dijk 1988, 1989, 1991) have contributed to CDS's development and allowed it to create an extensive toolkit for the analysis of political communication (for an overview of the contribution of CDS to the study of political communications, see Tileagă 2013). The original focus on passive versus active grammatical forms and particular syntactic and semantic choices[5] has been replaced by modern approaches (van Dijk 2008, 2009; Chilton 2004) inspired by the cognitive revolution in psychology and linguistics (Lakoff and Johnson 1980). Key insights in CDS emphasise how political knowledge is organised in and by networks of conceptual and metaphorical frames (cf. Chilton and Ilyin 1993; Wodak 2011) and mental models (van Dijk 2009). Moreover, the interest in oratory (see, e.g., Isaksen 2011) and the micro-analysis of politicians' rhetorical styles (see Bull 2002, 2003) in other disciplines dedicated to the study of political communication have been more than matched by CDS' attention to pragma-linguistic practices (e.g. Sowinska 2013; Wodak 2011; Fairclough 2000, 2010), recontextualisation through the media (Erjavec and Volcic 2007; Fairclough and Fairclough 2011; Hodges 2008) or role of context models (van Dijk 2009) in political rhetoric. Innovative inroads in the study of political communication are also made by ethnographies of political processes (Wodak 2011) and approaches to global political communication (Schäffner 2010).

Regardless of home discipline or field, the study of political communication is, we argue, about understanding the processes of actual politics and not of some abstract entity that towers over and influences inexorably our lives. Although the political sphere exerts an extraordinary influence on how we perceive and engage with and in politics, it is only one social and cultural domain among several others. Communication itself, with its forms and contents, is one other such domain—namely, a domain that is the foundation of culture (political or otherwise). If Edelman was right, in that politics "confer wealth, take life, imprison and free people,

---

[5] See, for instance, the seminal work of Fowler et al. (1979) on the role of power and control in the language of reporting of disturbances at the Notting Hill festival in London.

1 The Discursive Psychology of Political Communication 7

and represent a history with strong emotional and ideological associations" (1967, p. 5), then new frameworks for the study of politics as complex form of communicative activity are needed. This book is an attempt to show how that project might look like.

Communication and Domains of Social Practice in the Age of Information

Contemporary work on political communication is not confined to the political sphere. As Castells argues,

> the organizations of communication operate within the diverse cultural patterns of our world. These patterns are characterized by the opposition between globalization and identification, and by the tension between individualism and communalism. (2011, p. 136)

However, it is still commonly supposed that the essential *locus* of political communication scholarship is the political stage or the political spectacle. The predominance of this focus on politics relegates communication to a secondary role.

Although the subject of political communication pertains to forms of spoken, written and symbolic language, empirical research has generally proceeded independently of methodological advances in the analysis of communication. Ironically, the majority of research on political communication works with an outdated and impoverished metatheory of communication. "There is a tendency in some recent quantitative research", Bennett and Entman (2001) argue, "to reduce political communication to an anaemic relationship between abstracted message content and equally abstracted individual or aggregate responses" (pp. 5–6).

Media democracies (Franklin 2004) are important "domains of social practice" (Fairclough 2010). The political communication community has long since moved beyond charting the effects of mass communication, "that is, communication that takes place predominantly one-way, from a small number of professional communicators to a vast number of amateur 'receivers'" (Kinder 2003, p. 357). Mass communication has been replaced by mediated communication. Flows of political communications do not circulate unrestrained—mediation is the reflecting mirror of contemporary social processes. Mediation enables new shapes and forms of social and political process dependent on communication flows. As Blumler argues, "communication flows are relating to community boundaries and societal cleavages in new mixes" (2001, p. 205).

Mediated communication is the foundation for understanding old and new domains of social practice, for example, nationhood (Mihelj 2011) or dysfunctional news sharing (Chadwick et al. 2018), to name just a few of the more influential areas of development. Politics itself is "largely a mediated experience" (Delli Carpini and Williams 2001, p. 161). In the era of mediated communication, political communicators as well as audiences are described as "strategic actors who operate with particular goals in a rapidly changing socio-political environment" (Stanyer 2007, p. 176). Mediation ensures that political communications are not directed by the "political public relations industry" (McNair 2011, p. 34) but by the values, beliefs and motives of actual people, producers of everyday communications. Mediated communication pinpoints to the democratisation of communication practices and opens the way towards mass self-communication.

> Micro-electronics-based information and communication technologies make the combination of all forms of mass communication possible in a digital, global, multimodal, and multichannel hypertext. The interactive capacity of the new communication system ushers in a new form of communication, mass self-communication, which multiplies and diversifies the entry points in the communication process. (Castells 2011, p. 135)

"Domains of social practice" (Fairclough 2010) are manifest at other, more specific levels of communication practices too. Take, for instance, the ubiquitous practice of news/press reporting. What makes news/press reporting a social practice is, as Macmillan and Edwards (1999) contend, that

> normative, ethical, and political issues concerning press reporting are not only widely discussed and analysed outside of the activity of news report-

1 The Discursive Psychology of Political Communication 9

ing, but are also, and importantly as far as its readers are concerned, attended to in various analysable ways as an endemic feature of press reporting itself. (p. 154)

Researching communicative domains of social practice presupposes an analysis of a number of fundamental practices that describe the social expression of those practices.[6] Whether you are analysing news/press reporting or news interviews, what matters empirically is attention to describing "fundamental ground rules" (Clayman and Heritage 2002, p. 344) that govern conduct in those settings. Both news reporting and news interviews belong to the contemporary public sphere—they both enact and sustain other practices that, in turn, constitute what we call political communication more generally.

There is a further angle to researching communicative domains of social practice. The logics and formation of "large-scale action networks" (cf. Bennett and Segerberg 2013) are becoming a prominent tool in the analysis of causes and consequences of contentious politics in uncertain times. What Bennett and Segerberg (2012) call "connective action" enables new forms and consequences of both incivility (see Tileagă 2019, on misogyny) and progressive ideas and ideals (see Bennett and Segerberg, 2013, on protest networks), to be spread across media networks.

The electronic age has transformed political speechmaking (Jamieson 1988) as well as taught us how to "break the spiral of cynicism" (Cappella and Jamieson 1997) by disentangling the subtle links between media framing and the public good. The electronic age has also transformed the expression of politics and ushered us into a new age of visual mediation. The old rhetoric of the political image (Barthes 1977) has taken on new meanings and forms. The reception, interpretation and critique of political communications have changed too. Political communications embed "visual means of signification" (McNair 2011, p. 4)—from political advertising (Kaid and Holtz-Bacha 2006) and posters (Burgess 2011) to different other forms of mediation (see, e.g., visual satire in Richardson et al. 2011) visual and other semiotic forms shape and alter the

---

[6] For an excellent example, see Clayman and Heritage's (2002) approach to dissecting interactions in the modern news interview.

traditional delineations of political communications. Modern political communications are no longer one-sided or one-directional; they are multimodal in both semiotic (Kress 2009) and embodied (Mondada 2019) senses.

Discursive Psychology, Political Discourse and Situated Social Practices

The received wisdom argues that researching mass communication is being able to say how citizens "make sense of politics", how they "decide what is important in politics" and how they "evaluate the alternatives that politics puts before them" (Kinder 2003, p. 358). That empirical task is still one of the most pressing for researchers across disciplines. The essence of the chapters in this volume revolves around how to answer empirically these "how" questions. These questions imply the existence of a wealth of assumed beliefs, motives, ideas and experiences that people carry along with them. This book and chapters therein propose a reversal of that idea: "rather than asking is there a way of seeing below the surface to motives, ideas, thoughts and experiences, we can ask: are there procedures that participants have, for dealing with those notions?" (Edwards 2006, p. 43).

A discursive psychology (DP) of political communication recommends examining the "rich surface" (Edwards 2006) and the rich inter-textual field (Tileagă 2009) of informal and formal communicative practices. This richness, Edwards notes,

> is unimagined by those whose first move is not to record and examine it, but to invent tidy examples of it to illustrate conceptual points, discover causal connections with other things, or to immediately look through it to what lies beneath and beyond. (ibid., p. 43)

Instead of trying to resolve the issue of how communication works as a problem of psychological or neural entities, DP reframes the problem as a matter of "descriptive practices" (Edwards 1997, p. 317). However, DP is not based on a model of communication but rather on the paradigm of discourse as social action (Edwards 1997). Its focus is language "primarily

1 The Discursive Psychology of Political Communication   11

as a medium of social action" (Edwards 1997, p. 84). Thus, the substance of any discursive analysis is to locate psychological and communicative issues of any nature in "participants' own practices of accountability". The operative assumption is that "whatever people say is always action-oriented, specific to its occasion, performative on and for its occasion, selected from a indefinite range of options, and always indexically tied to particulars" (Edwards 2006, p. 46). This rings particularly true in the case of political language. Political language allows for a multitude of indexical interpretations and possibilities of expression by both elites and ordinary social actors (Edelman 1988, 2001).

For the majority of political communication researchers, cognitive and affective structures "constrain the complexity of interpretations that people produce" (Crigler 1996, p. 9). Situated communicative practices are said to replicate cognitive and affective frames (Marcus et al. 2000) or predispositions (Becker and Scheufele 2011). Language is the *representational* vehicle that serves as a mirror onto individual and collective psychology. In DP the representational function of language is replaced by a conception of language as a "tool that creates worlds and versions of worlds" (Edelman 2001, p. 82; cf. Billig 1996; Wittgenstein 1953).

DP focuses on social accomplishments of active users of talk and texts. Language is primarily a medium for action (for overviews of DP's main theoretical and methodological principles, see Hepburn and Wiggins, 2007; Augoustinos and Tileagă 2012; Tileagă and Stokoe 2015). DP has, since its inception, had a strong affinity with the systematic analysis of political discourse and political events. The seminal early text of DP (Edwards and Potter 1992) was a convincing illustration of a then nascent interest in understanding the "torrent of media coverage" (Edwards and Potter 1992, p. 1) on key political events of the times by understanding the "psychology" (memory, attribution, motive) that was thus made available. As Edwards and Potter were arguing, "the events [the 1990–1991 Gulf War] that took place were, to us, inextricable from their various constructions, each of which allowed for inferences about motives and morality, about strategy and politics" (ibid., p. 1). However, Edwards and Potter (1992) also consider other controversial political events in both the UK (e.g. the events that lead to the resignation of

Chancellor Lawson) and the USA (e.g. the Iran-Contra hearings and Watergate testimonies) as illustrations and case-tests of a newly developing discursive psychology. Public political discourse was providing an "arena in which to consider the operation of interest management, fact construction and accountability" (ibid., p. 7). Other early discourse analytic projects were concerned with the elucidation of the complex nature of racism (Wetherell and Potter 1992) and the issue of how speakers manage their talk to avoid being heard as "prejudiced" (Billig 1988). Early DP work has been an unassailable source for contemporary DP studies on political identities and prejudice (e.g. Goodman and Johnson, 2013), accusations and denials of racism in public discourse (Augoustinos and Every 2010), racial discourse (Edwards 2003), producing and responding to -isms in interaction (see papers in special issue by Whitehead and Stokoe 2015) as well as work on extreme forms of prejudice and moral exclusion (e.g. Tileagă 2007, 2015).

DP recommends an analytical focus that is not only about political events or political personalities *per se* but on the nature of public communication and public political discourse. For example, matters of "fact" and "truth" are analysed in terms of the rhetorical part they play in political argumentation rather than treated as matters of objective "truth" or "untruth" (Burke and Demasi 2019; Demasi 2019). Indeed, we should not lament that we live in an era of "post-truth politics". Rather, it is perhaps time that we recognise that "truth", in discourse, is a rhetorical matter and, therefore, an empirically tangible one (Demasi 2020).

DP, with its strong history of recognised academic and empirical work in analysing public political discourse, can help generate new insights into the subtleties of public forms and manifestations of politics in the public sphere. Insights developed by discursive psychologists "can help make sense of features of different sorts of discourse" (Edwards and Potter 1992, p. 7), ranging from ordinary talk to the affordances of the latest new media technologies. Early discursively oriented media studies (e.g. Ashmore 1993; MacMillan and Edwards 1999) have shown that DP can be used persuasively to recontextualise and redescribe mediated communication in the public sphere.

The coming of age of DP saw its focus move to the analysis of specific tropes or commonplaces of political rhetoric as substantive and separate

1 The Discursive Psychology of Political Communication   13

phenomenon of interest (e.g. Rapley 1998; Augoustinos et al. 2002; Tileagă 2008), albeit not exclusively. Other contributions in DP looked at the link between argumentation and political participation (Condor and Gibson 2007), national identity (Condor 2011), use of rhetoric in parliamentary debates about immigration and citizenship (e.g. Every and Augoustinos 2007) and textual analyses of historical documents (Tileagă 2009, 2011).

DP's eclecticism on topics in political communication is now morphing into a systematic and more encompassing approach to political communication—from the analysis of political speeches to mediated action in institutional settings and wider social issues and social problems. The two main trajectories of DP—CA-inspired and critical/post-structuralist (cf. Tileagă and Stokoe 2015)—need not be separated in the study of political communication. Both trajectories rest, to some greater or lesser extent, on a "non-causal conception of what makes social actions orderly and intelligible" (Edwards 2012, p. 432).

DP of political communication widens the intellectual reach of DP by incorporating and transforming approaches with which is sharing elective affinities: critical discourse studies (Lennon and Kilby, this volume), multimodal communication (Pettersson and Sakki, this volume) and rhetorical psychology (Andreouli, this volume; Murray, this volume). The chapters in this book attest to what is particular and original about discursive psychology: its diversity (Tileagă and Stokoe 2015). This is a book that emphasises DP's diversity of topics, issues, variety and breadth of assumptions and connections with other programmes of research in other disciplines and in the broader expanse of discourse analytic scholarship. Some caricature DP as lacking analytic depth and breadth in order to engage analytically with issues of power, politics, mediated communication and social problems more generally (Stokoe et al. 2012). DP engages directly with such issues regardless of topic—whether it is concerned with researching and unpacking interactional practices (Stokoe et al. 2012), unequal power relations (Tileagă 2005) or citizen engagement (Hofstetter and Stokoe 2015), DP, in its various guises, continues to promote a critical agenda.

Outline of Chapters

This book is an introduction to the variety of discursive research carried out in the sphere of political communication. It is not intended as a comprehensive overview of the state of discursive psychological research on political communication. Each chapter offers an illustration of how DP is engaging with the forms and nature of mediated communications in specific settings and across several national contexts. The book is divided into three broad sections: political communication of contentious politics, political communication and new media and, finally, discursive psychology, discourse and social problems.

The first section—political communication of contentious politics—focuses on DP's concern with analysing contentious political topics and issues. Chapters in this section discuss pressing contemporary political concerns with racism, nationalism, wealth inequality and the Brexit referendum.

The chapter by Stephen Gibson explores the dialogical nature of racism. The chapter begins with a brief review of the discursive literature on racism. Gibson then proceeds to look at how what he calls a "spectre of racism" is both expressed and resisted during the UK's 2015 General Election campaign, a time when the UK Independence Party (UKIP) received a large number of votes. Gibson analyses an episode of the BBC4 political discussion radio programme *Any Questions?* from March 2015 where anti-discrimination laws were being debated. Gibson demonstrates how being heard to be racist and being heard to make an accusation of racism are oriented to as difficult positions for speakers. In this sense, racism, then, becomes not only a problem for the person defending the contestable position but also for the person criticising that position. Gibson concludes with three points about the communication of racism: (a) the importance of attending analytically to what is treated as racist and when, especially when accusations are made implicitly, (b) the appreciation of the wider ideological climate as well as the more local interactional context that go into making sense of racism and (c) the crucial role of the context of debate, including a focus on aspects that transcend the local interactional context. Gibson's latter point is particularly apposite

1 The Discursive Psychology of Political Communication   15

analytically in the case of broadcast political debates, with politicians not only orientating to the face-to-face debate but also appealing to the values and attitudes of the overhearing and wider audience.

Eleni Andreouli uses rhetorical psychology to reveal the dilemmatic discourses used by laypeople to make sense of Brexit. Andreouli analyses talk from focus groups conducted just before the June 2016 EU referendum and in early 2017. Andreouli identifies two sets of ideological dilemmas: nationalism/internationalism, on the one hand, and prejudice/tolerance, on the other hand, that are used to frame individual lay perspectives. Andreouli discusses the lay perspectives of people describing themselves as either Remainers or Leavers. Remainers construct Leavers as prejudiced, whilst Leavers employ the argument that Britain would be more cosmopolitan once free from the constraints of the EU. The chapter contributes to a discursive political communication of lay perspectives on Brexit, as well as providing a contemporary example of how people engage with ideological dilemmas. In particular, Andreouli argues that it is not enough to study what politicians argue for and against in the political arena of today but also highlights the importance of studying, in detail, lay perspectives on Brexit—how non-politicians in the UK make sense of Brexit. Crucially, thanks to her rhetorical approach, one can appreciate that political reasoning on contentious politics, and the answer to the question "what people really think", does not always get a straightforward answer.

Philippa Carr demonstrates that television programmes that are arguably non-political can be discursively analysed as a form of political communication. She discusses the example of talk used in entertainment, documentary-style, programming to legitimise extreme wealth. In particular she looks at how the presence of the dominant ideology of our times—neoliberal individualism—is drawn on by the super-rich talk about domestic staff. She also looks at how the domestic staff account for their jobs. She finds interesting differences between the two sets of accounts. For example, the super-rich root their argument for the need of domestic staff on matters of necessity whereas staff themselves tend to be more tentative when asked the same question. Carr shows how TV editing can be used to introduce ambiguity to question the deservingness of the super-rich and how humour is used to criticise the discourse of the super-rich. Yet, both super-rich and staff demonstrate their positions as being ultimately justified and justifiable—the super-rich by focusing on their need for help in order to focus on their careers and the staff on the collective benefit of helping those around them. Ultimately, wealth inequality itself is not addressed but rather treated by both documentary participants and documentary producers as an everyday, natural, feature of the world. The chapter closes with a discussion of what counts as political communication in these settings. Carr argues that entertainment media genres, like reality-show docu-dramas, can be thought of as a form of political communication and analysed for what they reveal as much as for what they conceal.

Henry W. Lennon and Laura Kilby use multimodal critical discourse analysis to analyse political cartoons, as prime sites of visual and textual semiosis. Lennon and Kilby analyse media articles in *The Guardian* and *Politico* on the UK's membership of the European Union referendum. These political cartoons provide an excellent example of how political meaning is constructed and interpreted through prevailing social and political contexts. Lennon and Kilby show how national identity as well as "otherness" and "belonging" were constructed in the cartoons. They analyse in detail two particular semiotic tropes: "boundedness and isolation", and "uncertain waters". What is significant about these tropes, Lennon and Kilby argue, is that they are used to ultimately portray Brexit as a particularly British (as opposed to English, Scottish, Welsh or Irish) challenge whilst at the same time downplaying the role of the EU and Europe. They also discuss the ambiguous nature of visual satire in these cartoons—the humour cannot be interpreted as entirely disciplinary or entirely rebellious (see Billig 2005). This ambiguity gives the cartoons a degree of rhetorical ambiguity, meaning they can be interpreted in a multitude of ways (with the authors cautiously favouring the rebellious angle). This chapter contributes to the growing body of discursive research on Brexit (e.g. Krzyżanowski 2019; Meredith and Richardson 2019; Andreouli, this volume; Andreouli and Nicholson 2018). The chapter concludes with a cautionary note on the interpretation of both visual and linguistic forms of ambiguity.

The second section—political communication and new media—focuses on DP's contribution to analysing mediated practices: online

1 The Discursive Psychology of Political Communication 17

mobilisation, online far-right communication techniques and mediated racist encounters.

Petra Sneijder, Baukje Stinesen, Maartje Harmelink and Annette Klarenbeek analyse online mobilisation related to political issues and the interactional work in online mobilisation. The analysis of Facebook event pages of three Dutch social movements reveals three discursive strategies people use to achieve mobilisation and create public engagement: 1) questioning the integrity of authorities (in order to legitimise the cause), 2) presenting oneself as genuinely committed to the cause (as opposed to being "merely" interested in activism) and 3) constructing the idea of "togetherness". Discursive attempts at mobilisation involve people presenting themselves online as reasonable persons rather than "activists" or "victims". Presenting an image of reasonableness is a feature of other political communication research (e.g. Goodman and Johnson 2013). The chapter demonstrates the contribution that DP makes as a perspective to the study of mobilisation—and shows the part played by psychological categories (particularly in this case, emotion and identity) in wider social practices of mobilisation.

Katarina Pettersson and Inari Sakki return to the analysis of texts and iconic representations. Pettersson and Sakki combine Critical Discursive Psychology and visual rhetorical analysis to produce a case analysis of how a populist radical right politician's blog in Finland discusses the Syrian refugee "crisis". Radical right political blogs have been particularly well-followed in the Nordic countries and have played a significant role in the rise of other radical and far-right organisations. The analysis shows how the blog is used to embed populist arguments in alternative discourses that draw upon the reasonableness of writing on behalf of "the people". In particular the analysis highlights how the combination of content and form serves to enable the politician to present negative views of immigrants and minorities without coming across as prejudiced or populist. Pettersson and Sakki's analysis pays analytic attention to various non-verbal, especially visual, forms of online political communication and persuasion. This approach directs the analytic gaze towards appreciating the multifaceted nature of political communication—verbal aspects of political communication do not tell the full story. The work of Pettersson and Sakki, alongside other DP work (e.g. Burke 2018; Burke et al. 2020), is particularly important in highlighting the usefulness and need of discursive analyses that engage with multimodal frameworks.

Shani Burke and Mirko Demasi use DP to analyse racist encounters captured by members of the public on a personal phone. Using a case study approach of two encounters in the public domain, one in the UK and one in Finland, the analysis reveals how speakers use language that can be construed as explicitly racist, while also trying to frame such talk as in some way justifiable. Thanks to phone technology and social media, one can now access publicly interactions that may have been previously harder to access and, as Burke and Demasi argue, have been historically understudied: cases of face-to-face racist abuse. They found that "dehumanising and depersonalizing categorisations coexist with displays of reasonableness" (this volume). The same strategies identified in previous DP literature whereby speakers try to disguise talk as "not racist" are also used by speakers when the talk is explicitly racist, for example, by presenting one's views as consensual. Rationalisations and justificatory discourse enable veiled threats that are violent in and of themselves. Burke and Demasi show how detailed discursive analysis of actual encounters can expose the subtle dynamics of violent bigotry. The chapter shows how everyday justificatory tropes are used in the perpetuation of extreme prejudiced discourses.

The third section—discursive psychology, discourse and social problems—focuses on discursive psychology's engagement with present and past social problems, specifically the Syrian refugee crisis and the apartheid past of South Africa. While other chapters in this book also bear relevance to understanding and engaging with social problems, in this section these issues are discussed explicitly.

The chapter by Lise Marie Børlie and Simon Goodman explores how Syrian refugees are presented in online discussion forums in both the UK and Norway, revealing strategies that are used to challenge rarer positive representations of refugees. One such discursive move was to criticise public institutions within the European society for spreading propaganda. The media was constructed as manipulative, whilst supporters of refugees were constructed as naïve. This chapter provides empirical evidence of "eroding trust" towards the more traditional sources of news, as argued by Marshall and Drieschova (2018), but does so from the

1 The Discursive Psychology of Political Communication   19

perspective of people that actively engage with discussing the refugee crisis as a social problem. The other strategy, of treating those with pro-refugee posts as "naïve" or "lefties", was used to silence any pro-refugee sentiment in these particular online forums—these accusations were rarely responded to. The construction of "fake news" allows speakers to continue their opposition to refugees even in the face of "facts" that do not support their views. The findings build upon previous research that has shown online discourse about refugees can be hostile (e.g. Burke and Goodman 2012), by revealing that hostility can also be displayed towards supporters of refugees.

Lia Figgou and Dimitra Anagnostopoulou focus on how ideology is used to negotiate the responsibility of the refugee "crisis" in Greece, in the context of the country's bailout and the refugee movement through the Aegean Sea. Using a combination of rhetorical and discursive psychology, the analysis considers two debates in the Greek parliament. The analysis reveals how Greek politicians mobilise various argumentative moves in order to warrant their political choices and to downgrade the practices of their political opponents. Notably both the governing and opposition parties tended to use similar argumentative moves to justify their positions and actions. Both parties argued their positions were based on practical concerns as well as realpolitik. In particular this was done by downplaying one's party allegiance in favour of national interest and by accounting for decisions based on "indisputable" political realities. These types of arguments enabled politicians to make rhetorical moves that potentially present refugees as a social threat while, at the same time, carefully distancing themselves from making controversial claims on migration of vulnerable people. Implications for Greek political discourse and wider political context are also discussed.

In the final chapter, by Amy Jo Murray, we return to the spectre of racism. The chapter addresses the political communication of the said and the unsaid. The context is post-apartheid South Africa and talk about domestic labour relationships. This is the kind of talk that, as Murray argues, implicates both speaker and hearer as "ghosts" of the apartheid past. What is routinely said and what is routinely not said carry equal analytic weight. Data comes from nine interviews with white employers of domestic labour. The analysis uses the concept of dialogic repression

20   C. Tileagă et al.

(Billig 1997, 1999) to show how speakers explicitly avoid expressing "typical" madam-like (a stereotype of white dominance in South Africa) expressions. Murray shows how "white" and "employer" identities are enacted in talk in the context of domestic labour and how the interviewees avoid morally contestable identities. Particularising moves (Billig 1996) from the interviewer (inviting a discussion of participants' identity as whites employing black staff) are met by generalising moves, responses that position employees as "part of the family", omitting to mention what this entails in practice. Likewise, humour is used to smooth over awkward moments in the interviews, such as accounts of "scolding" employees. Murray argues that these types of discourses, which are both expressive and repressive, enable the participants to manage, or at least attempt to, a delicate rhetorical balance between having domestic staff and not being seen to be similar to the past, apartheid-era, white rulers. The irony here is that in downplaying one's conformity to the stereotype of "the madam", one can observe the construction of white accountability in post-apartheid South Africa. The spectre of "the madam" becomes expressed in the very discursive moves designed to conceal it.

Final Remarks

Researchers are drawn to DP because of its sophisticated understanding of language as mind and world-building. As the chapters in this book show, language is not an independent variable or the expression of inner cognitive processes (cf. also Tileagă 2013). If we strip language of its constructive and constitutive properties, we risk ending up with a limited worldview of political communication—a one-sided picture of a multi-faceted phenomenon (Billig 1996). A focus on politics should not have to mean that communication is relegated to a secondary role.

We showcase in this book work that provides an empirically robust and analytically rich inroad to making sense of a variety of political communications as mediated social practices. In this "age of media abundance" (Blumler and Kavanagh 1999), the effectiveness and influence of political communications depend on their discursive and sociocultural patterning and the range of settings, activities and practices that they are

1 The Discursive Psychology of Political Communication   21

part of. This suggests that discursive approaches to political communication may have a significant contribution to make—we can learn more about the social organisation of political communications by looking at the various ways in which political communications are publicly accomplished in texts, talk and various old and new media.

Political communication is complex and contextual. However, its manifestations are not universal, but, rather, particular. As Tileagă and Stokoe have noted, "DP offers particularistic answers to general questions" (2015, p. 5). The chapters in this book show how DP is able to describe the cultural patterning of political communications not only through selected case studies but also by offering particularistic answers to problems brought about by working with small-scale as well as large-scale qualitative data (Stokoe et al. 2012). DP opens new avenues for cross-fertilisation between fields concerned with both politics and the nature of communication. That project is underway. Discursive perspectives to political communication have enabled the rekindling of a dialogue between discourse and communication and media studies, on the one hand, and psychological approaches to political communication, on the other hand. Discursive psychology, we argue, is able to overcome the most common kinds of determinisms (technological, on the one hand, and psychological/cognitive, on the other hand) that seem to influence political communication scholarship (cf. Tileagă 2013).

It is not easy to place the study of political communication into an uncontroversial academic category or in one single discipline. Our aim in this chapter has been to provide a coherent rationale for the inclusion of DP in the toolbox of political communication researchers. This book provides an overview of theoretical and empirical work that was conducted in the spirit of researching political communication as a social accomplishment. The studies in this volume originate in the systematic, incremental, research programme of DP in conversation with other approaches. This is a research programme that is ready for rigorous innovation in a field that, until very recently at least, has been perceived as the province of only certain disciplines.

At a time when demands that both traditional and new media take a long look at how they discuss political issues of public interest have never

22   C. Tileagă et al.

been more cogent, we argue that political communication scholars ought to diversify their approaches to understanding the substance rather than the game or the spectacle of politics. Discursive psychology, we argue, can contribute to this project of diversification. The challenges posed by social media specifically—the increasingly offensive (Levmore and Nussbaum 2012), the sexist and misogynistic (Bates 2014) or the more progressive intersectional (Noble and Tynes 2016) Internet—are challenges that can be addressed with the tools and perspective of discursive psychology. Discursive psychologists themselves will need to broaden their horizons and produce more and more analyses that draw directly or indirectly upon the analysis of multimodal communications, as well as communications and media theories of mediated communication and connective action. Calls for dialogues between fields and areas of practice are of course not devoid of challenges.[7]

Discursive psychologists and political communication scholars alike should not make the mistake of thinking of politics

> as a separate field of human activity … without taking full account of the sense in which it is only one perspective or one facet of a system of closely linked activities … As soon as one considers the ties of political activities to other activities, it takes on different meanings. (Edelman 2001, pp. 56–57)

In the new language of digital media scholarship, what Edelman is akin to what Bennett and Segerberg (2013) call "connective action". Connective action underpins deliberative and participatory innovations in digital communications that, in turn, are enabling forms of social hostility that are making some of the most enduring and practised norms against the expression of public prejudice obsolete (e.g. antisemitism). Innovations are, increasingly, redrawing the boundaries of what is acceptable in the public sphere, mostly by producing new moral evaluative schemes for judging the dignity of people, communities and nations (cf. Tileagă 2019).

The importance of researching political communications in the public sphere has not declined. It has, nonetheless, and perhaps inevitably, changed.

---

[7] See, for instance, Tileagă and Byford (2014) on some of the pitfalls of interdisciplinarity.

This change is an important change. It is a change that has a lot to do with how we research public issues in public life as phenomena that go beyond mere disagreement on political matters. Political communications, both emancipatory and toxic, cross ideological lines and take a variety of forms, including ambiguous forms, more often than not and to a larger extent than we tend to assume.

References

Anderson, J. (1983). *The architecture of cognition*. Cambridge, MA: Harvard University Press.

Andreouli, E., & Nicholson, C. (2018). Brexit and everyday politics: An analysis of focus group data on the EU referendum. *Political Psychology, 39*(6), 1323–1338.

Ashmore, M. (1993). The theatre of the blind: Starring a Promethean Prankster, a Phoney Phenomenon, a Prism, a Pocket, and a Piece of Wood. *Social Studies of Science, 23*, 67–106.

Augoustinos, M., & Every, D. (2010). Accusations and denials of racism: Managing moral accountability in public discourse. *Discourse and Society, 21*, 251–256.

Augoustinos, M., LeCouteur, A., & Soyland, J. (2002). Self-sufficient arguments in political rhetoric: Constructing reconciliation and apologizing to the stolen generations. *Discourse and Society, 13*(1), 105–142.

Augoustinos, M., & Tileagă, C. (2012). Twenty five years of discursive psychology. *British Journal of Social Psychology, 51*, 405–412.

Barthes, R. (1977). *Image-music-text*. London: Fontana.

Bates, L. (2014). *Everyday sexism*. London: Simon & Schuster.

Becker, A. B., & Scheufele, D. A. (2011). New voters, new outlook? Predispositions, social networks, and the changing politics of gay civil rights. *Social Science Quarterly, 92*, 324–345.

Bennett, L., & Entman, R. M. (2001). *Mediated politics: Communication in the future of democracy*. New York: Cambridge University Press.

Bennett, W. L., Breunig, C., & Givens, T. (2008). Communication and political mobilization: Digital media and the organization of Anti-Iraq war demonstrations in the US. *Political Communication, 25*(3), 269–289.

Bennett, W. L., & Iyengar, S. (2008). A new era of minimal effects? The changing foundations of political communication. *Journal of Communication, 58,* 707–731.

Bennett, W. L., & Segerberg, A. (2012). The logic of connective action. *Information, Communication and Society, 15*(5), 739–768.

Bennett, W. L., & Segerberg, A. (2013). *The logic of connective action: Digital media and the personalization of contentious politics.* Cambridge University Press.

Benson, R. (2004). Bringing the sociology of media back in. *Political Communication, 21*(3), 275–292.

Benson, R. (2013). *Shaping immigration news: A French-American comparison.* New York: Cambridge University Press.

Billig, M. (1987). *Arguing and thinking: A rhetorical approach to social psychology.* Cambridge: Cambridge University Press.

Billig, M. (1988). The notion of "Prejudice": some rhetorical and ideological aspects. *Text, 8,* 91–110.

Billig, M. (1996). *Arguing and thinking: A rhetorical approach to social psychology* (2nd ed.). Cambridge: Cambridge University Press.

Billig, M. (1997). The dialogic unconscious: Psychoanalysis, discursive psychology and the nature of repression. *British Journal of Social Psychology, 36,* 139–159.

Billig, M. (1999). *Freudian repression: Conversation creating the unconscious.* Cambridge: Cambridge University Press.

Billig, M. (2005). *Laughter and Ridicule – Towards A Social Critique Of Humour.* London: Sage Publications.

Blumler, J. G. & Fox, A. (Eds) (1983). *Communicating to voters: Television in the First European Parliamentary Elections.* London: Sage Publications.

Blumler, J. G. (2001). The third age of political communication. *Journal of Public Affairs, 1,* 201–209.

Blumler, J. G., & Kavanagh, D. (1999). The third age of political communication: Influences and features. *Political Communication, 16,* 209–230.

Bull, P. (2002). *Communication under the microscope: The theory and practice of microanalysis.* New York: Psychology Press.

Bull, P. (2003). *The microanalysis of political communication: Claptrap and ambiguity.* London: Routledge.

Burgess, C. (2011). 'This election will be Won by people not posters' … advertising and the 2010 general election. In D. Wring, R. Mortimore, & S. Atkinson (Eds.), *Political communication in Britain* (pp. 181–197). Palgrave Macmillan.

1 The Discursive Psychology of Political Communication 25

Burke, S. (2018). The discursive "othering" of jews and muslims in the Britain first solidarity patrol. *Journal of Community and Applied Social Psychology, 28*(5), 365–377.

Burke, S., & Demasi, M. A. (2019). Applying discursive psychology to 'fact' construction in political discourse. *Social and Personality Psychology Compass, 13*(5), e12449.

Burke, S., Diba, P., & Antonopoulos, G. (2020). You sick, twisted messes': The use of argument and reasoning in islamophobic and anti-semitic discussions on facebook. *Discourse and Society, 31*(4), 374–389.

Burke, S., & Goodman, S. (2012). "Bring Back Hitler's Gas Chambers": Asylum seeking, Nazis and Facebook: A discursive analysis. *Discourse and Society, 23*(1), 19–33.

Byford, J. (2011). *Conspiracy theories: A critical introduction.* London: Palgrave Macmillan.

Cappella, J. N., & Jamieson, K. H. (1997). *Spiral of cynicism: The press and the public good.* New York: Oxford University Press.

Castells, M. (2011). *Communication power.* Oxford: Oxford University Press.

Chadwick, A., & Vaccari, C. (2019). *News sharing on UK social media: Misinformation, disinformation, and correction. survey report.* Loughborough: Online Civic Culture Centre, Loughborough University.

Chadwick, A., Vaccari, C., & O'Loughlin, B. (2018). Do tabloids poison the well of social media? Explaining democratically dysfunctional news sharing. *New Media and Society, 20*(11), 4255–4274.

Chilton, P. (2004). *Analysing political discourse: Theory and practice.* London: Routledge.

Chilton, P., & Ilyin, M. (1993). Metaphor in political discourse. *Discourse and Society, 4,* 7–31.

Chilton, P., & Schäffner, C. (1997). Discourse and politics. In T. van Dijk (Ed.), *Discourse as social interaction* (Vol. 2, pp. 206–231). London: Sage Publications.

Clayman, S., & Heritage, J. (2002). *The news interview: Journalists and public figures on the air.* New York: Cambridge University Press.

Condor, S. (2011). Rebranding Britain? Ideological Dilemmas in political appeals to "British multiculturalism". In M. Barrett, C. Flood, & J. Eade (Eds.), *Nationalism, ethnicity, citizenship: Multidisciplinary perspectives.* Cambridge Scholars.

Condor, S., & Gibson, S. (2007). Everybody's entitled to their own opinion': Ideological dilemmas of liberal individualism and active citizenship. *Journal of Community and Applied Social Psychology, 6,* 178–199.

Condor, S., Tileagă, C., & Billig, M. (2013). Political rhetoric. In L. Huddy, D. O. Sears, & J. S. Levy (Eds.), *Oxford handbook of political psychology* (pp. 262–300). New York: Oxford University Press.

Converse, P. (1964). The nature of belief systems in mass publics. In D. Apter (Ed.), *Ideology and discontent* (pp. 206–261). Free Press.

Crigler, A. N. (1996). Making sense of politics: Constructing political messages and meanings. In A. N. Crigler (Ed.), *The psychology of political communication* (pp. 1–10). University of Michigan Press.

Dalton, R. J. (2008). *Citizen politics: Public opinion and political parties in advanced industrial democracies* (5th ed.). CQ Press.

Deacon, D., & Wring, D. (2011). Reporting the 2010 General Election: Old media, new media – old politics, new politics. In D. Wring, R. Mortimore, & S. Atkinson (Eds.), *Political Communication in Britain*. London: Palgrave.

Delli Carpini, M. X., & Williams, B. (2001). Let us Infotain you: Politics in the new media environment. In L. Bennett & R. Entman (Eds.), *Mediated politics: Communication in the future of democracy* (pp. 160–191). New York: Cambridge University Press.

Demasi, M. A. (2019). Facts as social action in political debates about the European Union. *Political Psychology, 40*(1), 3–20.

Demasi, M. A. (2020). Post-truth politics and discursive psychology. *Social and Personality Psychology Compass*. https://doi.org/10.1111/spc3.12556

Downey, J., & Mihelj, S. (2012). *Central and Eastern European Media in comparative perspective: Politics, economy and culture*. Ashgate.

Downey, J., & Stanyer, J. (2010). Comparative media analysis: Why some fuzzy thinking might help. Applying fuzzy set qualitative comparative analysis to the personalization of mediated political communication. *European Journal of Communication, 25*(4), 331–347.

Edelman, M. (1967). *The symbolic uses of politics*. Urbana: University of Illinois Press.

Edelman, M. (1988). *Constructing the political spectacle*. Chicago: Chicago University Press.

Edelman, M. (2001). *The politics of misinformation*. New York: Cambridge University Press.

Edwards, D. (1997). *Discourse and cognition*. London: Sage Publications.

Edwards, D. (2003). Analyzing racial discourse: The discursive psychology of mind-world relationships. In H. van den Berg, M. Wetherell, & H. Houtkoop-Steenstra (Eds.), *Analyzing race talk: Multidisciplinary approaches to the interview* (pp. 31–48). Cambridge: Cambridge University Press.

Edwards, D. (2006). Discourse, cognition and social practices: The rich surface of language and social interaction. *Discourse Studies, 8*(1), 41–49.

Edwards, D. (2012). Discursive and scientific psychology. *British Journal of Social Psychology, 51*, 425–435.

Edwards, D., & Potter, J. (1992). *Discursive Psychology.* London: Sage Publications.

Erjavec, K., & Volcic, Z. (2007). 'War on terrorism' as a discursive battleground: Serbian recontextualization of G.W. Bush's discourse. *Discourse and Society, 18*, 123–137.

Every, D., & Augoustinos, M. (2007). Constructions of racism in the Australian parliamentary debates on asylum seekers. *Discourse and Society, 18*, 411–436.

Fairclough, I., & Fairclough, N. (2011). Practical reasoning in political discourse: The UK government's response to the economic crisis in the 2008 pre-budget report. *Discourse and Society, 22*, 243–268.

Fairclough, N. (2000). *New labour, new language.* London: Routledge.

Fairclough, N. (2010). *Critical discourse analysis: The critical study of language.* London: Longman.

Fiske, S., & Taylor, S. (1984). *Social cognition.* Longman Higher Education.

Fowler, R. (1991). *Language in the news: Discourse and ideology in the press.* Routledge.

Fowler, R., Hodge, R., Kress, G., & Trew, T. (1979). *Language and control.* London: Routledge & Kegan Paul.

Franklin, B. (2004). *Packaging politics: Political communications in Britain's media democracy.* Bloomsbury Academic.

Gamson, W. A., & Wolfsfeld, G. (1993). Movements and media as interacting systems. *Annals of the American Academy of Political and Social Science, 528*, 114–125.

Goodman, S., & Johnson, A. J. (2013). Strategies used by the far right to counter accusations of racism. *Critical Approaches to Discourse Analysis Across Disciplines, 6*, 97–113.

Hepburn, A., & Wiggins, S. (2007). *Discursive research in practice: New approaches to psychology and interaction.* Cambridge: Cambridge University Press.

Hodges, A. (2008). The politics of recontextualization: discursive competition over claims of Iranian involvement in Iraq. *Discourse and Society, 19*, 483–505.

Hofstetter, E., & Stokoe, E. (2015). Offers of assistance in politician-constituent interaction. *Discourse Studies, 17*(6), 724–751.

Huckfeldt, R. (2009). Information, persuasion, and political communication networks. In R. J. Dalton & H.-D. Klingemann (Eds.), *The Oxford handbook of political behavior* (pp. 100–122). New York: Oxford University Press.

Isaksen, J. (2011). Obama's rhetorical shift. *Communication Studies, 62*, 456–471.

Jamieson, K. H. (1988). *Eloquence in an electronic age*. New York: Oxford University Press.

Kaid, L., & Holtz-Bacha, C. (2006). *The SAGE handbook of political advertising*. Thousand Oaks: Sage.

Kinder, D. R. (2003). Communication and politics in the age of information. In D. O. Sears, L. Huddy, & R. Jervis (Eds.), *Oxford handbook of political psychology* (pp. 357–393). New York: Oxford University Press.

Klandermans, B. (2003). Collective political action. In D. O. Sears, L. Huddy, & R. Jervis (Eds.), *Oxford handbook of political psychology* (pp. 670–709). Oxford University Press.

Kreiss, D., & McGregor, S. C. (2018). Technology firms shape political communication: The work of Microsoft, Facebook, Twitter, and Google with Campaigns during the 2016 US presidential cycle. *Political Communication, 35*(2), 155–177.

Kress, G. (2009). *Multimodality: A social semiotic approach to contemporary communication*. London: Routledge.

Krzyżanowski, M. (2019). Brexit and the imaginary of "crisis": A discourse-conceptual analysis of European News Media. *Critical Discourse Studies, 465*(4).

Lakoff, G., & Johnson, M. (1980). *Metaphors we live by*. Chicago: Chicago University Press.

Lasswell, H., & Leites, N. (1949). *Language of politics: Studies in quantitative semantics*. New York: George W Stewart.

Lau, R., & Redlawsk, D. (2001). Advantages and disadvantages of cognitive heuristics in political decision making. *American Journal of Political Science, 45*(4), 951–971.

Levmore, S., & Nussbaum, M. (2012). *The offensive internet: Speech, privacy, and reputation*. Cambridge, MA: Harvard University Press.

MacMillan, K., & Edwards, D. (1999). Who killed the princess? Description and blame in the British Press. *Discourse Studies, 1*, 151–174.

Marcus, G., Neuman, W., & MacKuen, M. (2000). *Affective intelligence and political judgment*. Chicago: University of Chicago Press.

Margolis, M., & Resnick, D. (2000). *Politics as usual: The cyberspace "revolution"*. Thousand Oaks: Sage.

1 The Discursive Psychology of Political Communication 29

Marshall, H., & Drieschova, A. (2018). Post-truth politics in the UK's Brexit referendum. *New Perspectives, 26*(3), 89–105.

McGraw, K. M. (2003). Political impressions: Formation and management. In D. O. Sears, L. Huddy, & R. Jervis (Eds.), *Oxford handbook of political psychology* (pp. 394–432). New York: Oxford University Press.

McNair, B. (2011). *An introduction to political communication* (5th ed.). London: Routledge.

Meredith, J., & Richardson, E. (2019). The use of the political categories of Brexiter and Remainer in online comments about the EU referendum. *Journal of Community and Applied Social Psychology, 29*, 43–55.

Mihelj, S. (2011). *Media nations: Communicating belonging and exclusion in the modern world.* London: Macmillan.

Mondada, L. (2019). Contemporary issues in conversation analysis: Embodiment and materiality, multimodality and multisensoriality in social interaction. *Journal of Pragmatics, 145*, 47–62.

Mutz, D. (2001). The future of political communication research: Reflections on the occasion of Steve Chaffee's retirement from Stanford University. *Political Communication, 18*(2), 231–236.

Mutz, D. (2009). Political psychology and choice. In R. J. Dalton & H.-D. Klingemann (Eds.), *The Oxford handbook of political behavior* (pp. 80–99). New York: Oxford University Press.

Negrine, R. (2008). *The transformation of political communication. Continuities and changes in media and politics.* London: Palgrave Macmillan.

Negrine, R., & Stanyer, J. (2007). *The political communication reader.* London: Routledge.

Nisbet, M. C., & Feldman, L. (2010). The social psychology of political communication. In D. Hook, B. Franks, & M. Bauer (Eds.), *The social psychology of communication* (pp. 284–299). London: Palgrave Macmillan.

Noble, S. U., & Tynes, B. M. (2016). *The intersectional internet: Race, sex, class, and culture online.* New York: Peter Lang.

Osgood, C. (1978). Conservative words and radical sentences in the semantics of international politics. *Studies in the Linguistic Sciences, 8*, 43–61.

Rapley, M. (1998). Just an ordinary Australian: Self-categorisation and the discursive construction of facticity in "racist" political rhetoric. *British Journal of Social Psychology, 37*, 325–344.

Reisigl, M., & Wodak, R. (2001). *Discourse and discrimination: Rhetorics of racism and antisemitism.* London: Routledge.

Richards, B. (2004). The emotional deficit in political communication. *Political Communication, 21*(3), 339–252.

Richardson, K., Parry, K., & Corner, J. (2011). Genre and the mediation of election politics. In D. Wring, R. Mortimore, & S. Atkinson (Eds.), *Political communication in Britain* (pp. 304–324). London: Palgrave Macmillan.

Schäffner, C. (2010). Political communication mediated by translation. In U. Okulska & P. Cap (Eds.), *Perspectives in politics and discourse* (pp. 255–278). Amsterdam: John Benjamins.

Scheufele, D., & Tewksbury, D. (2007). Framing, Agenda setting, and priming: The evolution of three media effects models. *Journal of Communication, 57*, 9–20.

Schudson, M. (2004). The place of sociology in the study of political communication. *Political Communication, 21*(3), 271–273.

Semetko, H. (2009). Political communication. In R. J. Dalton & H.-D. Klingemann (Eds.), *The Oxford handbook of political behavior* (pp. 123–143). New York: Oxford University Press.

Sowinska, A. (2013). A critical discourse approach to the analysis of values in political discourse: The example of freedom in president Bush's State of the Union Addresses (2001–2008). *Discourse and Society, 24*(6), 792–809.

Stanyer, J. (2007). *Modern political communication.* Cambridge: Polity.

Stokoe, E., Hepburn, A., & Antaki, C. (2012). Beware the "Loughborough School" of social psychology: Interaction and the politics of intervention. *British Journal of Social Psychology, 51*, 486–496.

Suedfeld, P., Conway, L. G., & Eichhorn, D. (2001). Studying Canadian Leaders at a distance. In O. Feldman & L. O. Valenty (Eds.), *Profiling political leaders: Cross-cultural studies of personality and political behavior* (pp. 3–19). Praeger.

Taber, C. (2003). Information processing and public opinion. In D. O. Sears, L. Huddy, & R. Jervis (Eds.), *Oxford handbook of political psychology* (pp. 433–476). New York: Oxford University Press.

Tetlock, P. E. (1984). Cognitive Style And Political Belief Systems in the British house of commons. *Journal of Personality and Social Psychology, 46*, 365–375.

Tetlock, P. E. (2005). *Expert political judgment: How good is it and how can we know?* Princeton: Princeton University Press.

Tileagă, C. (2005). Accounting for extreme prejudice and legitimating blame in talk about the romanies. *Discourse and Society, 16*, 603–624.

Tileagă, C. (2007). Ideologies of moral exclusion: A critical discursive reframing of depersonalization, delegitimization and dehumanization. *British Journal of Social Psychology, 46*, 717–737.

Tileagă, C. (2008). What is a revolution? National commemoration, collective memory and managing authenticity in the representation of a political event. *Discourse and Society, 19,* 359–382.

Tileagă, C. (2009). The social organization of representations of history: The textual accomplishment of coming to terms with the past. *British Journal of Social Psychology, 48,* 337–355.

Tileagă, C. (2011). (Re)writing biography: Memory, identity, and textually mediated reality in coming to terms with the past. *Culture and Psychology, 17,* 197–215.

Tileagă, C. (2013). *Political psychology: Critical perspectives.* Cambridge: Cambridge University Press.

Tileagă, C. (2015). *The nature of prejudice: Society, discrimination and moral exclusion.* London: Routledge.

Tileagă, C. (2019). Communicating misogyny: An interdisciplinary research Agenda for social psychology. *Social and Personality Psychology Compass, 13*(7). https://doi.org/10.1111/spc3.12491

Tileagă, C., & Byford, J. (2014). *Psychology and History: Interdisciplinary Explorations.* Cambridge: Cambridge University Press.

Tileagă, C., & Stokoe, E. (2015). *Discursive psychology: Classic and contemporary issues.* London: Routledge.

Tversky, A., & Kahneman, D. (1981). The framing of decisions and the psychology of choice. *Science, 211,* 453–458.

van Dijk, T. A. (1988). *News as discourse.* Erlbaum.

van Dijk, T. A. (1989). Mediating racism: The role of media in the reproduction of racism. In R. Wodak (Ed.), *Language, power and ideology.* Amsterdam: John Benjamins.

van Dijk, T. A. (1991). *Racism and the press.* Routledge.

van Dijk, T. A. (2008). *Discourse and context: A sociocognitive approach.* Cambridge: Cambridge University Press.

van Dijk, T. A. (2009). *Society and discourse: How social context influence text and talk.* Cambridge University Press.

Valentino, N. A., & Nardis, Y. (2013). Political communication: Form and consequence of the information environment. In L. Huddy, D. O. Sears, & J. S. Levy (Eds.), *The Oxford handbook of political psychology* (pp. 559–590). New York: Oxford University Press.

Wetherell, M., & Potter, J. (1992). *Mapping the language of racism: Discourse and the legitimation of exploitation.* Harvester Wheatsheaf.

Whitehead, K., & Stokoe, E. (2015). Producing and responding to -isms in interaction. *Journal of Language and Social Psychology, 34*(4), 368–373.

Wilson, J. (1990). *Politically speaking: The pragmatic analysis of political language.* Oxford: Blackwell.

Wittgenstein, L. (1953). *Philosophical investigations.* Oxford: Blackwell.

Wodak, R. (1989). *Language, power and ideology: Studies in political discourse.* Amsterdam: John Benjamins.

Wodak, R. (2002). Friend or Foe: The defamation or legitimate and necessary criticism? Reflections on recent political discourse in Austria. *Language and Communication, 22,* 495–517.

Wodak, R. (2011). *The discourse of politics in action: Politics as usual.* London: Palgrave.

Part 1

Political Communication of Contentious Politics

2

Accusations and Denials of Racism in Dialogical Context

Stephen Gibson

Introduction

Much recent social psychological work on prejudice and racism has been characterised by a conceptual richness that has begun to move beyond some of the more individualistically oriented approaches which characterised earlier work. This has recently led to the suggestion that the discipline is at a point where it might be able to move 'beyond prejudice' (Dixon and Levine 2012), or in other words beyond the assumption that some form of individual process of judgement ('prejudice') lies at the root of myriad forms of social exclusion, oppression and disadvantage (see also Howarth and Hook 2005 and Tileagă 2016). A major aspect of this shift has involved the theorising of racism as a social accomplishment rather

---

I would like to acknowledge the research assistance of Rachael Booth in the project on which this chapter is based, which also benefitted from funding from the British Psychological Society.

S. Gibson (✉)
Heriot-Watt University, Edinburgh, UK
e-mail: S.gibson@hw.ac.uk

© The Author(s), under exclusive license to Springer Nature Switzerland AG 2020
M. A. Demasi et al. (eds.), *Political Communication*, Palgrave Studies in Discursive
Psychology, https://doi.org/10.1007/978-3-030-60223-9_2

than as an individual cognitive process. At the empirical level, researchers adopting the analytic tools of discursive and rhetorical psychologies (Billig 1996; Potter and Wetherell 1987) have sought to work through the implications of such a view of racism and have produced a voluminous literature on the way in which racism is enacted in talk and text (for reviews, see Augoustinos and Every 2007 and Goodman 2014).

Augoustinos and Every (2007) outlined five key findings from this literature, all of which revolve around the well-established idea that discursive actors seek to avoid the implication that they may be racist, xenophobic or otherwise prejudiced. First, racism is the subject of explicit denial (van Dijk 1992), exemplified in the form of the classic disclaimer, 'I'm not racist, but…'. Such denials serve as an attempt to inoculate the speaker against anticipated charges of racism and signal that a speaker is orienting to what they are about to say as being potentially hearable as racist. Second, people work up their claims as being grounded in external, observable reality. This construction of factuality (Potter 1996) functions to militate against the inference that one's views are the product of irrational prejudice but are instead a rational outcome of observing the world-as-it-is. Third, the self is presented positively, whilst the other is presented negatively. Notably, the speaker or a group of which the speaker is a member (e.g. 'we British') is presented as tolerant and reasonable. In contrast, it is the intolerance and unreasonableness of the other that makes their exclusion necessary. Fourth, discursive deracialisation refers to the downplaying or removal of 'race' categories from discourse which constructs negative images of minority groups. Thus, arguments against immigration might be presented as having nothing to do with 'race', but as instead being based solely around, for example, economic concerns. Finally, the use of liberal principles such as freedom, choice, equality and individualism can be identified in many cases where the upshot of the argument is to deny that racism is a problem, or to maintain a status quo characterised by racist social policies.

Over a decade since Augoustinos and Every's (2007) review, these five core findings can be understood as the foundations of the first wave of research on discourse and racism. Subsequent work has sought to expand on this, with a focus on how racism is denied accompanied by a concern for how accusations of racism are made and responded to and a concern for the dialogical nature of race and racism, which has led to increasing analytic attention being paid to the way in which social actors treat particular utterances as racist.

Accusations of Racism

In his classic exposition of the way in which the denial of racism has become a defining feature of new racism, van Dijk (1992) also drew attention to the difficulties in making accusations of racism. Yet it is only relatively recently that the analytic implications of this observation have come to be fully spelled out, with a number of empirical studies exploring in detail how accusations of racism are made and avoided (Augoustinos and Every 2010). For example, Riggs and Due (2010) considered a high-profile example of racism on the UK television programme *Celebrity Big Brother* and noted how interviews with those accused of racism in fact avoided making direct accusations of racism, instead using terms such as 'bullying'. There is clearly an interactional difficulty in making a direct accusation of racism—it is a highly face-threatening act that rides roughshod over norms of politeness—and yet Riggs and Due note that there is a more ideological dimension to the indirectness of these accusations. Specifically, they suggest that the interviewer

> is rendered complicit in the relationships of power which enable racism to continue unchecked by not naming it as a relationship between privilege and disadvantage, whereby those of us who occupy privileged locations within racial hierarchies stand to benefit from them, regardless of our individual intent. (Riggs and Due 2010, p. 269)

Other research has explored the way in which those accused of racism have responded. For example, in his analysis of the construction of racism in debates concerning asylum and immigration in the UK, Goodman (2010) quotes a newspaper article by Robert Kilroy-Silk, a former Labour Member of Parliament and television personality whose media career foundered after he became the subject of controversy over anti-Islamic comments. In response to his castigation for his original remarks, Kilroy-Silk responded:

38   S. Gibson

> The trouble with this country is that we are not allowed to tell the truth about certain things – such as immigration, asylum, multiculturalism and race – without being pilloried. But straight talk is needed. (Goodman 2010, p. 7)

Thus, the problem is not constructed as being racism itself, but rather the existence of taboos against the discussion of certain topics. In invoking race, immigration and so on, readers are told that such topics are typically beyond what one is allowed to discuss. Liberal values of free speech and the dangers of censorship are instead foregrounded, and the alternative view—Kilroy-Silk's own—is constructed in factual terms: it is the unpalatable but necessary 'truth'. Somewhat ironically, the very invocation of a taboo against speaking about these matters appears to function as a device for warranting extensive discussion of the subject, while also looking to stifle criticism.

Importantly, this concern with accusations highlights the way in which the analytical purview of research on racist discourse has been expanded in recent years, a project that has been developed most fully in the work of Susan Condor (2006; Condor et al. 2006; Condor and Figgou 2012).

A Dialogical Perspective

As Condor (2006) has noted, much of the early social psychological work on racist discourse tended to focus on individual actors 'dodging the identity of prejudice' (Wetherell and Potter 1992, p. 211) on their own behalf. Such work thus implicitly assumed a focus on the individual even at the same time as it sought to challenge the individualistic assumptions of social-cognitive approaches. By contrast, Condor (2006; Condor et al. 2006) has drawn on a number of key analytic resources—most notably the work of Goffman (e.g. 1981)—to argue for the exploration of how racism is produced dialogically:

> a consideration of the process by which charges of racism are made, accepted, challenged, denied or ignored in the course of social interaction might afford a perspective in which the status of any particular utterance, action or event as 'racist' or 'prejudiced' may itself be treated as a social accomplishment. (Condor et al. 2006, p. 445)

2 Accusations and Denials of Racism in Dialogical Context   39

More recent studies of racist discourse have indeed begun to explore the dialogical context in which the status of utterances as racist or prejudiced becomes a participants' concern (e.g. Durrheim et al. 2016; Every and Augoustinos 2007; Figgou and Condor 2006; Gibson 2017; Goodman and Rowe 2014; Whitehead and Stokoe 2015). For example, Whitehead (2015) analysed the way in which racism was responded to in a corpus of talk radio data. In many cases the hosts of the talk shows could effectively provide callers with the benefit of the doubt and in doing so work collaboratively with them to enable them to downgrade hearably racist complaints. However, in other cases that benefit of the doubt could be withheld or withdrawn.

Condor (2006) also highlights how the same utterance can perform multiple functions across the differing contexts in which it is presented. For example, she notes how a sample of racist discourse reproduced in a social scientific paper can—somewhat paradoxically—be seen to perform an *anti-racist* function by virtue of its very reproduction in the context of a critique of racist discourse. This can be understood in terms of Leudar and Nekvapil's (2004) notion of dialogical networks. This concept, developed in the study of political argumentation in the media, highlights the ways in which dialogical analysis needs not only to engage with the discourse produced in a single context but also with the ways in which contexts can relate to one another, with intertextual references considered as part of a wider network:

> Politicians and other individuals speaking on a theme in the media frequently address others who are not present. The media are networked in that newspapers report what has been said on the radio or television, and people 'on the air' refer to newspaper reports. (Leudar and Nekvapil 2004, p. 248)

This points back to Goffman's (1981) ideas about the multiplicity of audiences in any given setting. Thus, as Leudar and Nekvapil (2004, p. 248) note, 'Participants are sometimes involved in two "conversations" at the same time – with those present and those absent'.

In the present chapter, I want to flesh out some of these ideas through the use of an example of a political debate in which the racist (or

40   S. Gibson

otherwise) status of a third party becomes the object of debate. The case is drawn from a wider project that focussed on political discourse in the UK's 2015 General Election.

The Research Context

The 2015 UK General Election was notable—amongst other things—for the relatively large number of votes cast for the radical right-wing United Kingdom Independence Party (UKIP) under the leadership of Nigel Farage. Founded in 1993 as an avowedly anti-European Union party, UKIP had grown in prominence during the years leading up to 2015, in part as a result of the Liberal Democrats—who had previously been the 'third party' in UK politics—becoming partners in coalition government with the Conservatives (Ford and Goodwin 2014). With UKIP having won the largest share of the vote in the UK's 2014 European Parliamentary elections ('UK European election results' 2014), the Conservatives made a commitment in their General Election manifesto to hold a referendum on the UK's membership of the European Union. Although UKIP's 12.6% share of the vote was their largest ever at a General Election, it only resulted in one member of parliament, and the decision to offer the referendum was seen by some commentators as instrumental in the Conservatives winning a slim overall majority (Cowley and Kavanagh 2016).

UKIP's election campaign was notable for its focus on immigration and in particular for the way in which the party linked arguments for a reduction in immigration with their longstanding aim of withdrawing the UK from membership of the EU. While this drew criticism from opponents, focussing on EU membership has been described as providing a 'reputational shield' for UKIP (Ivarsflaten, cited in Ford and Goodwin 2014, p. 198) in that it has generally been considered a legitimate topic for debate in British politics and is thus a useful inoculation against potential accusations of prejudice. Indeed, UKIP has turned such accusations around in order to position mainstream politicians as out-of-touch. This is illustrated in UKIP's 2015 election manifesto, which highlighted two high-profile occasions on which British Prime Ministers had made accusations of racism:

2 Accusations and Denials of Racism in Dialogical Context 41

> Surveys consistently show immigration as one of the top three issues for voters. Yet, instead of listening, the old parties have responded with insults and contempt: even our prime ministers have labelled good, decent people 'closet racists' and 'bigots.' Immigration is not about race; it is about space. Immigrants are not the problem; it is the current immigration system that is broken. (UKIP 2015, p. 11)

The quotes from David Cameron ('closet racists') and Gordon Brown ('bigots') are attributed only to 'our prime ministers', indicating that readers are not expected to require any reminder of the context of these remarks.[1] Taken together, they function to demonstrate UKIP's claim that both major parties not only have failed to control immigration but have dismissed and besmirched 'good, decent people' in the process.

The analytic goal of the wider project was to explore how immigration was discussed in broadcast political debates during the election campaign, with a specific focus on how UKIP's position was constructed, challenged and defended (see Gibson and Booth 2018). In line with previous research, it was apparent that accusations of racism were indeed made indirectly and that responses to those accusations emphasised rationality, objectivity and factuality. However, in contrast to much previous research (Augoustinos and Every 2007; Goodman 2014), it was found that UKIP typically avoided negative evaluations of outgroups and instead sought to reject any implication that their position on immigration had anything to do with a dislike of outgroups. The present chapter explores these issues in the context of an extended case example from a broadcast political debate.

Empirical Example

My example is taken from an episode of the British Broadcasting Corporation's radio programme *Any Questions?*, broadcast on BBC Radio 4 on 13 March 2015. *Any Questions?* is a long-established political

---

[1] In 2006, David Cameron described UKIP supporters as 'fruitcakes, loonies and closet racists, mostly' ('UKIP demands apology from Cameron' 2006); in 2010, Gordon Brown referred to a member of the public, who had asked him questions about—amongst other things—immigration, as a 'bigoted woman' (see 'Gordon Brown "bigoted woman" comment caught on tape' 2010).

discussion programme, in which a panel of politicians and other commentators discuss political issues of the day in response to questions from members of a studio audience. The edition considered here is chaired by Jonathan Dimbleby, who was the regular host of the programme between 1987 and 2019, and features on the panel Ken Clarke (a former Conservative Chancellor of the Exchequer and at the time still a Member of Parliament), Suzanne Evans (then Deputy Chairman [sic] of UKIP), Tim Farron (a Liberal Democrat MP who had previously served as the President of his party and who would go on to lead it between 2015 and 2017) and Phil Redmond (a television writer and producer).

The stretch of discussion that concerns us here followed from the first question asked by an audience member, 'are anti-discrimination laws no longer needed?' This was itself a reference to a then-current controversy that had arisen as a result of comments made by Nigel Farage, UKIP's leader, in a television documentary made by Trevor Phillips—a former head of the Commission for Racial Equality and its successor the Equality and Human Rights Commission—in which Farage had suggested that he would favour the removal of many of the UK's anti-discrimination laws. Extract 2.1 is taken from the point immediately after Dimbleby has invited Farron to open the debate:

Extract 2.1

```
1  TF   (.h) yeah I er (.) >s- I was (.) on the road in<
2       (.) my (.) patch yesterday? (.) on the way up to: er
3       (.) Grasmere and I heard the (.h) er interview (.)
4       erm (.) er with Nigel Farage and he's claimed obviously
5       since that he was misreported and misquoted (.h) he
6       absolutely wasn't (.h) >er it< was very clear:
7       what he meant (.) and what he said (.h) er in
8       politics sometimes (.) you get people (.) very
9       often on the f- o-o (.) on the very right end of
10      (.h) British politics who will use (.h) what we call
11      (.) d-dog whistle messages (.h) >in other words<
12      subtle↑ (.) pretty nasty messages (.h) to be picked
13      up by a certain (.h) er audience shall we say (.h)
14      this was not dog whistle politics this was foghorn
15      politics (.h)  this  is  about    making  abso-
        lutely clear
```

2 Accusations and Denials of Racism in Dialogical Context   43

```
16      (.h) where (.) Nigel Farage's Party stands (.h) on the
17      issue >of a< diverse (.) and racially equal Britain
18      (.) the notion that we don't now need (.h) race
19      equality laws in the workplace >or anywhere else<
20      (.h) is absolutely nonsense (.h) and utterly (.)
21      offensive and it is a reminder (.h) that nationalists
22      of all kind (.h) are a huge danger to our country
23      because it's al- (.) nationalism is all: about (.h)
24      pitting one group (.h) against another (.h) rather
25      than all of us (as) standing together to try and
26      make a better Britain (.h) that we can all get behind
```

It is notable that Farron opens his turn by working up a description of how he came to hear of Farage's statements. His opening description of himself as having heard the interview while 'on the road in my patch yesterday' (lines 1–2) functions as a device for legitimating Farron's claims based on the fact that he has actually heard the interview himself (and thus is not, for example, reacting to second-hand glosses on Farage's statements; Pomerantz 1984). Farron is then able to position himself as challenging Farage's claims to have been 'misreported and misquoted', and he goes on to do this through a series of extreme case formulations (lines 5–6: 'he absolutely wasn't'; line 6: 'it was very clear'; lines 8–9 'very often'; line 9: 'the very right'; Pomerantz 1986). He subsequently uses the term 'dog whistle politics' to describe the way in which right-wing politicians may subtly seek to communicate 'pretty nasty messages' to 'a certain audience' (lines 11–13), but rejects this as inadequate to describe Farage's comments, which he instead glosses as 'foghorn politics'. Farron rejects Farage's and UKIP's position, describing it as 'absolutely nonsense and utterly offensive', and suggests that it makes it 'absolutely clear' what UKIP's position is regarding 'the issue of a diverse and racially equal Britain' (lines 16–17).

Here, then, we have a set of circumstances which would appear to be highly conducive to an accusation of racism. The topic of discussion is clearly and unambiguously related to matters of 'race', and Farron presents particularly strident criticisms of UKIP and Farage. And yet there is no straightforward, unambiguous accusation of racism. Instead, Farron describes UKIP as 'nationalists' who are concerned with 'pitting one group against another'. Moreover, though Farron states that UKIP's position on diversity and racial equality is 'absolutely clear', he does not specify what that position actually is. On the one hand, this highlights the extent to which Farron can treat his arguments as common sense and thus rely on his audiences to understand what he is saying. On the other hand, however, this highlights the potential delicacy of direct accusations, even if the person who is being accused (in this case, Farage) is not physically present.

Condor et al. (2006) note that speakers not only manage their own identities but the identities of others, and in this example it is Suzanne Evans, representing UKIP, who is in the position of having to respond to Farron's comments:

Extract 2.2

```
1  SE (.h) thank you (.h) erm (.) Nigel was asked a
2     question he wasn't involved in dog whistle
3     politics (.) he was doing an interview and >he was
4     actually doing the interview< that (.) took
5     place quite some few months ago (.h) he was
6     asked in UKIP (.) land (.) he wasn't asked in
7     reality as much as I like the sound of UKIP land
8     (.h) I don't think we're ever going to have (.)
9     UKIP land (.h) erm (.) and (.) he wasn't talking
10    about race (.) he was talking about nationality
11    (.h) and I think what I find (.) particularly
12    worrying (.) about what's happened over the last
13    couple of days (.h) is that when Nigel said
14    British (.h) the media heard the words (.) white
15    (.h) now (.) we are not (.) white (.) British (.)
16    anymore (.) across the patch (.h) and haven't
17    been (.) probably since about the: fifteenth
18    century (.h) British (.h) is a combination of all
19    colours (.h) creeds (.h) religions (.) and UKIP as
20    much as any other political party in Britain completely
21    (.) welcomes that
```

Here we see Evans defending Farage and articulating—on behalf of UKIP as a whole—a rejection of the principle and desirability of racial homogeneity. This account can be understood in terms of the dialogical

2 Accusations and Denials of Racism in Dialogical Context   45

frameworks of Condor (2006) and Leudar and Nekvapil (2004). Following Condor et al. (2006), we have a speaker who denies racism not on behalf of herself as an individual, but on behalf of another individual. However, this other individual is not physically co-present, but rather his words are re-constructed here in the form of a dialogical network through which the Phillips-Farage interview is made to 'speak' to, and is the subject of contestation within, the present debate (Leudar and Nekvapil 2004).

Evans first seeks to contextualise Farage's comments by asserting that he 'was asked a question' and that 'he was doing an interview … that took place quite some few months ago' (lines 1–5). This puts Farage's comments in a particular genre of talk and places the emphasis on the question(s) to which he was responding as much as the content of what Farage himself said. The temporal reference also seeks to position the comments as possibly out-of-date in an attempt to suggest that the criticism of Farage is also outdated. The relevance of the invocation of this context then becomes clearer as Evans states that 'he was asked in UKIP land he wasn't asked in reality' (lines 5–7). This refers to a particular phrase used in the interview by Phillips (*UKIP land*) in an attempt to gloss Farage's comments as referring to a hypothetical world in which everything could be organised according to UKIP's principles (for more on the use of hypotheticals in political discourse, see Demasi 2019). Evans goes on to de-emphasise 'race' by suggesting that 'he wasn't talking about race he was talking about nationality', thus denying racism on the grounds that one cannot be accused of racism if one is not explicitly dealing with matters of 'race'. Such rhetorical moves can be understood as examples of discursive deracialisation and are familiar from studies of new racism in which categories of 'race' are replaced with categories of nation (Augoustinos and Every 2007; Reeves 1983).

However, from line 11 Evans changes tack and moves from a defensive positioning to work up an accusation of her own. Evans attributes the hearing of Farage's comments as being concerned with 'race' to the media. This serves as an implicit accusation of racism insofar as it censures the media for equating 'British' with 'white', and Evans then works up UKIP's non-racist credentials by constructing a multicultural version of British identity (ll. 18–19) which 'UKIP as much as any other political party in Britain completely welcomes'. What is striking about this is that it involves an appropriation of the language of multiculturalism and anti-racism. Not only are strategies of deracialisation employed, but the accusation of racism is turned on its head—it is those who criticise who should, in fact, be challenged on the grounds of equating Britishness with whiteness. This is not the well-worn trope of anti-racism having gone too far, or of whites being victims of a 'reverse racism' (e.g. Johnson and Goodman 2013; Wood and Finlay 2008), but is instead a right-wing politician, representing a party that argues for strict controls on immigration, suggesting that her party embraces multicultural Britain and that it is 'the media' who are in fact racist (although, again, note that no direct accusation of racism is actually made). Such strategies were used time and again in the wider dataset from which this example is drawn (Gibson and Booth 2018).

However, a short while later, Evans continues by adopting precisely some of those familiar strategies of right-wing political discourse identified in previous research (e.g. Johnson and Goodman 2013; Wood and Finlay 2008), but attributes them to Trevor Phillips:

Extract 2.3

```
1  SE =and let me make it absolutely clear (.h)
2     he UKIP manifesto (.) which I'm writing (.h)
3     ill not be abolishing (.) discrimination (.)
4     of any kind (.h) it will absolutely (.) stand up
5     (.h) and reiterate the (.) universal declaration
6     of human rights (.) which I'm sure every one of us
7     in this room (.h) is very proud to have and very
8     happy to sign up to (.h) >and I think< what we've
9     had here is a situation and Trevor Phillips (.h)
10    er (.) who was actually making this programme
11    has said it his- his self (.h) we have got
12    so obsessed (.) with anti-racism now (.h) of
13    trying to- to weed out racism >wherever (we
14    find)< it and these are his words he said we've
15    developed this ugly (.) new doctrine that has
16    endangered lives (.h) and encouraged abuse (.h) and
17    we only have to look at various other issues like
18    we've had all manner (.h) of child sex abuse cases
19    (.h) when a deliberate↑ blind eye was turned to
```

2 Accusations and Denials of Racism in Dialogical Context   47

```
20    the issues of race (.h) now my concern is (.h) is
21    that (.) stopped (.) girls getting help (.h) er: it
22    has shut down debate (.h) and (.) the whole (.)
23    reason Trevor Phillips was making this programme
24    (.h) it was to ask that question (.) why won't we
25    discuss race (.) anymore (.h) and we have seen a
26    very classic example of why we don't discuss race
27    anymore because when people talk about it and they
28    actually have a debate about it (.h) e- it there
29    is this hu- torrent (.) of vile abuse that comes out
```

Evans works up UKIP's continued commitment to anti-discrimination legislation and invokes the universal declaration of human rights, constructing consensus with 'every one of us in this room'.[2] Moreover, she draws on category entitlement (Sacks 1995) in order to position herself as having a particular authority to be able to make these claims (line 2: 'the UKIP manifesto *which I'm writing*'). Subsequently, however, she constructs the nature of the problem not as racism, but rather as *anti-racism*. In suggesting that 'we have got so obsessed with anti-racism' (lines 11–12), Evans implies a lack of rationality (*obsession*) clouding the collective judgement. However, though she begins by speaking from a personal footing (lines 8–9: 'I think what we've had here…'; Goffman 1981), in order to inoculate herself against charges of racism, she also attributes this position to Trevor Phillips, thus aligning herself with his views (Dickerson 1997). Evans then invokes child sex abuse cases in which 'a deliberate blind eye was turned to issues of race' (lines 19–20), again making it clear that this is not only her own, or UKIP's, position but also that of Phillips—a noted anti-racism campaigner. This formulation not only involves a form of moral hierarchy, with the sexual abuse of children trumping racism, but also implies that race is actually a factor in some child sex abuse cases. In this context, Evans describes what has happened following Farage's comments as 'a very classic example of why we don't discuss race anymore' (lines 25–27). She works up a contrast between

---

[2] In context, her comment on lines 2–4 that the UKIP election manifesto will 'not be abolishing discrimination of any kind' can be heard as referring to anti-discrimination *legislation*. In other words, she was not suggesting that *discrimination* would not be abolished, but that *anti-discrimination laws* would not be abolished.

48   S. Gibson

people who 'talk about it and they actually have a debate' and the resulting 'torrent of vile abuse' (ll. 27–29). Those who wish to discuss race are thus merely wishing to engage in reasonable debate, whereas their opponents are irrationally and unreasonably spewing abuse. The image of anti-racism as the *real* problem is thus complete, with the *real* abuse not being racism itself, but those who accuse others of racism.

However, the debate does not end there, and Evans's remarks do not go unchallenged. In the following extract, the then Conservative MP Ken Clarke makes further veiled accusations, but like Farron in Extract 2.1, he does so without making an explicit accusation of racism:

Extract 2.4

```
1   KC   w-w-w-well (.) personally I-I think (.) straight to
2        answer the question yes we do (.) I think we are
3        the most tolerant (.) and: er (.h) er: (.) most
4        inclusive society (.) in >western Europe< (.)
5        we're very tolerant (.) to visitors↑ (.h) but
6        there's a minority >of the< population who are
7        bigoted (.h) and prejudiced (.) and a society like
8        ours (.) nee-needs the equality laws↓ (.) it's absurd
9        (.h) to say: (.) that we (.) don't er (.) we also
10       need  very  strict  (.)  c-controls  (.)  on  immi-
         gration (.)
11       combined (.) with a sensible approach to the needs of
12       a modern economy and the globalised economy (.h)
13       er and (.) we're very good at welcoming people who're
14       doing jobs we want (.) taking (.) p-working in
15       international companies (.h) people who come here
16       to work (.) people who behave themselves (.)
17       people who contribute (.h) er and obviously we'd all
18       like to deter people (.h) who are coming here for
19       (.h) reasons that aren't (.) very helpful (.h) th-
20       tha-tha-tha (.) both those are statements of the
21       obvious (.) I think (.h) on the question of what
22       Nigel said (.) textual analysis doesn't (.) really
23       what er (.h) w-what is called for (.) I think (.h)
24       I mean firstly I think (.) Nigel Farage (.) er
25       does sometimes just speak off the top of his head
26       (.h) er he's having a whale of a time
27       [you know he (.) he-he never=]
```

2 Accusations and Denials of Racism in Dialogical Context   49

```
28  SE  [you've never done that of course have you]
29  KC  =not of course he never (.) he never expected to
30      be er in the public eye: like this he loves it (.h)
31      a-a-[and: so he's just enjoying himself        ]
32  Au  ((laughter 3 secs))]
33  KC  (.h) he has no particular policies on most things
34      [(.h) e- he-he-he (.) he-he (.) he-he doe-     ]
35  Au  [((laughter 3 secs))                ]
36  KC  he does have a view: (.) about race and immigration
37      though there is the dog whistle effect to use the
38      (.h) th-the jargon which er: I quite agree Tim's
39      already used he he (.h) h-he-he-he-he: he li- he
40      likes to (.h) r-right let's face it (.) t-he
41      core of his vote is all those people who used
42      to vote for BNP and the en- English
43      [national defence league (.h)]
44  SE  [oh that's not true Ken] you kep-
45      [that's a ridiculous]=
46  KC  [(the- they do all-)]
47  SE  [=statement to make (.h) you=]
48  KC  [they vanished cause they all vote-]
49  SE  =have no idea
50  KC  [they all- they all vote for you=]
51  SE  [(.h) and as you very well know    ]
52  KC  =and some of their activists work for you
53      [( ) (.) the-the↑-]
54  SE  [ the reason UKIP] exists is because
55      [precisely of people like you:]
```

Clarke begins by referring back to the initial question concerning whether anti-discrimination laws are needed by suggesting that 'yes we do' need them (line 2), and he builds on this initial invocation of the collective deixical referent *we* (Billig 1995) by subsequently constructing an image of *us* as 'the most inclusive society in western Europe' (lines 3–4). This then allows him to frame anti-discrimination laws as being needed not because 'we' are habitually racist and discriminatory, but rather because of a 'minority of the population who are bigoted and prejudiced' (lines 6–7). This direct attribution of bigotry and prejudice may be unusual, but it is notable that it is attributed not to any specific individual or group, but to a vaguely defined minority. As Condor et al. (2006,

p. 445) noted, in exploring the dialogical context of racism, we adopt 'a perspective in which the status of any particular utterance, action or event as "racist" or "prejudiced" may itself be treated as a social accomplishment', and Clarke's formulation here individualises discrimination by framing it as being the result of a small number of people who possess these undesirable psychological characteristics. Thus in making an argument in favour of anti-discrimination legislation (and indeed in characterising opposition to it as 'absurd'), Clarke nevertheless works up a description of racism and discrimination as a minority problem set against the backdrop of a fundamentally non-racist society.

Having set out his position in favour of anti-discrimination legislation, he then goes on to assert the need for 'very strict controls on immigration' (line 10) but which allow a 'sensible approach to the needs of a modern economy' (lines 11–12). He develops this point further over the next few lines, building a contrast between categories of good and bad immigrants (lines 14–19; Augoustinos and Every 2007). He then concludes that his points thus far are 'statements of the obvious' (lines 20–21), thus framing his views regarding both the necessity of anti-discriminations laws and a strict but sensible approach to immigration controls as common sense. Addressing Farage's comments directly, he frames them as unsubtle in that 'textual analysis' (line 22) is not needed to interrogate their meaning. Instead, he works up an image of Farage as unthinkingly 'speak[ing] off the top of his head' and 'having a whale of a time' (lines 25–26). In this rendering, Farage is not a serious politician, but someone who 'never expected to be in the public eye' and is thus simply 'enjoying himself' (lines 29–31). This serves to undermine Farage's stake in the debate in that he is positioned as having no principled commitment to any particular course of action (Edwards and Potter 1992). In the midst of this characterisation of Farage, the first challenge from Evans is received as she implicitly chides Clarke for having double standards (line 28). Continuing his theme, Clarke suggests that Farage has 'no particular policies on most things' (line 33), before alighting upon the issue once again of 'race and immigration', on which he asserts that Farage 'does have a view' (line 36). He refers back to, and agrees with, Farron's earlier criticism of Farage's use of the 'dog whistle effect' before prefacing his elaboration on this with a bottom-line formulation (line 40: 'let's face it'; Potter 1996). Clarke

2 Accusations and Denials of Racism in Dialogical Context 51

subsequently suggests that UKIP have attracted the support of people on the extreme right (i.e. supporters of the British National Party and the English Defence League), which immediately attracts a rebuttal from Evans (line 44).

Again, we see what might be glossed as an accusation of racism that is delivered in such a way as to avoid making an explicit accusation of racism, and yet the immediacy and vociferousness of Evans's rebuttal (lines 44–45: 'that's not true'; 'ridiculous') indicates that the insinuation is not one that can be allowed to pass. Contrast, for example, the much milder response to the criticism directed at Farage's lack of seriousness (line 28). This is followed by an exchange in which the veracity of the statement regarding the far-right support for UKIP is further asserted by Clarke and challenged by Evans. Whereas Clarke suggests that these extremist parties have 'vanished' because of UKIP's success, Evans suggests Clarke is being disingenuous (line 51: '…as you very well know') and suggests instead that UKIP's popularity is instead a function of 'people like you' (line 55), indicating once again that it is those who would highlight racism as a problem who are, in fact, the problem.

Following this exchange, Clarke subsequently goes on to expand on his criticisms of Farage:

Extract 2.5

```
1   KC   there are things what he does: is he raises
2        (.h) it's very helpful to UKIP what's got them
3        going made them credible is raising (.h)
4        immigration (.) >and it's< very difficult
5        to have a sensible balanced (.) debate (.) about
6        the immigration in this country you'd think it's
7        easy (.h) to say we (.) gonna leave (.) out
8        people who are antisocial or have no right to be
9        here (.) but let in (.) and benefit those who our
10       economy needs but (.h) the the the it's hardly it's
11       a very difficult subject to have a sane conversation
12       on (.h) a-and (.) he LOVES arousing controversy
13       about it (.h) a-a-and then as you s- then a- as
14       you've heard from (.) my right from Suzanne who (.h)
15       I'm sure doesn't (.) share half of Nigel's views
16       (.h) er: but a-a-and is (.) very much nicer but the
```

```
17     (.) fact is
18  Au ((laughter 4 secs))
19  KC the the the the fact is y- then bring in all kinds
20     of reference to Asian gangs molesting women and how
21     we've taken anti-racism too far: and all the rest
22     of it
23  SE that was Trevor Phillips [said that not me]
24  KC [ that that keeps] your
25     hard line core vote
```

In the first part of Extract 2.5, Clarke argues that Farage, while motivated by a love of 'arousing controversy', has been able to make UKIP a 'credible' force by highlighting immigration. Clarke subsequently suggests that there are particular difficulties in having a 'sensible balanced debate about the immigration in this country' (lines 5–6), echoing his formula from Extract 2.4 about meeting the needs of the economy while excluding those who may be 'antisocial' or 'have no right to be here'. The implication is that Farage—who 'LOVES arousing controversy' (line 12)—is at least partly to blame for the difficulty in having a 'sane conversation'. In fleshing this out from line 13, he attends to one possible implication of his argument, which is that the criticisms of Farage could be taken as criticisms of Evans. To anticipate and inoculate against this, Clarke suggests that Evans is both 'very much nicer' than Farage and 'I'm sure doesn't share half of Nigel's views' (lines 14–16). This phrase in particular is striking in that it not only functions to avoid accusing Evans of holding the same views as Farage, but it does so while simultaneously implying that she may be being less than candid—she is defending Farage even though she does not, in fact, agree with him. In this respect, while Clarke's use of 'as you've heard from my right from Suzanne' makes Evans accountable for the statements attributed to Farage in that she has voiced them, she is not held accountable for holding the views implied by the statements themselves.

Despite this, when Clarke goes on to outline the statements that have aroused controversy (lines 19–22), Evans steps in to defend *herself*. However, she does so not by attributing the statements to Farage, but by attributing them to Trevor Phillips (line 23). Again, the deployment of Phillips is used to inoculate against implicit charges of racism (Dickerson

2 Accusations and Denials of Racism in Dialogical Context   53

1997), but this time Evans does so on her own behalf rather than UKIP as a party.

Following this exchange between Clarke and Evans, in the final extract we see Ken Clarke himself being held to account not for something he has said in this particular debate, but for a previous accusation of racism:

Extract 2.6

```
1   JD    can I just ask you this hold it (.h) can I ask
2         you this (.) you you (.) e- made it very clear:
3         (.) last year that you (.) shared the view that
4         was expressed (.) by David Cameron (.) some
5         time before that six years before that (.h)
6         that the Party (.h) er that UKIP (.) is full
7         of (.) am-amongst others er (.) fruitcakes loonies
8         and (.) closet racists
9   KC    I [didn't say that]
10  JD    [ erm (.) no no ] you
11        didn't but he said it and you said I've met
12        people in UKIP last year you said who
13        satisfy (.h) that description (.) closet
14        [racists]
15  Au    [((laughter 3 secs))]
16  KC    erm-
17  JD    do you-
18  KC    that was probably when I was last being pressed
19        for do you [agree with the Prime Minister=]
20  SE    [I tell you what I-]
21  KC    =but I↑ (.) w- all parties have a few: er people
22        [who fit that er: category (.h)]
23  SE    [I've met a few of the Tory Party Ken]
24  KC    absolutely (.h) but the-the the: the the-
25        the we- we're a broad church (.h) the-the
26        the: erm-
27  Au    ((laughter 3 secs))
28  KC    no no no but a-the the the the t-serious thing
29        about UKIP is it is (.h) it's one of these protest
30        Parties every Western democracy (.h) has about
31        fifteen twenty per cent of the population now (.h)
32        it's the Tea Party in America Le Pen it's
33        Syriza in- in Greece (.h) who (.) want to get off
34        (.) you know it's all the fault of the damn
```

```
35      politicians it's all the foreigners (.) it's
36      all Brussels (.h) there's nice simple solutions
37      (.h) er a- and actually the modern world which
38      I think is very exciting (.h) is one we've got to
39      join: (.) and reject that >and i-it< (.h) and we
40      happen to have a right wing nationalist one (.h)
41      Farage is a great campaigner (.) but he does go in
42      for dog whistle politics (.h) and he has ousted the
43      other rather nastier (.h) extreme right wing Parties
44      (.h) whose voters are now his core vote.
```

Dimbleby uses direct reported speech (Holt 1996) from David Cameron to suggest that Clarke has previously 'made it very clear' (line 2) that he agreed with Cameron's 'fruitcakes, loonies and closet racists' comment. This subtly implies that Clarke's criticisms of Farage may be accompanied by a more general impression of UKIP members as irrational and racist and provides a further example of the accountability of making an accusation of racism (Augoustinos and Every 2010). Clarke's immediate denial (line 9) is, in one sense, ambiguous in that it could be referring to the 'closet racists' comments (i.e. he is denying that he said the words attributed to Cameron), or it could be referring to the suggestion that he had 'made it very clear' that he agreed with the comments. Dimbleby pursues this by clarifying that he is not suggesting that Clarke had made the 'closet racists' comment, but—in a further use of direct reported speech, but this time *Clarke's* own speech—that he had concurred with Cameron. Indeed, it is notable that Dimbleby repeats only the term 'closet racists' (lines 13–14), indicating that it is the implication that UKIP members are racists—rather than mentally unstable—that is particularly accountable.

Clarke's response to this on lines 18–19 is telling—and rhetorically skilful—in that it neither rejects nor accepts Dimbleby's suggestion, but instead creates an impression of the remarks as attributable to stake and interest (Edwards and Potter 1992). By suggesting that his remarks may have been 'when I was last being pressed for do you agree with the Prime Minister', Clarke implies that he may simply have agreed with Cameron's statement because he was duty-bound to demonstrate agreement. The use of the term 'Prime Minister' (rather than using Cameron's name) is

2 Accusations and Denials of Racism in Dialogical Context   55

notable in that it makes relevant a relationship of authority (i.e. MPs of the same party are expected not to overtly disagree with their Prime Minister). The term 'pressed' is also potentially significant here as it implies that his remarks may have been a response to repeated and insistent questioning on the matter, creating an impression of his remarks as having been produced merely to satisfy journalists. Clarke then proceeds to minimise the apparent criticism of UKIP party members (lines 21–22) by suggesting that UKIP is not exceptional in having members who 'fit that category'. This is taken up by Evans who suggests that this is indeed true of the Conservative (Tory) Party (line 23), which is readily acknowledged by Clarke who then ironically draws on the notion of the party being a 'broad church', eliciting laughter from the audience. There is a rich tradition of scholarship on laughter and humour in political discourse (e.g. Billig 2005; Demasi and Tileagă 2019), and this use of humour functions to underplay any criticism of the Conservative Party, while also skilfully moving the debate even further away from Clarke's accusation of racism. Indeed, Clarke subsequently explicitly marks this exchange as non-serious (lines 28–29: 'but the serious thing about UKIP'), framing the preceding debate over the 'closet racists' remark as frivolous and insubstantial and allowing him to move on to provide his own analysis of UKIP's support which places it in the context of broader international social trends (lines 29–44). Space constraints prohibit a full analysis of this stretch of talk, but in working up this image of UKIP as part of a recognisable trend, he constructs the party's position as oversimplistic (line 36) and thereby at odds with the complex reality of 'the modern world' (line 37). Towards the end of the extract, Clarke remains critical of UKIP, but studiously avoids anything approaching a direct accusation of racism: UKIP is a 'right wing nationalist' party; Farage engages in 'dog whistle politics'; and UKIP has taken voters from other 'rather nastier extreme right wing parties'. The implication is again clear, but in skilfully moving away from the invitation to stand by what Dimbleby constructs as a previous more direct accusation of racism, Clarke again avoids explicitly labelling UKIP, its policies, its members, its leader or its voters as racist. Ultimately, this follows from Clarke's earlier image of racism as a matter of individual bigotry and prejudice (Extract 2.4) and ensures that while his criticisms of UKIP are strident, the party

56   S. Gibson

is nevertheless not explicitly treated as reaching the threshold required for it to be described as racist.

Discussion

The analysis of this extended sequence of debate highlights not only the difficulties for speakers who risk being accused of racism but also the difficulties faced by those who might seek to make such accusations. This analysis is, of course, only a single example from a single genre that prioritises dialogue and debate. In this respect, it is an ideal context in which to make the case for dialogical analysis. Yet a debate that could have focussed on whether policies advocated by Nigel Farage are racist becomes as much about the legitimacy of accusations of racism themselves. Racism is thus not simply a problem for Evans—who defends Farage—but also for Clarke, who is explicitly criticising Farage's policies on 'race and immigration'.

The use of a single extended case example allows for the debate to be followed through at greater length than might be possible in the typical empirical report, and this makes a number of broader observations possible. First, the analysis of accusations and denials of racism in dialogic context necessitates a focus on what, precisely, racism is taken to be at any given moment. As Condor et al. (2006, p. 445) noted, a focus on the dialogical construction and enactment of racism highlights that 'the status of any particular utterance, action or event as "racist" or "prejudiced" may itself be treated as a social accomplishment'. In this context, it is notable that Ken Clarke relies on an individualistic conception of prejudice and bigotry (Extract 2.4), whilst refraining from overtly labelling Farage, UKIP, or any specific utterance or action issued by them as racist. Moreover, we can note how even the most seemingly strident of criticisms, such as Farron's (Extract 2.1), stop short of making a direct accusation of racism.

This leads to a second observation, which is that in order to make sense of this debate, it is necessary to consider both the ideological and interactional structuring of discourse. The relative merits of micro and macro approaches to analysis have been debated at length over

2 Accusations and Denials of Racism in Dialogical Context 57

the years (e.g. Billig 1999; Wetherell 1998; Schegloff 1997, 1999; Weatherall 2016), and it is not my intention to rehearse these debates here. However, it is notable that both ideological and micro-analytic lenses are needed here in order to understand what is going on. There are clearly interactional norms against accusations of racism that arise as the function of the interactional trouble that may be occasioned by attributing such an opprobrious category. But equally, the ideological framing of racism as a matter of individual prejudice and/or bigotry means that labelling something as racist is, by definition, to impugn the morality of an individual. Indeed, these ideological assumptions of individualism underpin arguments on both sides of these debates, with exclusionary policies designed to limit immigration being tied to neoliberal ideas around individual merit and ability (Gibson and Booth 2018), just as critics challenge such policies as revealing the individual prejudices of their advocates. Here we can move from the analysis of how racism is understood to a suggestion for alternative understandings: if racism can be conceived in more social terms (e.g. as institutional racism, or as a cultural property), then to attribute racism may be less interactionally delicate. Such a possibility is, of course, a matter for empirical analysis, and future research would do well to explore how socio-cultural conceptions of racism are articulated and received.

Third, it is notable that in responding to implicit charges of racism, Evans not only defends herself, her party and its leader, but she turns the rhetorical tables, suggesting that it is those who criticise who are in fact racist (Extract 2.2). Two things are worthy of note about this: (1) Evans, like Farron and Clarke, makes this accusation implicitly—that is, she conforms to the general norm against accusations of racism; (2) in contrast to many analyses of how right-wing speakers and writers make counter-accusations of racism (e.g. Johnson and Goodman 2013; Wood and Finlay 2008), Evans does not suggest that white people are now victims of racism, but instead appropriates one of the tropes of anti-racism—that people treat the category 'British' as synonymous with 'white'—and attributes it to those in the media who are critical of UKIP. Yet by invoking Trevor Phillips, Evans is nevertheless able to rehearse some of the standard tropes of racist discourse (i.e. the linking of 'race' and paedophilia). Thus, Evans articulates the familiar argument of anti-racism having gone too far, whilst also adopting the very language of anti-racism in order to position UKIP's critics as racist.

Finally, the dialogical nature of the interaction is highlighted not only by the consideration of an extended example of broadcast political debate but by the intertextual nature of the discussion. The debaters are not simply debating with themselves, but are addressing their remarks to multiple audiences—Goffman's (1981) *ratified overhearers*—the physically present studio audience, the imagined public listening on the radio and their party colleagues (Condor 2006). The recipient design of their talk can therefore only be understood in terms of the immediate face-to-face interactional context *in combination* with a more distal—and necessarily more ill-defined—set of contexts. Moreover, physically present participants—Farron, Evans, Clarke and Dimbleby—are joined by rhetorically invoked figures such as Trevor Phillips, Nigel Farage and David Cameron. The views and utterances of the physically present debaters can be problematised, but similarly the utterances of these absent others are also a matter for contestation. They can be used to say things that might not otherwise be sayable, to manage stake and interest and to corroborate assertions. The debate can thus embed earlier texts (such as Phillips's interview with Farage) in a dialogical network (Leudar and Nekvapil 2004) that stretches beyond the confines of the particular stretch of talk under consideration. Indeed, as the dialogical perspective on racist discourse develops further, the next logical step is to use the networks approach to actually recover these disparate interactional episodes and explore the unfolding debate longitudinally—an approach which, with a few notable exceptions (e.g. Goodman et al. 2017; Popoviciu and Tileagă 2020), is relatively rare in discursive psychological research.

References

Augoustinos, M., & Every, D. (2007). The language of "Race" and prejudice: A discourse of Denial, reason, and liberal-practical politics. *Journal of Language and Social Psychology, 26,* 123–141. https://doi.org/10.1177/0261927X07300075

Augoustinos, M., & Every, D. (2010). Accusations and Denials of racism: Managing moral accountability in public discourse. *Discourse and Society, 21*, 251–256. https://doi.org/10.1177/0957926509360650

Billig, M. (1995). *Banal nationalism.* Sage Publications.

Billig, M. (1996). *Arguing and thinking: A rhetorical approach to social psychology* (2nd ed.). Cambridge University Press.

Billig, M. (1999). Whose terms? Whose ordinariness? Rhetoric and ideology in conversation analysis. *Discourse and Society, 10,* 543–558. https://doi.org/10.1177/0957926599010004005

Billig, M. (2005). *Laughter and ridicule: Towards a social critique of humour.* Sage Publications.

Condor, S. (2006). Public prejudice as collaborative accomplishment: Towards a dialogic social psychology of racism. *Journal of Community and Applied Social Psychology, 16,* 1–18. https://doi.org/10.1002/casp.845

Condor, S., & Figgou, L. (2012). Rethinking the prejudice problematic: A collaborative cognition approach. In J. Dixon & M. Levine (Eds.), *Beyond prejudice: Extending the social psychology of conflict, inequality and social change* (pp. 200–221). Cambridge University Press.

Condor, S., Figgou, L., Abell, J., Gibson, S., & Stevenson, C. (2006). "They're not racist": Prejudice denial, mitigation and suppression in dialogue. *British Journal of Social Psychology, 45,* 441–462. https://doi.org/10.1348/014466605X66817

Cowley, P., & Kavanagh, D. (2016). *The British general election of 2015.* Palgrave Macmillan.

Demasi, M. A. (2019). Facts as social action in political debates about the European Union. *Political Psychology, 40,* 3–20. https://doi.org/10.1111/pops.12496

Demasi, M. A., & Tileagă, C. (2019). Rhetoric of derisive laughter in political debates on the EU. *Qualitative Psychology.* Advance online publication. https://doi.org/10.1037/qup0000156

Dickerson, P. (1997). 'It's Not Just Me Who's Saying This…': The deployment of cited others in televised political discourse. *British Journal of Social Psychology, 36,* 33–48. https://doi.org/10.1111/j.2044-8309.1997.tb01117.x

Dixon, J., & Levine, M. (Eds.). (2012). *Beyond prejudice: Extending the social psychology of conflict, inequality and social change.* Cambridge University Press.

Durrheim, K., Quayle, M., & Dixon, J. (2016). The struggle for the nature of "Prejudice": "Prejudice" expression as identity performance. *Political Psychology, 37,* 17–35. https://doi.org/10.1111/pops.12310

Edwards, D., & Potter, J. (1992). *Discursive psychology*. Sage Publications.

Every, D., & Augoustinos, M. (2007). Constructions of racism in the Australian parliamentary debates on asylum seekers. *Discourse and Society, 18*, 411–436. https://doi.org/10.1177/0957926507077427

Figgou, L., & Condor, S. (2006). Irrational categorization, natural intolerance and reasonable discrimination: Lay representations of prejudice and racism. *British Journal of Social Psychology, 45*, 219–243. https://doi.org/10.134 8/014466605X40770

Ford, R., & Goodwin, M. (2014). *Revolt on the right: Explaining support for the radical right in Britain*. Routledge.

Gibson, S. (2017). Everyday politics, everyday racism: Censure and management of racist talk. In C. Howarth & E. Andreouli (Eds.), *The social psychology of everyday politics* (pp. 34–48). Routledge.

Gibson, S., & Booth, R. (2018). 'An Australian-Style Points System': Individualizing immigration in radical right discourse in the 2015 UK General Election Campaign. *Peace and Conflict: Journal of Peace Psychology, 24*, 389–397. https://doi.org/10.1037/pac0000267

Goffman, E. (1981). *Forms of talk*. Blackwell.

Goodman, S. (2010). "It's Not Racist to Impose Limits on Immigration": Constructing the boundaries of racism in the asylum and immigration debate. *Critical Approaches to Discourse Analysis Across Disciplines, 4*, 1–17.

Goodman, S. (2014). Developing an understanding of race talk. *Social and Personality Psychology Compass, 8*, 147–155. https://doi.org/10.1111/spc3.12095

Goodman, S., & Rowe, L. (2014). "Maybe it is Prejudice… But it is NOT Racism": Negotiating racism in discussion forums about gypsies. *Discourse and Society, 25*, 32–46. https://doi.org/10.1177/0957926513508856

Goodman, S., Sirriyeh, A., & McMahon, S. (2017). The evolving (Re)categorisations of refugees throughout the "Refugee/Migrant Crisis". *Journal of Community and Applied Social Psychology, 27*, 105–114. https://doi.org/10.1002/casp.2302

'Gordon Brown 'bigoted woman' comment caught on tape'. (2010). *BBC News*. Retrieved from http://news.bbc.co.uk/1/hi/8649012.stm

Holt, E. (1996). Reporting on talk: The use of direct reported speech in conversation. *Research on Language and Social Interaction, 29*, 219–245. https://doi.org/10.1207/s15327973rlsi2903_2

2 Accusations and Denials of Racism in Dialogical Context   61

Howarth, C., & Hook, D. (2005). Towards a critical social psychology of racism: Points of disruption. *Journal of Community and Applied Social Psychology, 15*, 425–431. https://doi.org/10.1002/casp.840

Johnson, A. J., & Goodman, S. (2013). Reversing racism and the elite conspiracy: Strategies used by the British National Party Leader in Response to Hostile Media Appearances. *Discourse, Context and Media, 2*, 156–164. https://doi.org/10.1016/j.dcm.2013.04.006

Leudar, I., & Nekvapil, J. (2004). Media dialogical networks and political argumentation. *Journal of Language and Politics, 3*, 247–266. https://doi.org/10.1075/jlp.3.2.06leu

Pomerantz, A. (1984). Giving a source or basis: The practice in conversation of telling 'How I Know'. *Journal of Pragmatics, 8*, 607–625. https://doi.org/10.1016/0378-2166(84)90002-X

Pomerantz, A. (1986). Extreme case formulation: A way of legitimizing claims. *Human Studies, 9*, 219–229. https://doi.org/10.1007/BF00148128

Popoviciu, S., & Tileagă, C. (2020). Subtle forms of racism in strategy documents concerning Roma inclusion. *Journal of Community and Applied Social Psychology, 30*, 85–102. https://doi.org/10.1002/casp.2430

Potter, J. (1996). *Representing reality: Discourse, rhetoric and social construction.* Sage Publications.

Potter, J., & Wetherell, M. (1987). *Discourse and social psychology: Beyond attitudes and behaviour.* Sage Publication.

Reeves, F. (1983). *British racial discourse: A study of British political discourse about race and race-related matters.* Cambridge University Press.

Riggs, D. W., & Due, C. (2010). The management of accusations of racism in *Celebrity Big Brother. Discourse and Society, 21*, 257–271. https://doi.org/10.1177/0957926509360652

Sacks, H. (1995). *Lectures on conversation.* Basil Blackwell.

Schegloff, E. A. (1997). Whose text? Whose context? *Discourse and Society, 8*, 165–187. https://doi.org/10.1177/0957926597008002002

Schegloff, E. A. (1999). Schegloff's texts as 'Billig's Data': A critical reply. *Discourse and Society, 10*, 558–572. https://doi.org/10.1177/0957926599010004006

Tileagă, C. (2016). *The nature of prejudice: Society, discrimination and moral exclusion.* Hove: Routledge.

'UK European election results'. (2014). *BBC News.* Retrieved fromhttps://www.bbc.co.uk/news/events/vote2014/eu-uk-results

UKIP. (2015). *Believe in Britain: UKIP Manifesto 2015.* Retrieved fromhttps://
d3n8a8pro7vhmx.cloudfront.net/ukipdev/pages/1103/attachments/origi-
nal/1429295050/UKIPManifesto2015.pdf

'UKIP demands apology from Cameron'. (2006). *BBC News.*Retrieved from
http://news.bbc.co.uk/1/hi/4875026.stm

van Dijk, T. A. (1992). Discourse and the Denial of Racism. *Discourse and
Society, 3,* 87–118. https://doi.org/10.1177/0957926592003001005

Weatherall, A. (2016). Interpretative repertories: Conversation analysis and
being critical. In C. Tileagă & E. Stokoe (Eds.), *Discursive psychology: Classic
and contemporary issues* (pp. 15–28). Routledge.

Wetherell, M. (1998). Positioning and interpretative repertoires: Conversation
analysis and post-structuralism in dialogue. *Discourse and Society, 9,* 387–412.
https://doi.org/10.1177/0957926598009003005

Wetherell, M., & Potter, J. (1992). *Mapping the language of racism.* Harvester
Wheatsheaf.

Whitehead, K. A. (2015). Everyday antiracism in action: Preference organization in responses to racism. *Journal of Language and Social Psychology, 34,*
374–389. https://doi.org/10.1177/0261927X15586433

Whitehead, K. A., & Stokoe, E. (2015). Producing and responding to *-isms* in
interaction. *Journal of Language and Social Psychology, 34,* 368–373. https://
doi.org/10.1177/0261927X15586432

Wood, C., & Finlay, W. M. L. (2008). British national party representations of
Muslims in the month after the London bombings: Homogeneity, threat,
and the conspiracy tradition. *British Journal of Social Psychology, 47,* 707–726.
https://doi.org/10.1348/014466607X264103

3

Lay Rhetoric on Brexit

Eleni Andreouli

Brexit Ruptures

In June 2016, in the UK's second[1] European Union membership referendum, British voters opted for leaving the EU. The vote was close, with 52% of the voters voting to leave against 48% voting to remain. Nonetheless, this was a surprising result: the leadership of the major political parties supported remaining in the EU, and most polls leading up to the vote suggested that Remain would win. Brexit, thus, has been taken to signify a rupture with "politics as usual".

Much has been written about the kind of rupture that the Brexit vote represents. On the one hand, Brexit is seen as representing a shift away

---

[1] The first EU membership referendum in the UK was in 1975 when remaining in what was at then the European Community (EC) won.

E. Andreouli (✉)
The Open University, Milton Keynes, UK
e-mail: eleni.andreouli@open.ac.uk

© The Author(s), under exclusive license to Springer Nature Switzerland AG 2020
M. A. Demasi et al. (eds.), *Political Communication*, Palgrave Studies in Discursive Psychology, https://doi.org/10.1007/978-3-030-60223-9_3

63

from the liberal establishment that has dominated politics over the past few decades. Brexit has been cast as a nationalistic and illiberal project, with academic research suggesting that support for leaving the EU is related with anti-immigration attitudes (Goodwin and Milazzo 2017) and with authoritarianism (Surridge 2019). But what is a sign of intolerance for some, for others it is a manifestation of democracy in action bringing the "will of the people" into the political centre stage.

The aim of the chapter is not to say which side of the argument is right or wrong. The chapter starts from a different premise: it sees politics as a field of contestation where multiple political agents, with diverse agendas, identities and power positions, struggle to institute their own versions of political reality. What is of significance from this perspective is not whether citizens should support leaving or remaining in the EU, but how particular versions of political reality are constructed to support particular political projects over others. Edelman's (1988) symbolic approach to politics is useful here. Edelman draws attention to political language and studies the ways in which political issues (such as social problems, leaders and enemies) are brought into existence through political rhetoric. For Edelman, political language is performative. It does not describe reality; it creates reality. Taking this point further, Edelman moreover argues that "this performative function of language is all the more potent in politics when it is masked, presenting itself as a tool for objective description" (1988, p. 115). Edelman's view of politics chimes with the approach of rhetorical psychology, which I will draw upon in this chapter.

In the following sections of the chapter, I will first discuss the "rise of the people" as a common explanatory narrative for the Brexit vote. I will then argue that, particularly in the current populist political climate, it is crucial that "what the people think" is studied in its depth and complexity, which, I argue, can be achieved with a rhetorical psychological approach. In the fourth and more substantive section, I discuss findings from a qualitative study on lay views on Europe and the European Union in the context of the 2016 referendum. In discussing these findings, I highlight both the entrenched polarities of Brexit and also the dilemmas and ambivalence of lay views on this issue. This analysis challenges an either/or understanding of Leave/Remain political positions and suggests that there are possibilities for creating new positions and moving beyond polarisation. In the final section, I conclude the chapter with some reflections on the implications of this work.

Explaining Brexit: The Rise of "the People"?

As a first step in understanding what led to Brexit, there has been a lot of work on the different characteristics of Leave and Remain voters. Leave voters have been often described as "left-behind" and "losers of globalisation". They have been found to be, on the whole, less educated, less ethnically diverse and older, and they tend to reside in smaller towns than cities. Remainers are the mirror image of that. They have been described as the "winners of globalisation": they have been found to be, overall, more educated and more ethnically diverse and they tend to live in cities rather than towns (Goodwin and Heath 2016; Hobolt 2016; Swales 2016). Another difference that has received much scholarly attention has been that Remainers tend to be more liberal in their views as opposed to Leavers who tend to be more authoritarian (Surridge 2019; Peitz et al. 2018). This finding resonates with the idea that contemporary political cleavages, in England and the West more generally, are no longer only class-based, but they are also culture-based, particularly along a cosmopolitan/communitarian axis (Kriesi 2010; Wheatly 2015). This, alongside the finding that left- and right-wing orientation was not found to be significantly associated with how people voted in the referendum (as has been the case with previous UK elections), has led some scholars to suggest that the political cleavages of Brexit are cultural rather class-based and economic (Surridge 2019). This means that political views have more to do with one's cultural values and identity rather than their "objective" class position (as measured traditionally by income and other measures of economic capital).[2]

As interesting as these new trends are, they should be approached with an acknowledgement that political identities are much more complicated than simple schemas suggest they might be. As Surridge (2019) notes, the

---

[2] It is worth noting that recent approaches to class have also embraced a more cultural analysis of class, highlighting the intersections between economic, social and cultural capital (Savage 2015).

"relationship between values and political behaviour is complex and depends critically on the context of the vote in question" (p. 8). Several authors have stressed that the misuse of the left-behind concept advances polarising "culture wars" (Koch 2017), which juxtapose liberal cosmopolitans against conservative communitarians, patronises the working classes (Mckenzie 2017) and prioritises the white working classes to the exclusion of other ethnic groups (Bhambra 2017).

However problematic, such polarising constructions of social groups serve as tools of political rhetoric. They are employed by politicians to make group-based appeals (Thau 2019) to the electorate, for example by claiming to speak on behalf of "the people" against the interests of the elites and the establishment. As an example, below is an extract from Nigel Farage's (a UK righwing politician and leading Brexit campaigner) comments following the 2016 referendum:

> This, if the predictions now are right, this will be a victory for real people, a victory for ordinary people, a victory for decent people. We have fought against the multinationals, we have fought against the big merchant banks, we have fought against big politics, we have fought against lies, corruption and deceit. And today honesty, decency and belief in nation, I think now is going to win.

In the extract, Farage constructs a bipolar categorisation. On the one side, there are "the people": "real", "ordinary" and "decent" people, as he describes them. On the other side, there are "the elites": the multinationals, the big merchant banks and the big politics. This is a typical "us/them" construction which presents one pole as positive and the other as its negative mirror image (see, e.g., Said 1995). The two are presented as in conflict with each other: in this battle, only one can win—and, in the referendum, it was "the people" who won. Farage claims Brexit as the victory of the good against the bad, of the democratic will of "real" people against the interests of corrupt economic and political elites. Farage here constructs an image of himself as an "aspirant leader" of the people, and to do this, he constructs the political and economic elites ("multinationals", "big merchant banks", "big politics") as the enemy (Edelman 1988). Importantly, as Edelman notes (1988, p. 82), when leaders or "aspirant" leaders name enemies, they also invoke specific ideologies upon which the us/them categorisation of political order can be based. As Reicher and Haslam (2017) have argued in relation to Donald Trump's rhetoric that contains similar tropes, Farage acts here as an identity entrepreneur. He constructs an in-group identity, "the people", which is seemingly inclusive, and an out-group identity, "the elites". According to Farage's line of argument here, the two sides are incommensurable and there is no effort to seek a common ground. Rather, Farage is clearly only appealing to "the people", claiming to be one of them (as shown in his use of "we"), and seeking to gain their support. In contrast, the elite "other" is placed "beyond the bounds of legitimate discourse" (Billig 1987, pp. 267–277), which further reinforces polarisation.

Despite its seeming "innocence", the category of "the people" is deeply ideological. Are "the people" in Farage's extract those who voted for Brexit and not the rest 48% who did not? This would, for instance, include the majority of English and Welsh voters, but it would exclude the majority of Scottish and Irish voters. And are "the elites" those who live in cosmopolitan cities such as London or Manchester who voted predominantly for Remain and who are often dismissively described as out-of-touch metropolitans? And what about those who did not or could not vote in the referendum, such as migrants? The seemingly inclusive category of "the people" does not apply to everyone. Farage hints at this in the extract by referring to "belief in nation", thereby alluding that those who are seen as not belonging to the nation also fall outside the category of "the people" and, consequently, are excluded from his vision of Brexit Britain. In Farage's talk, then, "people" means British people, thus invoking a banal assumption of nationhood as the basis of identity (cf. Billig 1995). Further to this, Farage appeals to "real" British people, which, in this context, invokes a racialised construction of the working classes (Bhambra 2017), packaged in what has become a commonplace "culture wars" explanation of Brexit, one that pits "cosmopolitan elites" against the left-behind (Mckenzie 2017). Needless to say, this account ignores the range of issues and grievances that contributed to Brexit and sidesteps the specificities of different groups, communities and contexts. This brief analysis illustrates the dangers of politically manipulating (cf. Billig and Marinho

68 E. Andreouli

2014) the category of the people in a way that polarises politics and excludes dialogue and engagement.

Taking "the People" Seriously: A Rhetorical Approach

Following on from the critical discussion above, the approach advanced in this chapter aims to explore the intricacies, complexities and dilemmas of lay or common-sense thinking as a form of knowledge produced by "thinking societies" (Moscovici 2000). From this perspective, people, rather than simply holding beliefs or opinions, are seen as actively constructing knowledge about their social world by communicating and engaging with others in their everyday lives. There are different strands of social psychology which take a social constructionist view on knowledge construction, mainly from the European "sociological" strand of the discipline (Farr 1996). Here, I draw predominantly on the tradition of rhetorical psychology as elaborated by Billig 1987; Billig 1991; Billig et al. 1988.

Rhetorical psychology sees thinking as a dialogical process of internal argumentation (Billig 1987). From this perspective, people are argumentative thinkers, that is, they are able to employ arguments and counter-arguments to make sense of the world around them. Importantly, thinking is not simply something that individual people do "inside their heads"; it is something that people do with others, through internal dialogue with other perspectives and through social debate. As scholars in cognate approaches, notably Marková (2003) in her elaboration of dialogicality, have also suggested, thinking is a dialogical process that involves both self and others. What makes rhetorical psychology particularly useful for this analysis of Brexit rhetoric is its emphasis on argumentation, especially in the context of everyday interactions and common sense. "Witcraft" (Billig 1987) is art of reasoning that does not require technical expertise; it is part and parcel of everyday "commonsensical" thinking whereby people mobilise and engage with different arguments and counter-arguments in the course of their everyday interactions as well as in their "internal" thinking. People, for example, are able to both categorise, and thus simplify the world around them, and to particularise special cases, and thus unsettle existing categories. The argumentative nature of thinking provides the seeds for further debate and for the creation of new ideas, which keep common sense moving and changing.

Importantly, common sense is not just a here-and-now process of everyday political or other debates. It has a culture and a history that grounds it in specific socio-political contexts. Contrary to the image of the apolitical layperson and to the notion that common sense is consensual and self-evident, it is argued here that there is a politics to common-sense knowledge, both because common sense deals with political matters—such as unemployment (Gibson 2011) and the European Union (Andreouli 2019b)—and because common sense is itself politicised (see also Andreouli 2019a, Andreouli and Figgou 2019). As Hall and O'Shea (2015) have argued, common sense is a contested arena: what is taken to be common-sensical is itself political and can be argued upon. To give an example from UK politics, David Cameron and George Osborne (the UK Prime Minister and Chancellor of the Exchequer, respectively, in 2010–2016) justified the austerity policies they imposed at the time by drawing a parallel to household economics. They argued that in the same way that a household would strive to live within its means, so should the state. This was presented as sufficient justification for introducing and tightening austerity in the years following the global financial crisis. Whilst presented as neutral common sense, this account of the UK's economy draws on conservative ideology, an important element of which is limiting public spending and reducing the role of the state in welfare provision whilst putting emphasis on individual responsibility.

Another point to note is the dilemmatic nature of common sense. Staying with the same example of the welfare, individualistic ideas about personal responsibility go hand in hand with more communitarian ideas. This is the case, for instance, with the National Health Service, through which the UK state provides free healthcare for all, and this is a source of national pride in the UK. This apparent paradox of the fact that individualism and communitarianism can appear equally common-sensical can be solved by acknowledging that common sense is dilemmatic (Billig 1987). It consists of a diverse range of, often opposing, commonplaces, such as serving justice and showing mercy. Whilst commonplaces as such carry different value and weight in different ideological configurations and by different socio-cultural milieux, there still remains the possibility of dilemma and argumentation.

It follows that ideologies themselves (both as part of everyday common sense and as intellectual formalisations; see Billig 1982) are dilemmatic. An example, which is commonly cited in relevant literature and which is of particular relevance to this chapter, is the ideology of nationalism (Billig 1995). According to Billig's thesis, nationalism, as an everyday ideology, contains both the theme of particularism (seeing one's nation as exceptional and different) and the theme of universalism (seeing one's nation as part of a universal system of nation-states). This has been shown by Condor, for instance, in her study of Official UK Labour Party discourses in 2006. Condor found that while Britain was represented as a non-nationalistic and multicultural society, this discourse implicitly presupposed a pre-existing natural order of ethnically homogenous nations. What is more, multiculturalism was constructed as a distinctively British trait, thereby reproducing the notion that nations are essentially different from each other. Billig (1995) has also discussed at depth the very "banal" (i.e. habitual and unquestioned) practices that reproduce the nation-state as a "natural" form of community (e.g. flags in public buildings) within a world of nation-states (each different from each other).

Work in rhetorical psychology has shed light on the intricate ways that laypeople in everyday talk draw upon and navigate such ideological dilemmas: such as between individualism and communitarianism (as shown above and discussed by Billig 1982), tolerance and prejudice (e.g. Augoustinos and Every 2007; see also below) and freedom and control of public space (Dixon et al. 2006; Gray and Manning 2013). As I have argued previously (Andreouli et al. 2019), what this work collectively shows is the creativity in everyday ideological thinking. As opposed to much social psychological work which traditionally focuses on how people achieve closure and cognitive balance, it is argued here people are able to engage with and employ diverse and opposing ideological themes in everyday interactions about political matters. They are also able to combine them in often unanticipated ways that build new lines of argument and new positions (see also Andreouli et al. 2019, 2020), defying the seeming incommensurability of political positions, such as Leave and Remain.

Everyday Rhetoric on Brexit: A Focus Group Study on the UK-EU Referendum

A rhetorical psychological approach was employed in the work presented in this chapter. The first study, discussed in the following two sections of this chapter, involved 9 focus groups with 38 participants, and it was conducted in June 2016, just days before the EU referendum. The aim of these focus groups was to study representations of Europe and the EU in the context of the forthcoming referendum. The data were collected across several locations in England and the participants were supporters of a range of political parties (Conservative, Labour, Green, Liberal Democrat and UK Independence Party). There was balance in the sample between individuals who intended to vote Leave and Remain. The sample was also balanced in terms of age, gender and socioeconomic background. A second smaller study explored representations of Brexit in the context of the referendum result at the start of the negotiations between the UK and EU. This study consisted of three focus groups of mixed Leave/Remain supporters and it was conducted in January–February 2017 in Wales and England.[3] This study is discussed in the next section.

First, a thematic analysis was conducted in order to map out important themes. This resulted in three "global" themes (politics, economy and culture/identity) which consisted of smaller themes (such as sovereignty, costs/benefits of Brexit and values of cosmopolitanism and tolerance) (for more details, see Andreouli and Nicholson 2018; Andreouli et al. 2020). This analysis allowed us to gain an overview of key ideas that structure lay understandings of Brexit; however, it was also constraining

---

[3] England and Wales differ from the other UK nations regarding support for Brexit. While voters in England and Wales (with the notable exception of metropolitan cities such as London) largely voted in the referendum to leave the EU, voters in Scotland and Northern Ireland voted to remain.

because it did not allow us to examine the nuances of and interconnections between ideas as they unfold through dialogue and argumentation. As such, at a second stage, we conducted a rhetorical analysis of the key dialectical theme of prejudice/tolerance which was particularly salient in across the dataset. In particular, we identified the different argumentative lines that participants employed to define the relationship between Brexit and prejudice. In doing so, we examined both the specific rhetorical strategies that shape the local micro-interactions and the wider ideological groundings and dilemmas upon which the relationship between Brexit and prejudice/tolerance was built (see Andreouli et al. 2019). In this chapter, I bring together the findings of these previous analyses and use extracts from publications related to this project, in order to discuss the polarisation of everyday rhetoric about Brexit. The extracts presented below have thus been selected for illustrative purposes because they are exemplary of the theoretical points made in the chapter. Full analyses of the dataset and methodological discussion can be found in Andreouli (2018), Andreouli and Nicholson (2018) and Andreouli et al. (2019). I discuss the value and identity polarities of Brexit, which shape the debate into a seemingly unbridgeable for/against dipole, but also the "crossings" from one side to the other through the rekindling of dilemmatic tensions. I show that these "crossings" open up a space for the emergence of new positions that can rejuvenate the ideational stalemate that characterises Brexit.

Brexit Polarities: Leave and Remain Positions as Incommensurable

As mentioned in the first section of this chapter, right- and left-wing orientation did not make a significant difference in how people voted in the EU referendum in the UK. Instead, cultural values, particularly liberalism/authoritarianism (also conceptualised in terms of cosmopolitanism/communitarianism), appeared to have been more significant (Surridge 2019). As argued above, this has fed into a "culture wars" representation of the social order (see Staerklé 2015) whereby Brexiter and

Remainer are represented as polarised and mutually exclusive identities. Arguably, this polarity owes much to the very heated and conflictual referendum campaigning, with the Remain camp, for instance, dubbing the Brexit campaign as "Project Hate" (due to its anti-immigration rhetoric) and the Leave side dubbing the Remain campaign as "Project Fear" (due to its alarmist rhetoric for post-Brexit UK economy).

The two sides have thus appeared to be deeply prejudiced against each other. Taking a rhetorical perspective, our research analysed how the relationship between support for Brexit and prejudice is discursively constructed in lay talk. We were particularly interested in looking at how constructions of the relationship between Brexit and prejudice are anchored in different ideological traditions and how they were negotiated in the context of focus group discussions conducted in June 2016 and January–February 2017 (Andreouli et al. 2019).

In the study, we approached prejudice as a social practice (Durrheim et al. 2016). In particular, we adopted a discursive psychology approach and we studied the different ways in which prejudice is constructed in everyday talk, how these constructions may be contested and negotiated in the course of social interaction and also how representations of prejudice are rooted in deeper ideological and cultural assumptions (see also Tileagă 2015). Our discursive approach was specifically rhetorical drawing on the research tradition of ideological dilemmas (Billig et al. 1988). Following this tradition, we located the ideological foundations of the concept of prejudice in the ideology of liberalism (itself rooted in the tradition of Enlightenment that foregrounds the value of logic and reason against "biased" thinking based on belief). What has been called the "norm against prejudice" is anchored in this ideological foundation, and it compels people not to be prejudiced against others on the basis of their group memberships, but to judge them in a rational and non-biased way.

In our focus group data, we found that support for Brexit was routinely related to prejudice—prejudice itself being often seen as the cause for Brexit support. This is not surprising considering that Leave-supporting arguments drew predominantly on anti-immigration themes, while the Remain side made more use of economy-type argumentation (Curtice 2016), thus foregrounding its credentials as the "pragmatic" reasonable voice. In this context, the repertoire of Brexit/prejudice versus

Remain/tolerance was commonplace in our data; it functioned as a symbolic resource for lay political reasoning about Brexit. That this schema was mobilised in the focus groups does not mean that it was accepted. Rather, it functioned as an organising principle that helped participants structure their reasoning for or against Brexit. Both Leave- and Remain-supporting accounts were oriented towards the norm against prejudice, and, in both, this norm was tacitly accepted. But in the specific interactional contexts of building up different arguments for/against Brexit and in the light of the different identities and political visions at stake, the norm was oriented to very differently. In particular, while supporters of remaining in the European Union commonly argued against Brexit on the basis that it is rooted in nationalistic prejudice, particularly xenophobia, participants who supported leaving the EU often cast this very idea as being itself a type of prejudice against Leavers.

Below is an illustration of the former from a participant who intended to vote Remain in June 2016:

In the extract, support for Brexit is explicitly attributed to prejudice against foreigners which is presented here as being more prominent in the countryside outside of metropolitan cities (l.3, ll.5–6). Thus, the extract illustrates a construction of support for Brexit as a biased political position that draws upon an outdated and traditional mentality as opposed to the tolerant outlook of people in metropoles. In other extracts from the data, Brexit was associated with bigotry, lack of intelligence, an outdated imperialism and the extreme right (Andreouli et al. 2019).

In the context of the liberal norm against prejudice, Leave supporters in the study employed identity management strategies to inoculate themselves from accusations of prejudice. One such strategy was, for example, making a distinction between being against migrants and being in favour of "controlling" immigration (Andreouli et al. 2019; see also Burke and Goodman 2012, for similar findings in the UK asylum-seeking debate). In addition to individualising strategies that separated oneself from the "typical" Leave voter, it was also common to discount the very idea that Brexit is based on anti-immigration prejudice. In some accounts, arguing that Brexit is a prejudiced political position was constructed as a prejudiced position itself. In the quote below, it is the very accusation of racism that is constructed as problematic because it is based on an "irrational"

3 Lay Rhetoric on Brexit   75

Extract 3.1

---

1 I think they're [Brexit supporters] not very good at foreigners [laughs]. It'd be quite
2 interesting to see on Thursday [the day of the referendum] where the proportion of
3 vote comes from, whether it's coming from the cities and outside that, I'm going to
4 find absolutely fascinating as to whether… Because I think, as I said before, I think that
5 the inner cities, we're extremely tolerant of foreigners. Whereas out in the countryside,
6 I don't' think they are quite so much.[a]

---

[a]Extracts in this section have been drawn from Andreouli et al. (2019)

Extract 3.2

---

1 Oliver: [F]or people to be branded racists, as a blanket term for everybody that votes
2 Leave [Connor: Yep yeah.] is absolute bollocks.

---

generalisation ("a blanket term", l.1) as opposed to measured rational thinking (see also Figgou and Condor 2006; see also Goodman 2010, 2014, on the taboo against accusations of prejudice on the basis that it limits reasonable debate).

What transpires from Extracts 3.1 and 3.2 is that the concept of prejudice, defined variously to serve different rhetorical ends, was key in structuring participants' understandings of Brexit and, also, their understandings of the relationship between the Leave and the Remain sides. As has been argued by Durrheim et al. (2016), struggles to define what counts and what does not count as prejudice are key for understanding the politics of intergroup relations. In our study, attributing prejudice to one or the other side was a way of legitimising some voices (those constructed as tolerant) and silencing others (those constructed as prejudiced). This hinges on who wins the discursive battle to define prejudice. Two prominent examples from the data are that prejudice could be constructed in terms of nationalistic Euroscepticism (consequently, Brexit is seen as a manifestation of prejudice towards foreigners, as per Extract 3.1), or it could be constructed in terms of an exclusionary and racist Eurocentrism (hence, consequently, Remain was seen as a

76 E. Andreouli

Extract 3.3

---

1 [It] seems to me like people who are on the left who want to leave, like
  almost can't
2 speak out, like they've lost a voice, because they just are scared of looking
  like they're
3 far-right and xenophobic.

---

manifestation of prejudice towards non-Europeans, as in Extract 3.8) (Andreouli et al. 2019).

The polarisation between these two "camps" meant that building an alternative position that cut through these dichotomies was discursively very difficult to achieve. This was particularly evident in the words of one of the Remain supporters in our study (Extract 3.3):

The quote illustrates the difficulty of finding connections across the Leave/Remain polarity: from a left Remain perspective, being a Brexiter is equated with xenophobia, leaving little space for making a case against the EU on a non-right-wing basis, such as criticising its neoliberal economic policies and its treatment of refugees from outside the EU.[4]

This rift between Remain and Leave has persisted and remains strong at the time of writing (three years following the referendum). Research by Hobolt and colleagues shows that the relevance of Brexiter and Remainer identities has remained strong in the years after the referendum. Far more people feel a strong attachment to Remain or Leave that consider themselves to be a supporter of a political party (Hobolt et al. 2019). These are, remain at the moment of writing (2019), dominant political identities. The two groups are polarised: Remainers and Leavers describe each other as "hypocritical", "selfish" and "closed-minded" and their own group as "honest", "intelligent" and "open-minded" (Hobolt et al. 2019). However, as will be shown in the following sub-section, this does not necessarily mean that there is no point of connection between the two sides.

---

[4] This us/them polarity partly explains perhaps to an extent the difficulty of advancing a "Lexit" position, which, for some, is the natural position of the anti-global capitalism left.

Beyond Either/or: Ambivalence and Dilemmas in Constructions of Brexit

Nationalism has provided a key ideological backbone in debates about Brexit. This has very often taken the form of associating Brexit with xenophobic nationalism, as shown in the previous sub-section, and also with national pride and protecting national sovereignty. The two can be said to represent the "bad" and "good" face of nationalism, respectively, and they echo sociological and psychological literature which has described the former as "nationalism" and the latter as "patriotism" (e.g. Bar-Tal 1993). Contrary to the idea that they correspond to different psychological states, Billig has argued that the distinction between "our patriotism" and "their nationalism" fails to acknowledge their common ideological anchoring (and, indeed, the distinction between patriotism and nationalism is itself ideological because it is used to construct the "Rest" as nationalist and the West as benignly patriotic). For Billig (1995), the distinction is not one of nationalism and patriotism, but one of "hot" and "banal" nationalism—the former being seen, for example, in national liberation movements and the latter in everyday, "forgotten" habits. Both, in their own ways, reproduce the idea of nationhood as a natural identity, which, for Billig (1995), is the core idea of nationalism. This section will show some of the ways that participants navigated the dilemmatic tensions of nationalism in their talk about the EU referendum and Brexit.

Extracts 3.4 and 3.5 are from Leave-supporting accounts and they are particularly oriented towards what was described above as "good" nationalism. Two aspects of this benign type of nationalism are touched upon, namely, pride and the protection of national sovereignty.

Extract 3.4 presents an account of national pride which is at odds with being European. Being British here is taken to mean non-European and

Extract 3.4

---

1 I don't want to be a European. We're British and I think we're a great country, I

2 think it could be better. But I do think we are- I would never want to live anywhere

3 else in the world.

---

78   E. Andreouli

Extract 3.5

---

1 You know, trading between the Americans, Europe, you know, all over the world. I

2 don't see it being an issue, it opens UK up to other countries what we can trade to

3 instead of being stuck in Europe [...] I think we're being held back, you know,

4 because of Brussels we have to have permission to do- to be told what to do.[a]

---

[a]Extracts 3.4 and 3.5 have been drawn from Andreouli (2018)

not living "anywhere else in the world" (ll.2–3). Extract 3.5 is also advancing an argument for a "good" type of nationalism, but this one is more "pragmatic" than "emotional", the focus being on protecting national interests over the interests of other countries. To do this, according to this account, the UK should remain open to other countries, but it should not be told "what to do" by "Brussels" (l.4). Here, what is at stake is the value of national sovereignty: having to ask permission from Brussels is presented as not only restricting ("we're being held back", l.3) but also as belittling ("we have to have permission to do- to be told what to do", l.4), echoing imperialistic narratives of British greatness that have historically anchored British Euroscepticism, not only in the far-right (as perhaps expected) but also in the political mainstream (Gifford 2006).

On the other hand, Remain-supporting accounts stressed the "bad" face of nationalism and advanced a universalistic position drawing on values of post-nationalism and cosmopolitanism, as the following extracts show:

Both aforementioned extracts negotiate the tension between a cosmopolitan and a national outlook in global politics—what Billig (1995) would describe as the tension between universalism and particularism in the ideology of nationalism. In Extract 3.6, the participant maps the cosmopolitan/national distinction onto the distinction between reason and bias. Cosmopolitanism, exemplified in the extract in terms international engagement and international institutions such as the European Court of Human Rights, is associated with reason, a "collective better wisdom" (ll.3–4). On the other hand, bias is associated with a national frame of reference. What the participant means with the phrase "discrimination of

3 Lay Rhetoric on Brexit   79

Extract 3.6

---

1 There's like, I guess, like the European Convention on Human Rights, and the

2 European Court of Human Rights, and, I mean, I personally think it's fabulous, and

3 its judgements are brilliant. It's kind of like, I see it as a kind of collective better

4 wisdom that can override the discrimination of certain countries.[a]

---

[a]Extract 3.6 has been drawn from Andreouli and Nicholson (2018)

Extract 3.7

---

1 I feel a bit embarrassed as well, like from a world point of view. I think I feel a bit

2 like, great, we've said to the world we just want to shut ourselves off and be a little

3 island.[a]

---

[a]Extract 3.7 has been drawn from Andreouli (2018)

certain countries" (l.4) is left unexplained in the extract, but we may speculate that this is a reference to "other" less tolerant countries or to the notion of nationalism as a form of prejudice more generally. In Extract 3.7, international engagement (or the lack thereof) is affectively invested. Very much in contrast to the view that Brexit is a positive vision of national pride, Brexit here is constructed as national embarrassment (l.1) because it advances an image of Britain in the world as a small-minded country "in retreat" of the world (ll.2–3).

It may appear unsurprising that Remainers would support cosmopolitan values whilst Leavers would support sovereignty values. However, the distinction between Remain and Leave positions was not as clear-cut: both Remain and Leave accounts were oriented to both sides of the argument. In Leave accounts, participants sought to abide by the "norm against prejudice" and presented themselves as non-prejudiced, building a narrative of cosmopolitan and tolerant Brexit, as in Extract 3.8 (also Andreouli 2018). In Remain accounts, on the other hand, participants did not question the principle and the value of national sovereignty and often went at lengths to present themselves as patriotic despite supporting EU membership, as in Extract 3.9. Extract 3.8 is from a Leave account:

80   E. Andreouli

Extract 3.8

---
1 [Brexit] means that people who are from Europe aren't in front of the
  queue. It will
2 be equal for everyone now, that's why it's less racist.[a]

---
[a]Extract 3.8 was previously published in Andreouli (2018) and Greenland and
  Figgou (2019)

Extract 3.9

---
1 I don't want to personally be involved in the EU for anything else but trade.
  But with
2 trade comes so many other things. So, like all the directives about how
  things
3 should be produced, and tariffs, and health and safety aspects of products,
  and the
4 free movement of people. That's all part of trade. I don't expect them to
  interfere
5 with any of our laws [...] And I'm no fan of the EU and I don't think many
  Brits are
6 particularly happy with the EU. But with a pragmatic head on, it's the trade
  and the
7 economy element.[a]

---
[a]Extract 3.9 has been drawn from Andreouli and Nicholson (2018)

In the extract above, supporting remaining in the EU is constructed as more racist than Brexit because it creates a two-tiered system that privileges some migrants (EU citizens) but not others (non-EU citizens). In this account, Brexit is perfectly aligned with a tolerant colour-blind vision of the world, thus abiding by the norm against prejudice which ingrained in the ideology of liberal democracies.

Below is an example of a Remain perspective, showing one of the ways that participants oriented both to the value of patriotism and national pride and to the value of international engagement.

Here, the participant builds up a "reluctant Remainer" position by employing a distinction between economy and politics: while the influence of the EU in the former domain (particularly trade) can be tolerated and is useful, it is the EU's political interference that the participant takes issue with. Directives, tariffs, free movement and health and safety regulations (ll.3–4) are all presented as relatively inconsequential and part of the generic category of trade (l.5), which does not appear to hold much value in terms of its effect on national sovereignty. But "interfering with any of our laws" (ll.4–5) (which can be understood as the domain of politics, not the economy) is presented as qualitatively different: it falls outside the remit of the EU (which is, in turn, constructed here narrowly as a trade alliance, l.1), and it violates UK sovereignty. This distinction between the economy and politics maps onto another dilemma, that of being pragmatic versus acting emotionally (see Andreouli and Nicholson 2018). In this account, the participant is positioned as a reasonable pragmatist. Her account draws a balance between managing the "practical" demands of international trade and the "identitarian" value of national sovereignty. Further, the fact that this fine balance between emotional and pragmatic concerns is only reluctantly arrived at ("I'm no fan of the EU… but") adds to the robustness of this argument (Edwards 2005).

Conclusions

This chapter has taken a rhetorical approach to lay views on Brexit, a particularly heated political topic in the UK since the 2016 EU referendum. Brexit has been seen as representing a rupture with the political status quo and, as such, it has received much scholarly attention. It is telling that a Web of Science search on the topic for the period 2016–2019 produced over 3000 sources and a Google Scholar search produced over 44,000 results. As discussed in the beginning of this chapter, much of this work has focused on explaining the reasons for the Brexit vote by studying the distinctive characteristics of Leave and Remain voters, but also it has sought to understand the "bigger" political realignments that are associated with Brexit.

The chapter contributes to this work by focusing specifically on political communication about Brexit. The study of political communication is a diverse area of research and it is rooted in several intellectual traditions: sociological theories of opinion formation, theories of the public sphere, the study of political language as well as work in social cognition (Bennett and Iyengar 2008; see also Nisbet and Feldman 2011). This chapter is positioned within the general approach of the study of political language and meaning-making processes. Murray Edelman, one of the key figures of this approach, summarises this theoretical perspective as follows:

> It is the language about political events, not the events in any other sense, that people experience; even developments that are close by take their meanings from the language that depicts them. So political language *is* political reality; there is no other so far as the meaning of events to actors and spectators is concerned. (1988, p. 104, original emphasis)

The chapter has explored lay talk about Brexit by adopting a rhetorical psychological perspective. This is a particularly valuable perspective in this context because it focuses on dilemmas and ambiguity in lay political thinking as opposed to fixity and closure. As such, it challenges the Remain/Leave dichotomy, which dominates existing work, and focuses instead on studying the nuances, commonalities and tensions between and within Leave- and Remain-supporting accounts. It was further argued in this chapter that such a nuanced analysis is crucial, particularly in the context of the rise of populist political projects which claim to represent "the people" against "others" of different kinds (such as economic elites, the political establishment and migrants).[5] Against this background, this chapter has sought to take seriously "what the people think" by exploring specifically the themes, arguments and counter-arguments that are at play when lay thinkers reason about the European Union and Brexit in the context of focus group discussions.

The analyses reported here showed that Brexit is indeed a polarised field. Taking the particular case of discourse about the relationship between Brexit and prejudice, it was shown that constructions of prejudice are an important anchor that grounds the polarity between Remain and Leave. For Remainers, it was the prejudice of Leavers that led to Brexit, which consequently was constructed as a symbol of Britain's closed-mindedness. On the other hand, in Leave-supporting accounts, a narrative of cosmopolitan Brexit was employed to argue that the UK

---

[5] Populism is a heavily debated and contentious term. It is also varied, as are the different categories of the "people" and its "others" (e.g. foreigners, elites, etc.). For a discussion of populism as a discursive repertoire that encompasses different us/them categories, see Brubaker (2017).

would be more open to the world after "unshackling" itself from the narrowness of the EU. However, in both sets of accounts, abiding by the "norm against prejudice" was commonplace, illustrating the common ideological roots across seemingly incommensurable positions. Similarly, both Leave- and Remain-supporting participants mobilised themes of nationalism in their talk and navigated an ideological dilemma between "good" and "bad" nationalism. In both Remainer and Leaver accounts, national sovereignty and love for one's country were taken as unquestionable values whilst the "bad" side of nationalism (e.g. bigotry and intolerance) was "othered" (Andreouli et al. 2016).

The relatively brief analysis of this chapter highlights the insufficiency of simplistic explanatory schemas of public opinions and illustrates the value of studying how people *reason* about significant socio-political issues such as Brexit. This addresses Nesbitt-Larking and Kinnvall's (2012) call for adopting a "global perspective" in political psychology, one which recognises that old dualisms (such as left/right) have become redundant; instead, to understand issues of political psychology today, we need to foreground hybridity, complexity and mobility. Paying attention to how people reason, rather on what opinions they hold, provides us with a processual and dialogical perspective for understanding tensions and conflicts but also dialogue and engagement and, ultimately, political change.

References

Andreouli, E. (2019a). Social psychology and citizenship: A critical perspective. *Social and Personality Psychology Compass, 13*(2). e12432.

Andreouli, E. (2019b). Constructions of Europe in the Run-up to the EU referendum in the UK. *Identities: Global Studies in Culture and Power, 26*(2), 241–259.

Andreouli, E., & Figgou, L. (2019). Critical social psychology of politics. In K. O'Doherty & D. Hodgetts (Eds.), *Sage handbook of applied social psychology*. Sage.

Andreouli, E., Greenland, K., & Figgou, L. (2020). Lay discourses about Brexit and prejudice: 'Ideological Creativity' and its limits in Brexit debates. *European Journal of Social Psychology, 50*(2), 309–322.

Andreouli, E., Greenland, K., & Howarth, C. (2016). 'I Don't Think Racism Is That Bad Any More': Exploring the 'End of Racism' discourse among students in English schools. *European Journal of Social Psychology, 46*(2), 171–184.

Andreouli, E., Kaposi, D., & Stenner, P. (2019). Brexit and emergent politics: In search of a social psychology. *Journal of Community and Applied Social Psychology, 29*(1), 6–17.

Andreouli, E., & Nicholson, C. (2018). Brexit and everyday politics: An analysis of focus group data on the EU referendum. *Political Psychology, 39*(6), 1323–1338.

Augoustinos, M., & Every, D. (2007). The language of "race" and prejudice. *Journal of Language and Social Psychology, 26*(2), 123–141.

Bar-Tal, D. (1993). Patriotism as fundamental beliefs of group members. *Politics and the Individual, 3*(2), 45–62.

Bennett, W. L., & Iyengar, S. (2008). A new era of minimal effects? The changing foundations of political communication. *Journal of Communication, 58*, 707–731.

Bhambra, G. K. (2017). Brexit, trump, and 'methodological whiteness': On the misrecognition of race and class. *The British Journal of Sociology, 68*(S1), S214–S232.

Billig, M. (1982). *Ideology and social psychology: Extremism, moderation and contradiction*. Blackwell.

Billig, M. (1987). *Arguing and thinking: A rhetorical approach to social psychology*. Cambridge: Cambridge University Press.

Billig, M. (1991). *Loughborough studies in communication and discourse*.Ideology and opinions: Studies in rhetorical psychology. Sage Publications.

Billig, M. (1995). *Banal nationalism*. Sage Publications.

Billig, M., Condor, S., Edwards, D., Gane, M., Middleton, D., & Radley, A. (1988). *Ideological Dilemmas: A social psychology of everyday thinking*. Sage.

Billig, M., & Marinho, C. (2014). Manipulating information and manipulating people. *Critical Discourse Studies, 11*(2), 158–174.

Brubaker, R. (2017). Why populism? *Theory and Society, 46*(5), 357–385.

Burke, S., & Goodman, S. (2012). "Bring back Hitler's gas chambers": Asylum seeking, Nazis and Facebook: A discursive analysis. *Discourse & Society, 23*(1), 19–33.

Condor, S. (2006). *Representing, Resisting and Reproducing Ethnic Nationalism: Official UK Labour Party Representations of 'Multicultural Britain'*. Paper Presented at the VIII International Conference on Social Representations, Rome, August 30, 2006.

Curtice. (2016). *The Two Poles of the Referendum Debate: Immigration and the Economy*. Retrieved from https://whatukthinks.org/eu/wp-content/uploads/2016/01/Analysis-paper-4-The-two-poles-of-the-referendum-debate.pdf (6/03/2019)

Dixon, J. A., Levine, M., & McAuley, R. (2006). Locating impropriety: Street drinking, moral order and the ideological dilemma of public space. *Political Psychology, 27*(2), 187–206.

Durrheim, K., Quayle, M., & Dixon, J. (2016). The struggle for the nature of "Prejudice": "Prejudice" expression as identity performance. *Political Psychology, 37*(1), 17–35.

Edelman, M. (1988). *Constructing the political spectacle*. The University of Chicago Press.

Edwards, D. (2005). Discursive psychology. In K. L. Fitch & R. E. Sanders (Eds.), *Handbook of language and social interaction* (pp. 257–273). Routledge.

Farr, R. (1996). *The roots of modern social psychology: 1872–1954*. Blackwell.

Figgou, L., & Condor, S. (2006). Irrational categorization, natural intolerance and reasonable discrimination: Lay representations of prejudice and racism. *British Journal of Social Psychology, 45*, 219–243.

Gibson, S. (2011). Dilemmas of citizenship: Young people's conceptions of un/employment rights and responsibilities. *British Journal of Social Psychology, 50*, 450–468.

Gifford, C. (2006). The rise of post-imperial populism: The case of right-wing Euroscepticism in Britain. *European Journal of Political Research, 45*, 851–869.

Goodman, S. (2010). "It's not racist to impose limits on immigration": Constructing the boundaries of racism in the asylum and immigration debate. *Critical Approaches to Discourse Analysis Across Disciplines, 4*(1), 1–17.

Goodman, S. (2014). Developing an understanding of race talk. *Social and Personality Psychology Compass, 8*(4), 147–155.

Goodwin, M., & Milazzo, C. (2017). Taking back control? Investigating the role of immigration in the 2016 vote for Brexit. *The British Journal of Politics and International Relations, 19*(3), 450–464.

Goodwin, M. J., & Heath, O. (2016). The 2016 referendum, Brexit and the left behind: An aggregate-level analysis of the result. *The Political Quarterly, 87*(3), 323–332.

Gray, D., & Manning, R. (2013). 'Oh my god, we're not doing nothing': Young people's experiences of spatial regulation. *British Journal of Social Psychology, 53*(4), 640–655.

Hall, S., & O'Shea, A. (2015). Common-sense neoliberalism. In S. Hall, D. Massey, & M. Rustin (Eds.), *After neoliberalism? The Kilburn Manifesto* (pp. 52–68). Lawrence and Wishart.

Hobolt, S., Leeper, T., & Tilley, J. (2019). Emerging Brexit identities. In A. Menon (Ed.), *Brexit and Public Opinion 2019*. London: The UK in a Changing Europe. Available at http://ukandeu.ac.uk/wp-content/uploads/2018/01/Public-Opinion.pdf

Hobolt, S. B. (2016). The Brexit vote: A divided nation, a divided continent. *Journal of European Public Policy, 23*(9), 1259–1277.

Koch, I. (2017). What's in a vote? Brexit beyond culture wars. *American Ethnologist, 44*(2), 225–230.

Kriesi, H. (2010). Restructuration of partisan politics and the emergence of a new cleavage based on values. *West European Politics, 33*(3), 673–685.

Marková, I. (2003). *Dialogicality and social representations: The dynamics of mind.* Cambridge University Press.

Mckenzie, L. (2017). The class politics of prejudice: Brexit and the land of no-hope and glory. *The British Journal of Sociology, 68*(S1), S265–S280.

Moscovici, S. (2000). In G. Duveen (Ed.), *Social representations: Explorations in social psychology.* Polity Press.

Nesbitt- Larking, P., & Kinnvall, K. (2012). The discursive frames of political psychology. *Political Psychology, 33*(1), 45–59.

Nisbet, M. C., & Feldman, L. (2011). The social psychology of political communication. In D. Hook, B. Franks, & M. Bauer (Eds.), *Communication, culture and social change: The social psychological perspective* (pp. 284–299). Palgrave Macmillan.

Peitz, L., Dhont, K., & Seyd, B. (2018). The psychology of supranationalism: Ideological correlates and implications for EU attitudes and post-Brexit preferences. *Political Psychology, 39*(6), 1305–1322.

Reicher, S., & Haslam, S. A. (2017). Trump's appeal: What psychology tells us. *Scientific American.* Retrieved from https://www.scientificamerican.com/article/trump-rsquo-s-appeal-what-psychology-tells-us/ (30/07/2019)

Said, E. (1995). *Orientalism.* Penguin.

Savage, M. (2015). *Social class in the 21st century.* Penguin Books.

Staerklé, C. (2015). Social order and political legitimacy. In G. Sammut, E. Andreouli, G. Gaskell, & J. Valsiner (Eds.), *The Cambridge handbook of social representations* (pp. 280–294). Cambridge University Press.

Surridge, P. (2019). The left-right divide. In A. Menon (Ed.), *Brexit and Public Opinion 2019* (pp. 6–8). London: The UK in a Changing Europe. Available athttp://ukandeu.ac.uk/wp-content/uploads/2018/01/Public-Opinion.pdf

Swales, K. (2016).*Understanding the Leave Vote*.NatCen. Retrieved from http://natcen.ac.uk/our-research/research/understanding-the-leave-vote/ (20/02/2017)

Thau, M. (2019). How political parties use group-based appeals: Evidence from Britain 1964–2015. *Political Studies, 67*(1), 63–82.

Tileagă, C. (2015). *The nature of prejudice: Society, discrimination and moral exclusion*. Routledge.

Wheatly, J. (2015). Restructuring the policy space in England: The end of the left–right paradigm? *British Politics, 10*, 268–285.

4

Extending the Boundaries of Political Communication: How Ideology Can Be Examined in Super-Rich Television Documentaries Using Discursive Psychology

Philippa Carr

Viewing Entertainment Programmes on Television as Political

The presentation of entertainment broadcasts as mundane means that they are not considered political. However, Livingstone (1998) places television as being part of everyday life and not part of a separate realm. Exploring how entertainment documentaries are political involves challenging how television media can be viewed as distinct from people's everyday lives as opposed to being part of conventional conversation and reflecting constructions of reality on screen. Television programmes refer to external events that draw upon viewers' social knowledge. Additionally, people refer to events from television programmes within their everyday

---

P. Carr (✉)
University of the West of England, Bristol, UK
e-mail: philippa2.carr@uwe.ac.uk

© The Author(s), under exclusive license to Springer Nature Switzerland AG 2020
M. A. Demasi et al. (eds.), *Political Communication*, Palgrave Studies in Discursive
Psychology, https://doi.org/10.1007/978-3-030-60223-9_4

89

talk. As such, television programmes are not distinct and are incorporated within individual's discourse. Similar to people's talk, television programmes contain differing positions to social issues. The differing presentations within the media draw upon differing ideology for rhetorical purposes (Edley 1993). Thus, television programmes are political as they contain opposing ideological stances and some ideologies are more dominant than others (Edelman 2001; Mihelj and Huxtable 2018). For example, soap operas contain difficulties about whether a character should act in their individual interest or for the benefit of the local community (Livingstone 1998).

> The salience of the social class issue in Britain means that there is a strong sense of valued working-class traditional culture to be lost by individual self-betterment that is celebrated in the soap operas. (Liebes and Livingstone 1994, p. 736)

Characters are positioned within a dilemma where they can either act in their own interest to experience social mobility or maintain their sense of belonging within their community. Soap operas reflect social changes in society as a form of social commentary and individual's negotiation of neoliberal positions around self-improvement. The presence of differing ideological positions within entertainment programmes presents an opportunity to explore how these broadcasts are political and draw upon ideology in people's talk about wealth inequality.

Despite researcher's emphasis on analysing news and current affairs programming, Mihelj and Huxtable (2018) state that entertainment programmes can also be viewed as a form of political communication. Historical analysis of entertainment programming in socialist Eastern Europe found that the programmes used rhetoric that drew upon the dominant ideology of the period (Imre 2016; Mihelj 2017). Documentaries as a genre can vary in terms of their seriousness and emphasis placed on entertainment (Miller 2010). Some forms of entertainment documentary meet the criteria for reality programming as they provide direct access to individuals (Casey 2008) such as the super-rich in wealth porn broadcasts. Reality programming follows a format with a narrative being formed in the post-production process after its subjects have been filmed (Miller 2010; Kelly and Boyle 2011). Lifestyle programming, another type of reality programme that uses a documentary format, has been found to draw upon neoliberal ideology as the programme places an emphasis on the individual who is presented as needing continual self-improvement to succeed (Färber and Podkalicka 2019). Despite their presentation as mundane entertainment, entertainment documentaries can be analysed as a form of political communication allowing for the analysis of how super-rich programming draws upon ideology to account for wealth inequality.

Neoliberalism as a Dominant Ideology

When exploring the ideology underlining discourse in wealth porn programming, neoliberalism and its emphasis on the individual need to be highlighted in relation to the value placed on wealth. Neoliberalism can be defined as the extension of free market economics into other spheres (Brown 2003) and, more specifically, the needs of corporations (Crouch 2011). An emphasis is placed on individual responsibility and the shrinking of the welfare state (Brown 2003). Neoliberalism is pervasive due to its use as 'common sense' or as a form of lived ideology (Sugarman 2015, p. 103). The focus on market values and individual responsibility within neoliberal ideology results in those who perform well and generate wealth are considered successful. By announcing the end of ideology (Harvey 2000), neoliberalism permits ideological ignorance preventing the consideration of more equitable ideological positions (Walsh-Bowers and Gokani 2014). Individualism is drawn upon in talk to legitimise the interests of the wealthy over the collective needs of poorer groups (Carr et al. 2018). Individualistic ideology places a focus on the individual presenting people as being autonomous and not constrained by their social environment. Individualism can be defined as placing the need of the individual ahead of the collective in the form of the nation-state (Abercrombie 1980) and a core tenet of neoliberal ideology. Equality is also drawn upon as an ideology in individuals' talk and is viewed as being historically significant since the eighteenth century (Billig et al. 1988). To manage the ideological tension with individualism in developed Western societies, the ideology drawn upon is negotiated to present 'an equality which allows the successful to be more equal than the rest' (Billig et al. 1988, p. 36). Billig (1982) explores how ideology at a theoretical level is inconsistent; explanations for poverty provide an example as speakers negotiate individual and structural explanations. Similarly, television broadcasts draw upon opposing ideological positions (Edelman 2001; Mihelj and Huxtable 2018). In programming about money-saving behaviour and minimalism, consumption is presented as both immoral and necessary to construct individual identities (Färber and Podkalicka 2019). Poorer individuals are presented as lacking self-discipline to need a budget whilst the more affluent warrant their budgeting as a moral decision. The analyses of lifestyle programming explore how differing forms of ideology are drawn upon in broadcasts although these programmes do not feature the extremely wealthy.

Individualism can be found in differing psychological concepts to explain wealth inequality, such as social class and the Protestant Work Ethic (PWE), that are used by researchers. When exploring social mobility and class, Walkerdine (2011) found that responsibility for class status and social mobility is placed on the individual. Working-class values such as acting in the community's interest are derided and middle-class norms about independence are presented as aspirational. Similarly, PWE is related to high levels of individualism and more prevalent in countries with high levels of inequality (Furnham et al. 1993). Kelvin and Jarrett (1985) argue that PWE has evolved into a 'wealth ethic' that prioritises individual self-sufficiency and not being dependent on the welfare state over work. These components of PWE also form key components of individualism within neoliberalism. Therefore, individualism is a common thread in psychological concepts used to explain wealth inequality that requires further exploration.

Representations of Economic Inequality

There is a need to explore the representation of the super-rich and wealth inequality given the detrimental consequences for all. The UK has the fifth highest levels of economic inequality in the 37 member countries of the Organisation for Economic Co-operation and Development (Keeley

2015). Economic inequality restricts social mobility by restricting access to resources such as education (Taylor 2010). Additionally, there is a negative impact on public health (Pickett and Wilkinson 2015), physical health (Wilkinson and Pickett 2010) and mental health (Pickett et al. 2006; Wilkinson and Pickett 2018). Wealthy individuals maintain wealth inequality through their disproportionate involvement in the financial sector (Medeiros and de Souza 2015) and employing managers to minimise their tax obligations restricting the funds available for public spending (Harrington 2016). Given the negative impact of economic inequality and the role of the super-rich in its maintenance, there is a need to explore how inequality is presented and accounted for in the media. Edelman (2001) states that inequality has a low profile in news broadcasts as differing levels of individual wealth are presented as deserved upon differing levels of effort. Items in news broadcasts about poverty hold people to account for their own poor status and not socio-economic conditions (Iyengar 1990). By presenting poverty as the result of individual effort, differing levels of wealth becomes common sense as some individuals are less deserving than others. These media constructions draw upon neoliberal ideology that places a focus on the individual and competing for resources (Brown 2003). In light of news broadcasts about poverty drawing upon neoliberal ideology, there is a need to examine how super-rich programming presents extreme wealth as a form of entertainment despite inequality's detrimental consequences to poorer groups in society.

'Wealth porn' has been used to describe media programmes about the super-rich (Poole 2000, p. 22). This genre shares some similarities with 'poverty porn' (Hester 2014) or 'Factual Welfare Television' (De Benedictis et al. 2017, p. 337) genre such as placing the viewer in a voyeuristic position (Feltwell et al. 2017) and places a focus on financial behaviours like spending (Paterson et al. 2017). Super-rich programming such as the *Rich Kids of Instagram* positions the individuals featured in both an aspirational and derisory manner (Marwick 2015). However, their self-presentation within the programmes focuses on their heightened work ethic to suggest that their purchases are the result of their labour (Littler 2018; Marwick 2015). In Littler's (2018) research, plutocratic elites featured on programmes such as the *Rich Kids of Instagram* are characterised as a 'luxury flaunter' due to their excessive spending (p. 115). She found two other characterisations of wealthy individuals: the 'normcore pluto-crat' is presented as ordinary onscreen; in contrast, the 'kind parent' is characterised as a well-meaning philanthropist. In contrast to poverty porn programming, these representations draw upon meritocratic values that are advantageous to the wealthy. Focus groups discussing audience's construction of poverty porn and wealth inequality included talk about wealthy groups (Paterson et al. 2017). Here, the extreme wealth of 'bank-ers' is presented as ethically challenging through being constructed as 'greed' (p. 226) that draws upon a contrasting ideology around the collec-tive good. Both super-rich programming and poverty porn genres reflect the neoliberal ideology underpinning depictions of wealth and poverty in the media where a focus is placed upon the actions of individuals. The financial status of the individuals featured places extreme inequality as acceptable in a competitive external environment. However, there is a need to explore how wealth inequality is presented in domestic settings where the super-rich interact with poorer groups such as their employees.

Media Representations of Domestic Staff

Period dramas broadcast depictions of extreme wealth and staff and employer relations. Media and historical researchers have focused on *Downton Abbey*, a British drama series that has an audience of 120 mil-lion worldwide (Copelman 2019). *Downton Abbey* draws upon individu-alistic ideology to present employers as benevolent and their domestic world as independent from wider society and state intervention (Littler 2018). The internal hierarchy is constructed as fair (Gullace 2019) with members of the household being aware of their position (Byrne 2014). For viewers, domestic inequality is represented through the use of accents with staff having regional accents and family members sounding upper class (Baena and Byker 2015). Gullace (2019) highlights how domestic staff exist for their aristocratic employers' benefit. The use of domestic staff is constructed as an uncontroversial part of British history (Baena and Byker 2015) that serves to justify the nation's colonial past (Littler 2018). The construction of domestic inequality in period dramas reflects the presentation of inequality in society as fair. Thus, there is a need to explore constructions of domestic staff in non-fiction and how inequality is accounted for in a contemporary situation.

Defining domestic staff is complex given their diverse roles globally; however, this can be described as people who undertake work in domestic settings on a regular basis with an employment arrangement (ILO 2011). Domestic work is presented as low status (Singha 2019) with workers having reduced rights, such as access to leave, compared to staff in other sectors (ILO 2013). In the UK, the reduced rights for employees of the super-rich on Overseas Domestic Worker visas (Fudge and Strauss 2014) have been highlighted in addition to the potential for the exploitation and trafficking of workers (Briddick 2019). In particular, the Overseas Domestic Worker visa has been criticised as decreasing employees' rights in order to attract the super-rich to the UK (Fudge and Strauss 2014). Given the problematic status and rights of domestic workers, there is a need to explore how they are presented in the media and their position is accounted for as employees of the super-rich. By exploring the presentation of contemporary domestic workers in super-rich programming, there is an opportunity to examine how extreme inequality is publicly accounted for in the home.

Method

Discursive Psychology (DP) has been used to explore how economic inequality is constructed in television and radio programming (Goodman and Carr 2017; Carr et al. 2018). A discursive approach examines how psychological constructs such as identity are used and how people manage their accountability (Edwards and Potter 1992). DP is social constructionist at a micro level (Burr 2015) that can be used to consider how talk is situated and how people draw upon ideology in their discourse (Edley and Wetherell 1997). When using DP, researchers can include both ideological concerns and the wider context in their analysis (Gibson 2016). Media data provides an opportunity to explore the construction of groups in society (Abell and Stokoe 2001) and analysing this data requires an approach such as DP where talk is viewed as situated and requiring the audience to draw upon socially shared knowledge (Abell and Stokoe 1999). Edley (1993) states that media representations are a discursive resource drawing upon differing ideological positions. DP provides a suitable methodology for researching data such as entertainment documentaries by allowing the analysis of a media corpus that is situated and draws upon ideology. For example, in my previous work (Goodman and Carr 2017), we found that televised debates about benefit claimants drew upon individualistic arguments to construct the unemployed as lacking work-based behaviours to account for their poverty.

With television broadcasts, the editing process adds a further layer of presentation management as narration and production decisions construct a cultural product. When using DP, the production of the programme becomes part of the analysis, although the researcher does not have access to the process itself, they can examine the editing as part of the completed broadcast. Billig (2007) demonstrates how this can be achieved when analysing voiceovers and presenters in general election news coverage. Voiceovers are used to challenge the accounts of politicians and to present them as untrustworthy to the electorate. The challenge to politicians' discourse is warranted by constructing an alternative position that questions the visual image on screen. This approach can be extended to television documentaries allowing the analyst to explore how contrasting constructions of the super-rich are accomplished. As a result, DP can be used to analyse highly edited television documentaries to explore how wealth inequality is constructed.

Attenborough (2016) acknowledges the decline in analysing media sources in DP since its early origins. He identifies the benefits of using DP to explore how psychological talk is situated and media accounts are used as social actions. Using DP to examine how media broadcasts are used allows for the consideration of how programmes about the super-rich account for wealth inequality by drawing upon ideology. Early DP used data from a range of media sources including television broadcasts such as *Spitting Image*, a satirical puppet show, to explore the construction of Margaret Thatcher's gender identity as the UK's first female Prime Minister (Edwards and Potter 1992). There is a need to analyse media data due to its influence on public opinion (Attenborough 2016) and how discourse from the media becomes part of everyday talk (LaMarre and Sutherland 2014). Media data provides information about the extremely wealthy as a group that can afford to live separately from others in society (Urry 2007, 2014). For example, the super-rich can use private aeroplanes that bypass conventional airport passenger channels. Less affluent groups do not have this type of choice regarding their visibility in society. The level of isolation chosen by the super-rich is dependent on their level of wealth as more affluent individuals have a more separate lifestyle (Beaverstock and Faulconbridge 2013). Whilst the use of discursive and rhetorical approaches to analyse news and current affairs programming is established (e.g. Edwards and Potter 1992; Billig 2007; Demasi 2019; Burke and Demasi 2019), there is a case to be made for using DP to examine entertainment broadcasts. This will be demonstrated through analysing wealth porn documentaries to explore how the domestic staff of the super-rich are constructed. In addition, this analysis will consider how the super-rich account for their employment of domestic staff for everyday tasks. Through this analysis, an example of how entertainment programming can be analysed will be provided including how ideology is drawn upon to account for inequality in the domestic sphere.

The data consists of 41.5 hours of free-to-air terrestrial television broadcast during 2016 featuring the term 'super-rich'. The usage of the term super-rich to describe extremely wealthy people in television documentaries was established when BBC2 had a super-rich season of five programmes in 2015 (Mumford and Wardell 2015). The corpus contains programmes from the main UK terrestrial broadcasters indicating that the term is widely used. Whilst there are other categories that can be used to refer to wealthy people, the term super-rich was used due to its current popularity within television media. A search was conducted for any programme aired on a terrestrial channel during 2016 with the term super-rich within the title, programme description or subtitling transcript. Programmes that did not refer to the super-rich in relation to their wealth in a non-fictional contemporary context were removed such as the Australian children's television programme *Bananas in Pyjamas*. A basic Jeffersonian notation was used to transcribe the corpus that is aligned with a DP approach (Wiggins 2017). Additional notations were added to reflect the edited nature of the programmes including the use of italic font to indicate the use of a voiceover and bold font to identify where speakers' talk is also subtitled on the screen (see Appendix 1). The corpus was then examined further to find examples featuring talk about or by domestic staff to allow for the exploration of the research aim.

Analysis

Wealth porn programming presents wealth inequality as banal and this is constructed through the positioning of staff and their employers in the programmes warranting a domestic hierarchy. The labour of domestic staff is presented as having a high emotional cost through the impact of their mobility upon family relations. The wealthy account for their use of staff through the use of talk about class and being 'super busy'. The use of 'strategic ambiguity' allows programme makers to present unclear arguments that offer differing translations (Condor et al. 2013). Vague arguments offer an alternative account to the gross inequality between wealthy employers and employees that is warranted as common sense and difficult to challenge.

Domestic Staff as Essential

The use of staff for everyday tasks is presented as a necessity for the extremely wealthy within the programmes. In Extract 4.1, Lucinda Croft (L), a dollhouse seller, discusses the type of product that is bought by her wealthiest clients. This extract is from *The World's Most Expensive Toys* broadcast on Channel 4 and also features the narrator (N).

A programme titled *The World's Most Expensive Toys* is not expected to be political yet the narration highlights the increasing economic inequality

Extract 4.1

1.	N:	*For the first time ever in full-sized Britain there are a million millionaires*
2.		*and as the super-rich are also getting richer Lucinda has seen the demand*
3.		*for more and more extras.*
4.	L:	*The clients said, 'You need to do me some staff'(.)* like a whole team o of
5.		staff for their dolls' house cos she says 'otherwise it's not realistic'

in the UK by mentioning the increased numbers of wealthy people ('*million millionaires*' (1)) and their heightened wealth. A common feature within the programmes is that the super-rich do not talk about their wealth directly to the camera. Instead, wealth is flagged through talk about consumption such as employing domestic staff. The use of talk about staff in the narration is objectifying through their presentation as '*extras*' (3) achieved through being followed by Lucinda's discourse. Lucinda uses reported speech to account for super-rich individuals' use of domestic staff as normal. Similar to Macmillan and Edwards (1999) where third-party reporting is used in newspapers to construct claims, in entertainment documentaries, edited footage of those working for the super-rich is used. A common feature within the programmes is to talk about the resources of the extremely wealthy to be used to flag their extraordinary levels of wealth without mentioning money. The warranting of employing domestic staff as a routine practice is achieved through the use of banal talk about a child's toy albeit an ostentatious version produced for those with extreme wealth.

Using Talk About Class to Account for Employing Staff

Extracts 4.2 and 4.3 from *Too Posh to Parent*, broadcast on Channel 4, examine how the super-rich themselves talk about employing domestic staff for everyday tasks. In Extract 4.2, a contrast is provided through featuring Mo (M), chauffeur and bodyguard, and his employer, Nina Naustdal (NN), fashion designer, plus Nina's child (C) and the narrator (N). Irene (I), 'millionairess' with five children, and Amanda Jenner (A), 'potty lady', are present in Extract 4.3. These extracts explore how wealthy people account for their use of staff through talk about class.

Extract 4.2 is edited to present a clear class distinction between the wealthy and their staff. Mo constructs this difference in relation to their class identity ('*I'm working-class I work for upper-class*' (4.2:4)). This is accentuated through the footage of social housing and central London as Mo travels to work. Additionally, the narrator refers to the location and

100   P. Carr

Extract 4.2

1.	N:	*((footage of social housing)) East London. Chauffeur and bodyguard*
2.		*Mo is about to start his day.*
3.	M:	Come out the door about six thirty to be at work *eight* o'clock, eight
4.		fifteen the latest *I'm working-class I work for upper-class.*
5.	N:	*((footage of central London)) Driver Mo works for thirty-four-year-old*
6.		*fashion designer Nina Naustdal who lives in a seven million pound*
7.		*townhouse in London's Chelsea.*
8.	C:	*If you had a mum and a dad, they can't do everything. If we didn't have*
9.		*(.) staff mummy's life would be so difficult.*
10.	NN:	I don't think there is a big taboo about using staff today.
11.	N:	*((children with staff members)) With three children, Nina spends two*
12.		*hundred thousand pounds a year on parental outsourcing.*
13.	NN:	*You can have* three nannies for one child *two tutors a day* just to make
14.		sure they're up to date with th, their homework. Chefs and butlers, three
15.		four drivers.
16.	M:	One of the things in my job is to look out for Nina's kids.
17.		I'm there to take em to school. If they're gonna go anywhere outside of
18.		school hours *I've gotta take 'em.* Yeah, I mean, you don't know who,
19.		who's out there, watching, you know? *((NN putting on earrings)) You*
20.		*hear stories every day.*
21.	NN:	*Today you know if there's something you want done you can get*
22		*someone else to do it.*

Extract 4.3

1.	I:	I have two butlers. I have somebody who *((staff working)) turns*
2.		*down all my beds we have a driver we have a tutor we have a*
3.		*nanny. It's always good to have a staff when* you're super busy like
4.		me *((footage of walking around room))*
5.	A:	What a beautiful [beautiful room]
6.	I:	[Thank you.] Do you like [it?]
7.	A:	[Oh I love]
8.	I:	*((to camera))* I have the best school I have the best help. You speak
9.		the best way as posh as possible. *((Irene trying on a hat and shoes))*
10.		*Why would you be ashamed to be posh? I mean if I can buy it like*
11.		*I'm* doing (.) why not?

cost of Nina's home to further indicate her extreme wealth ('*lives in a £7 million townhouse in London's Chelsea*' (4.2:6–7)). The flagging of wealth continues throughout the extract and is similar to Extract 4.3, where there is footage of Irene's large mansion and lavish interiors. By flagging extreme wealth throughout the extracts, the visuals support the speaker's discourse about their need for staff. The size of the properties and their lavish décor differ from the homes of less affluent people, and visually it is clear that their domestic tasks would be exponentially more than could be expected in a conventional household. Nina in Extract 4.2 uses hedging when presenting employing domestic staff as a norm for the super-rich ('I don't think there is a big taboo about using staff today' (4.2:10)). By using hedging, Nina can manage her accountability for this statement given that poorer individuals within the audience are required to carry out domestic tasks themselves. The name of programmes such as *Too Posh to Parent* challenges the presentation of the extremely wealthy having staff for domestic tasks as the norm. The construction of ambiguity through the production process allows the questioning of the inequality present within super-rich homes managing the difficulties of challenging everyday assumptions about wealth. In Extract 4.3, 'posh' is used to indicate class and superiority emphasised through using a three-part list repeating the word 'best' ('*I have the best school I have the best help. You speak the best way as posh as possible*' (4.3:8–9)). The acceptability of outsourcing domestic tasks is achieved by the use of rhetorical questions (4.3:9–11) that allows Irene to construct her purchasing of 'help' as something that others would do if they had sufficient funds. This talk is also present in Extract 4.2 where wealth is presented as allowing you to pay others to do tasks (4.2:21–22). This discourse warrants class as something that can be bought through activities such as hiring staff and aspirational. The concomitant flagging of wealth with speakers' talk further warrants the need for staff given the ostentatious surroundings of the super-rich.

Accounting for Unfairness and Sacrifices Made by Staff

Whilst the super-rich warrant their use of staff through presenting their actions as aspirational and due to them being 'super busy', they are also required to account for the inequality present within their households. Extract 4.4 from the *Rich Kids of Instagram* broadcast on E4 features Emir (E), an 'heir to a Turkish property empire', with his dog Boss, his

102   P. Carr

Extract 4.4

1.	N:	((Stella working while Emir watches in home)) *It's time for Emir to*
2.		*get ready for his own party (.2) and that means briefing the staff.*
3.	E:	Stella has been working with me for a few years now and she's
4.		literally I don't know what I would do without her (.) Boss loves
5.		her as well they they go on long walks on the Hudson River (.) She
6.		cooks for me, she cleans the apartment, she takes care of Boss, she
7.		takes care of me. (.2) Taking care of everything (h)
8.	N:	*And with Stella in charge of buffing up the flat*
9.	E:	OK, bye Boss bye Boss let's get ready for the gym
10.	N:	*Emir can focus on the more important task of buffing up himself*
11.	E:	((at gym)) How does the hat look? Pretty good. Huh? It looks good.
12.		**Do I look better with hat or without hat?**
13.	S:	*((walking dog)) Working with Mr Emir* ((to camera)) he tells me if
14.		he's going to have (.) a party or er friends over so that his house is
15.		pre-ready (.) t, to welcome (.) visitor (h)
16.	PT:	*((at gym)) Five more. Four, three, two, one.*
17.	S:	((to camera)) He likes to be organised and sometimes I forget the
18.		coffee table and he'll text me or call me like "Stella, you forgot
19.		the coffee." "I'm sorry, Mr Emir, I'm so tired!" (.2) He makes me
20.		work hard, but no complaints

housekeeper Stella (S), an unidentified Personal Trainer (PT) and the narrator (N). Extract 4.4 provides a further exploration of how the work practices of the super-rich and their staff are presented.

Similar to the above extracts, Emir is presented as enjoying leisure time through the editing and narration showing him watching Stella work and going to the gym while she walks his dog. Narration, editing and use of subtitles are used to ridicule employers using humour to lower their status (Billig 1992). Subtitles are not used for their traditional purpose to display speech for people with hearing impairments. Instead, subtitles are placed in the top right of the screen to emphasise Emir's talk about his appearance in the gym to ridicule his position (11–12). Within the *Rich Kids of Instagram* series, subtitling is used to emphasise specific talk by speakers. The use of talk and text demonstrates the use of multimodal communication (Kress 2010) structured via the use of non-traditional subtitling to construct humour. In particular, the emphasis on Emir's talk is used to present him as 'absurd' (Antaki 2003, p. 85). By positioning Emir's talk as absurd, the programme can provide an alternative

4 Extending the Boundaries of Political Communication...   103

construction of the extremely wealthy that if presented seriously could attract controversy. By using absurdity through the use of alternative subtitles, Emir's talk is highlighted and ridiculed whilst defending the programme makers' position as criticising the wealthy is controversial requiring speakers to manage their stake (Carr et al. 2018).

Emir presents Stella as an essential part of his life (*'I don't know what I would do without her'* (4)) reflecting the super-rich's need for domestic staff presented in Extract 4.1. Unlike Emir, the footage and her direct talk to the camera is used to present Stella as effortful. Stella's work ethic is presented through talk about Emir as a demanding employer as she recounts being reprimanded for forgetting the coffee (17–18), an everyday basic task. Stella is required to negotiate her position within this anecdote as it initially appears critical of her employer (*'I'm sorry, Mr Emir, I'm so tired!'* (.2) He makes me work hard, but no complaints' (19–20)). Stella manages her position through the use of 'quiescence' as what could be presented as unfair is negotiated through talk about her being comfortable about the arrangement (Fine and Gordon 1989). She needs to manage her stake as an employee yet by using quiescence Stella is able to construct her employer as overly demanding without warranting herself as a complainer. This allows Stella to manage her identity as an effortful worker for a needy wealthy employer. However, as above, the production process is more critical of the privileged as employers as they are presented as demanding.

The effect of the demands of the super-rich is explored further in relation to talk about the sacrifices made by migrant staff. In Extract 4.5, Connie (C) talks about her experience leaving her children in the Philippines to work for Irene from *Too Posh to Parent* in Extract 4.3.

Connie constructs her position as a nanny as requiring resilience as her talk is focused on leaving children with family. She draws upon assumptions about migration as an everyday part of working for the super-rich (*'Most Filipino womans we do that. We you know think about the future'* (9–10)). Connie warrants her mobility as having a delayed reward through her talk about her child at university. Footage of Connie playing with a child is interwoven with Connie's talk about leaving her own children (*'So you must be strong to leave my ba, my family'* (1)). Connie is constructed as resilient as she recounts children not recognising their

Extract 4.5

1.	C:	((to camera)) So you must be strong to leave my ba, my family
2.		((playing with Irene's child)) *It's different when you leave your kids*
3.		*like one year and then when you come back they are* three years
4.		old and it's sad because the k, kids (.) the child c, can't recognise
5.		you "That's your mum." Y, they can't even, "Oh, it's your mum."
6.		but they're just embarrassed and ashamed to come to you you can't
7.		even hug. ((to camera in playground)) People think (h) it's easy to
8.		leav, to leave your own family. It's very difficult but for now (.) i, it's
9.		a long time 20 years. *Most Filipino womans we do that.* We you
10.		know think about the future ((to camera)) I get my dreams come
11.		true because my er two child is already finished the university. *I*
12.		*have a friend, as well* ((to camera)) she just gave birth two weeks
13.		and then she went to work because she is a single mum and she
14.		leave her baby to her mum when she arrived, she *have still milk in*
15.		*her* you know breasts (h) so then she cried when when the milk
16.		come out. She'd just cry because she remember her baby behind
		she just left them

parents (2–4). This is achieved through using talk in the third person to present this as a shared experience for Filipino women. Connie uses discourse about her friend's experience as further evidence ('she just gave birth two weeks and then she went to work because she is a single mum and she leave her baby to her mum' (12–13)). A 'single mother' category is used by her to account for her friend's actions and negotiate her morality (Stokoe 2003) to present her choice as an economic necessity. However, Connie laughs and uses talk about crying (15) to construct the high emotional cost to her friend. Thus, entertainment programming about the super-rich draws upon talk about migration and employment that requires negotiation by speakers to account for the sacrifices involved by poorer groups.

Discussion

Entertainment documentaries are a form of political communication as wealth porn programming draws upon a dominant ideology, such as neoliberalism, meeting Edelman's (2001) criteria to manage accountability for the wealthy's employment of domestic staff. Entertainment documentaries present wealth inequality as banal through their construction of staff working in the domestic sphere of the super-rich. The construction of inequality as mundane is achieved through drawing upon individualism as a tenet of neoliberal ideology. Talk about class as 'posh' and visual images of wealth allow super-rich speakers to warrant employing staff as an aspirational practice that is deserved. However, the fairness of the position of staff is challenged through the production process by using humour to ridicule extremely wealthy people. By editing footage and providing narration, an ambiguous argument is constructed within the broadcasts through the use of humour. This ambiguity allows the economic inequality present within the homes of the super-rich to be challenged but not overtly questioned. An additional dilemma is present within the programmes themselves as staff are constructed as paying a high emotional cost for their employment but receive benefits for their individual families. By drawing upon neoliberalism, employing domestic staff is positioned as just and acceptable in entertainment documentaries.

Entertainment Documentaries as a Form of Political Discourse

Wealth porn broadcasts need to be researched as a form of political communication given the negative consequences of wealth inequality in society. Individualistic arguments allow wealthy speakers to account for the extreme inequality that is present within their homes through the employment of domestic staff. Gibson (2016) highlights the banal acceptability of capitalism in society and the importance for Discursive Psychologists to consider ideology within their analysis. The situatedness of the media (Attenborough 2016) such as within television programmes requires the audience to draw upon their own cultural knowledge (Abell and Stokoe 2001). By flagging their wealth through their location or talk about being 'posh', the programmes draw upon constructions of wealth without requiring the super-rich to state their net worth. Through discussing the employment of workers, entertainment documentaries become a site for the super-rich to account for their practices drawing upon individualistic ideology to manage their position. Whilst wealth porn programming may be presented as mundane entertainment, it draws upon neoliberalism to maintain the status quo of the super-rich employing domestic staff. Thus, entertainment documentaries are used as a vehicle for political rhetoric to account for wealth inequality in society.

Using Humour to Manage Stake

Programming about extreme wealth uses humour as a vehicle to argue against extreme wealth and to critique the discourse of the super-rich. Humour provides more than entertainment and can be used to ridicule individuals (Billig 2001). Marwick (2015) discussed how the *Rich Kids of Instagram* presents privileged individuals as both aspirational and derided. The ridicule of people featured in the programmes is achieved through the use of humour in the post-production process. Comedy involves challenging social norms (Billig 2001, 2005) and positioning the wealthy as ridiculous questions their construction as wealth generators through their employment of others. Reality television that involves direct access to people, such as the wealth porn genre, presents its subjects as both everyday and bizarre (Casey 2008). Warranting the super-rich as weird invokes ridicule to challenge their position in society as humour can be used to question competence (Goodwin 1990). The difficulties of challenging the rich are managed through the use of absurdity to manage stake as warranting an argument as funny is a protective strategy. Arguments that criticise the extremely wealthy are constructed as not serious and allow controversial statements to be made. Humour and, in particular, the presentation of the super-rich as absurd allow the discourse of the super-rich to be challenged. Therefore, entertainment documentaries use humour to create arguments against wealth inequality.

Negotiating Ambiguity About Employing Domestic Staff

Within the programmes, both staff and wealthy employers are positioned within dilemmas about their role. The super-rich present staff as a necessity within their lives as they are effortful (Gibson 2009). By using codes about class, wealthy speakers draw upon the aspiration of independence used by the middle classes as they benefit from more time (Walkerdine 2011). Talk about wealthy individuals in the media warrants their need to be free of restrictions due to their wealth and assumed economic productivity (Carr et al. 2018). Super-rich speakers draw upon neoliberalism, placing an emphasis on individual freedom and consumption, to account for employing staff as purchasing extra time for themselves. Unlike other representations of domestic staff on television such as period dramas, the hiring of domestic staff within the programmes is warranted as a modern everyday assumption for the more affluent. Wealthy speakers warrant the use of staff as aspirational by arguing that others would if they were in their position. However, the construction of staff as essential for the super-rich challenges their position as independent from others. Additionally, the editing of footage to show ostentatious lifestyles further emphasises the ambiguity within the documentaries as the super-rich are warranted as lacking financial restrictions yet dependent on staff for everyday tasks. The use of voiceovers to ridicule (Billig 2007) further questions the position of the super-rich to generate wealth when they do not perform basic tasks such as organising a party. Strategic ambiguity (Condor et al. 2013) is used to challenge the deservedness of the super-rich and, in addition to humour, offers further protection when challenging the deservedness of the super-rich.

Domestic staff featured within the programmes need to manage their accountability for working for the super-rich as their labour is constructed as demanding and involving sacrifices. Workers' talk uses quiescence to present themselves as comfortable with the arrangement despite being separate from their family and subject to the demands of the super-rich. Staff use this contrast to manage their position as an employee and to present themselves as hardworking and resilient. Whilst the labour of

108   P. Carr

staff is positioned as in the interest of others such as family member's educations, the super-rich account for being domestic employers as beneficial to them. For example, when wealthy mothers warrant the outsourcing of their role through talk about needing additional time. Employers' consumption of labour is constructed as fair as both sides benefit (Gullace 2019). Staff are objectified (Walker 2017) through their presence as 'extras' that also allow the super-rich to warrant their status in society (Steedman 2003) and to present these arrangements as fair. Talk about class is used to present poorer groups working for the super-rich as an everyday assumption. Just world arguments where individuals are positioned as responsible for their status (Goodman and Carr 2017), as people get 'what they deserve' (Lerner 1980, p. 11), are used to account for the employment of domestic staff. Talk about the world as just allows the extreme inequality with the programmes to be presented as acceptable. Presenting society as just involves drawing upon individualism as a tenet of neoliberalism to warrant people as deserving of their economic status. Entertainment documentaries about the super-rich draw upon neoliberal ideology to account for their use of domestic staff constructing extreme inequality within their homes. By including opposing ideological stances through the use of ambiguity, the broadcasts are a form of political communication.

Conclusion

This chapter establishes that entertainment documentaries can be analysed as a form of political communication as they draw upon dominant neoliberal ideology and negotiate differing ideological positions. Wealth porn documentaries present wealth inequality as an everyday assumption. Researchers' boundaries about what types of genres can be viewed as a form of political communication can be extended to include documentaries. A particular way of producing the televisual genre and content becomes part of the analysis. Narrative ambiguity challenges the dominant discourse legitimising extreme inequality within the home. Ambiguity questions the warranting of the super-rich as deserving of staff for basic tasks through the use of humour to ridicule their position.

Domestic staff account for their labour by drawing upon collective ideology as their work benefits others. The extension of the analysis of political communication needs to include DP. Documentaries provide an example of how DP can be used to analyse entertainment broadcasts as a form of political communication.

References

Abell, J., & Stokoe, E. H. (1999). 'I take full responsibility, I take some responsibility, I'll take half of it but no more than that': Princess Diana and the location of blame in the Panorama interview. *Discourse Studies, 1*(3), 297–319.

Abell, J., & Stokoe, E. H. (2001). Broadcasting the royal role: Constructing culturally situated identities in the Princess Diana Panorama interview. *British Journal of Social Psychology, 40*(3), 417–435.

Abercrombie, N. (1980). *Class, structure and knowledge*. Basil Blackwell.

Antaki, C. (2003). The uses of absurdity. In H. van den Berg, M. Wetherell, & H. Houtkoop-Steenstra (Eds.), *Analyzing race talk: Multidisciplinary approaches to interview discourse* (pp. 85–102). Cambridge University Press.

Attenborough, F. T. (2016). A forgotten legacy? Towards a discursive psychology of the media. In C. Tileagă & E. Stokoe (Eds.), *Discursive psychology: Classic and contemporary issues* (pp. 224–240). Routledge.

Baena, R., & Byker, C. (2015). Dialects of nostalgia: Downton Abbey and English identity. *National Identities, 17*(3), 259–269. https://doi.org/10.108 0/14608944.2014.942262

Beaverstock, J. V., & Faulconbridge, J. R. (2013). Wealth segmentation and the mobilities of the super-rich. In T. Birtchnell & J. Caletrío (Eds.), *Elite mobilities* (pp. 40–61). Routledge.

Billig, M. (1982). *Ideology and social psychology: Extremism, moderation and contradiction*. Blackwell.

Billig, M. (1992). *Talking of the royal family*. London: Routledge.

Billig, M. (2001). Humour and hatred: The Racist Jokes of the Ku Klux Klan. *Discourse & Society, 12*, 267–289.

Billig, M. (2005). *Laughter and Ridicule: Towards a social critique of humour*. Sage Publications.

Billig, M. (2007). Politics as an appearance and reality show: The hermeneutics of suspicion. In D. Wring, J. Green, R. Mortimore, & S. Atkinson (Eds.),

Political communications: The general election campaign of 2005 (pp. 215–229). Palgrave Macmillan.

Billig, M., Condor, S., Edwards, D., Gane, M., Middleton, D., & Radley, A. R. (1988). *Ideological dilemmas: A social psychology of everyday thinking.* SAGE.

Briddick, C. (2019). Precarious workers and probationary wives: How immigration law discriminates against women. *Social & Legal Studies, 29*(2), 201–224. https://doi.org/10.1177/0964663919839187

Brown, W. (2003). Neo-liberalism and the end of liberal democracy. *Theory and Event, 7*(1). https://doi.org/10.1353/tae.2003.0020

Burke, S., & Demasi, M. (2019). Applying discursive psychology to 'fact' construction in political discourse. *Social & Personality Psychology Compass, 13*(5). https://doi.org/10.1111/spc3.12449

Burr, V. (2015). *Social constructionism.* Routledge.

Byrne, K. (2014). Adapting heritage: Class and conservatism in Downton Abbey. *Rethinking History, 18*(3), 311–327. https://doi.org/10.108 0/13642529.2013.811811

Carr, P., Goodman, S., & Jowett, A. (2018). 'I don't think there is any moral basis for taking money away from people': Using discursive psychology to explore the complexity of talk about tax. *Critical Discourse Studies, 16*(1), 84–95. https://doi.org/10.1080/1745904.2018.1511440

Casey, B. (2008). *Television studies: The key concepts* (2nd ed.). Routledge.

Condor, S., Tileagă, C., & Billig, M. (2013). Political rhetoric. In L. Huddy, D. O. Sears, & J. S. Levy (Eds.), *Oxford handbook of political psychology* (pp. 262–300). Oxford University Press.

Copelman, D. M. (2019). Consuming Downton Abbey: The commodification of heritage and nostalgia. *Journal of British Cinema and Television, 16*(1), 61–77. https://doi.org/10.3366/jbctv.2019.0456

Crouch, C. (2011). *The strange non-death of neo-liberalism.* London: Polity.

De Benedictis, S., Allen, K., & Jensen, T. (2017). Portraying poverty: The economics and ethics of factual welfare television. *Cultural Sociology, 11*(3), 337–358. https://doi.org/10.1177/1749975517712132

Demasi, M. (2019). Facts as social action in political debates about the European Union. *Political Psychology, 40*(1), 3–20. https://doi.org/10.1111/pops.12496

Edelman, M. (2001). *The politics of misinformation.* Cambridge University Press.

Edley, N. (1993). Prince Charles- our flexible friend: Accounting for variations in constructions of identity. *Text, 13*(3), 397–422.

Edley, N., & Wetherell, M. (1997). Jockeying for position: The construction of masculine identities. *Discourse & Society, 8*(2), 203–217.

Edwards, D., & Potter, J. (1992). *Discursive psychology*. Sage Publications.

Färber, A., & Podkalicka, A. (2019). Thrift television: Narratives of enduring, saving, and living well. A thematic introduction. *Culture Unbound, 11*(3–4), 421–442.

Feltwell, T., Vines, J., Salt, K., Blythe, M., Kirman, B., Barnett, J., et al. (2017). Counter-discourse activism on social media: The case of challenging "poverty porn" television. *Computer Supported Cooperative Work, 26*, 345–385. https://doi.org/10.1007/s10606-017-9275-z

Fine, M., & Gordon, S. M. (1989). Feminist transformations of/despite psychology. In M. Crawford & M. Gentry (Eds.), *Gender and thought: Psychological perspectives*. Springer.

Fudge, K., & Strauss, K. (2014). Migrants, unfree labour, and the legal construction of domestic servitude: Migrant domestic workers in the UK. In C. Costello & M. Freedland (Eds.), *Migrants at work: Immigration and vulnerability in labour law*. Oxford University Press.

Furnham, A., Masters, J., Bond, M., Payne, M., Heaven, P., Rajamanikam, R., et al. (1993). A comparison of protestant work ethic beliefs in thirteen nations. *Journal of Social Psychology, 133*(2), 185–197. https://doi.org/10.1080/00224545.1993.9712136

Gibson, S. (2009). The effortful citizen: Discursive social psychology and welfare reform. *Journal of Community & Applied Social Psychology, 19*(6), 393–410.

Gibson, S. (2016). Banal nationalism, postmodernism and capitalism: Revisiting billig's critique of rorty. In C. Tileagă & E. Stokoe (Eds.), *Discursive psychology: Classic and contemporary issues* (pp. 289–302). Routledge.

Goodman, S., & Carr, P. (2017). Belief in a just world as an argumentative resource in debates about unemployment benefits. *Journal of Community and Applied Social Psychology, 27*(4), 312–323.

Goodwin, M. C. (1990). *He-said-she-said: Talk as social organization among black children*. Indiana University Press.

Gullace, N. F. (2019). A (very) open elite: Downton Abbey, historical fiction and America's Romance with the British aristocracy. *Journal of British Cinema and Television, 16*(1), 9–27. https://doi.org/10.3366/jbctv.2019.0453

Harrington, B. (2016). *Capital without borders: Wealth managers and the one percent*. Harvard University Press.

Harvey, D. (2000). *Spaces of hope*. University of California.

Hester, H. (2014). Weaponizing prurience. In B. Korte & F. Regard (Eds.), *Narrating poverty and precarity in Britain* (pp. 205–224). Berlin: De Gruyter.

Imre, A. (2016). *TV socialism*. Duke University Press.

International Labour Organization. (2011). *Domestic workers convention, 2011 (No. 189): Convention concerning decent work for domestic workers*. Retrieved July 26, 2019, from https://www.hrw.org/report/2014/03/30/hidden-away/abuses-against-migrant-domestic-workers-uk

International Labour Organization. (2013). *Domestic workers across the world: Global and regional statistics and the extent of legal protection*. Geneva: International Labour Office.

Iyengar, S. (1990). Framing responsibility for political issues: The case of poverty. *Political Behavior, 12*(1), 19–40.

Jefferson, G. (2004). Glossary of transcript symbols with an introduction. In G. H. Lerner (Ed.), *Conversation analysis: Studies from the first generation* (pp. 13–31). John Benjamins.

Keeley, B. (2015). Income inequality: The gap between rich and poor. *OECD Insights*. https://doi.org/10.1787/9789264246010-en

Kelly, L. W., & Boyle, R. (2011). Business on television: Continuity, change, and risk in the development of television's "business entertainment format". *Television & New Media, 12*(3), 228–247. https://doi.org/10.1177/1527476410372097

Kelvin, P., & Jarrett, J. E. (1985). Unemployment. *European Monographs in Social Psychology*.

Kress, G. (2010). *Multimodality: A social semiotic approach to contemporary communication*. Routledge.

LaMarre, A., & Sutherland, O. (2014). Expert opinion? A micro-analysis of eating disorder talk on Dr. Phil. *The Qualitative Report, 19*(43), 1–20.

Lerner, M. J. (1980). *The belief in a just world: A fundamental delusion*. Plenum Press.

Liebes, T., & Livingstone, S. (1994). The structure of family and romantic ties in the Soap Opera: An ethnographic approach. *Communication Research, 21*(6), 717–741. https://doi.org/10.1177/009365094021006004

Littler, J. (2018). *Against meritocracy: Culture, power and myths of mobility*. Routledge.

Livingstone, S. (1998). *Making sense of television: The psychology of audience interpretation* (2nd ed.). Routledge.

MacMillan, K., & Edwards, D. (1999). Who Killed the Princess? Description and Blame in the British Press. *Discourse Studies, 1*(2), 151–174. https://doi.org/10.1177/1461445699001002002

Marwick, A. E. (2015). Instafame: Luxury selfies in the attention economy. *Public Culture, 27*(1(75)), 137–160. https://doi.org/10.1215/08992363-2798379

Medeiros, M., & de Souza, P. H. F. (2015). The rich, the affluent and the top incomes. *Current Sociology Review, 63*(6), 869–895. https://doi.org/10.1177/0011392114551651

Mihelj, S. (2017). Memory, post-socialism and the media: Nostalgia and beyond. *European Journal of Cultural Studies, 20*(3), 235–251. https://doi.org/10.1177/1367549416682260

Mihelj, S., & Huxtable, S. (2018). *Media systems to media cultures: Understanding socialist television*. Cambridge University Press.

Miller, T. (2010). *Television studies: The basics*. Routledge.

Mumford, G., & Wardell, S. (2015). Catch-up TV Guide: Super-rich season, togetherness and more. *The Guardian*. January, 10. Retrieved July 20, 2018, from https://www.theguardian.com/tv-and-radio/2015/jan/10/catch-up-tv-guide

Paterson, L. L., Peplow, D., & Grainger, K. (2017). Does money talk equate to class talk? Audience responses to poverty porn in relation to money and debt. In A. Mooney & E. Sifaki (Eds.), *The language of money and debt* (pp. 205–231). https://doi.org/10.1007/978-3-319-57568-1_9

Pickett, K. E., James, O. W., & Wilkinson, R. G. (2006). Income inequality and the prevalence of mental illness: A preliminary international analysis. *Journal of Epidemiology and Community Health, 60*(7), 646–647. https://doi.org/10.1136/jech.2006.046631

Pickett, K. E., & Wilkinson, R. G. (2015). Income inequality and health: A causal review. *Social Science and Medicine, 128*(C), 316–326. https://doi.org/10.1016/j.socscimed.2014.12.031

Poole, G. A. (2000). 'Wealth porn' and beyond. *Columbia Journalism Review, 39*(4), 22.

Singha, L. (2019). *Work, labour and cleaning: The social contexts of outsourcing housework*. Bristol University Press.

Steedman, C. (2003). Servants and their relationship to the unconscious. *Journal of British Studies, 42*, 316–350.

Stokoe, E. H. (2003). Mothers, single women and sluts: Gender, morality and membership categorization in neighbour disputes. *Feminism and Psychology, 13*(3), 317–344. https://doi.org/10.1177/0959353503013003006

Sugarman, J. (2015). Neoliberalism and psychological ethics. *Journal of Theoretical and Philosophical Psychology, 35*(2), 103–116. https://doi.org/10.1037/a0038960

Taylor, P. (2010). *The careless state: Wealth and welfare in Britain today.* Bloomsbury.

Urry, J. (2007). *Mobilities.* Polity.

Urry, J. (2014). *Offshoring.* Polity.

Walker, T. J. (2017). Black skin, white uniforms: Race, clothing, and the visual vernacular of luxury in the andes. *Souls, 19*(2), 196–212. https://doi.org/10.1080/10999949.2016.1239158

Walkerdine, V. (2011). Neoliberalism, working-class subjects and higher education. *Contemporary Social Science, 6*(2), 255–271. https://doi.org/10.1080/21582041.2011.580621

Walsh-Bowers, R., & Gokani, R. (2014). The personal and political economy of psychologists' desires for social justice. *Journal of Theoretical and Philosophical Psychology, 34*, 41–55. https://doi.org/10.1037/a0033081

Wiggins, S. (2017). *Discursive psychology: Theory, method and applications.* Sage Publications.

Wilkinson, R., & Pickett, K. (2010). *The spirit level: Why equality is better for everyone.* Penguin Books.

Wilkinson, R., & Pickett, K. (2018). *The inner level: How more equal societies reduce stress, restore sanity and improve everyone's wellbeing.* Penguin Books.

5

A Multimodal Discourse Analysis of 'Brexit': Flagging the Nation in Political Cartoons

Henry W. Lennon and Laura Kilby

Constructing Nationhood and National Identity

Given the comparatively modern construction of the nation-state, the study of nationhood, nationalism and national identity has a relatively young history (Billig 1995). Nations are typically characterised as bounded, finite entities, with a sovereign right to act as a self-determining agent on an international stage (Anderson 2006). Nationalism, understood as the habitual identification and strong devotion to one's own nation, is an inseparable aspect of nationhood and closely linked to conflicts that centre on ethnic and political fault lines (Guibernau et al. 2010). Over the course of the twentieth century, national identity—a

---

H. W. Lennon (✉)
University of Derby, Derby, UK
e-mail: h.lennon@derby.ac.uk

L. Kilby
Sheffield Hallam University, Sheffield, UK

© The Author(s), under exclusive license to Springer Nature Switzerland AG 2020
M. A. Demasi et al. (eds.), *Political Communication*, Palgrave Studies in Discursive
Psychology, https://doi.org/10.1007/978-3-030-60223-9_5

115

sense of connectedness to the nation that is embedded in everyday civic life—has increasingly entered political thought (Anderson 2006). The nation can be understood as an 'imagined community', insofar that most members will never know each other, yet will share an 'image of their communion' (Anderson 2006, p. 6) irrespective of social, ethnic or economic inequalities within. Anderson (2006) further highlights that, regardless of how national identity is socially engineered or politically reworked in elite discourse, it always requires the emotional endorsement of its citizenry. Billig (1995) emphasises that national identity comprises a typology of commonplace narrative mechanisms such as values, achievements and everyday practices that facilitate the binding of a nation. These characteristics may reflect ambiguities and contradictions that can subtly change over time. Thus, overt and more implicit prejudice discourse towards different out-groups, such as immigrants, can gradually alter in shared societal discourse as some groups are assimilated or side-lined, whilst newer or more newsworthy out-groups take centre stage. Shared history is also pertinent to national identity, providing both a resource for the community to meet the future and an anchor that can provoke feelings of pride and, equally, feelings of shame or ambivalence (Parekh 2000).

Billig's (1995) thesis on 'banal nationalism' demonstrates that nationalism is endemic in the mundane language of the nation-state, largely unnoticed in the social psychology of everyday life. Rather than viewing nationalism as an 'identity' unique to individuals, it is an 'everyday ideology' that implicitly informs social life as a shared experience, unless circumstantial political events necessitate explicitly confrontational, expressive and/or proud rhetoric. Billig (1995) describes nationalism as a 'way of being in a world of nations' (p. 65), with the nation continually flagged in political and media discourse. Billig illustrates his argument via a 'day survey' of British national newspapers, which evidences how the nation is a repeated feature of news stories. In some cases, where the news concerns international current affairs, explicit reference to 'Britain' or discussions of 'Brits' serve to flag the nation. However, reminders of nationhood are also routinely embedded in the sports pages, in weather reports and in home news stories. For example, in the sports pages, individuals are regularly referred to through terms such as 'British hopeful', and images of the British flag are a common feature. Weather reports routinely feature a map of Britain and refer to weather variations across 'the country', and this is sometimes also contrasted with weather coming in from 'abroad' (Billig 1995). Billig's thesis on the mundane, everyday forms of nationalism is a particularly powerful argument when set against the pervasive narrative in 'Western' nations where nationalism is often framed as an exceptional perspective, on the edges of civilised or 'reasonable' political discourse (e.g. Goodman and Johnson 2013). Following Billig' s (1995) work, there is a body of discursive research interested in the dynamics of national identity and nationalism, much of which has been conducted around the British and Irish archipelago (e.g. Abell et al. 2006, 2007; Condor 2000, 2010; Joyce et al. 2012; Stevenson and Abell 2011). These studies explore national identity as 'ways of talking about nationhood' (Billig 1995, p. 8).

The UK and Brexit

The UK has long been constructed as a nation through discourses of Britishness. As befitting a national identity, Britishness is an overarching identity of civic and political status, subsuming a series of regions, nations and ethnic groups, set against a backdrop of a Protestant culture, recurrent war and an increasingly multicultural empire (Colley 1992). There are important debates regarding the relative dominance of Englishness within the construction of British national identity in relation to Scotland, Wales and Northern Ireland (see Cohen 1994; MacPhee and Poddar 2007; Ward 2009). Whilst rehearsing these debates is outside the scope of the current chapter, our analysis will explore how such issues play out where they are shown to be relevant in our data. Britishness has increasingly featured in social questions concerning globalisation, 'super' diversity, democratic deficit, social stratification, digitalisation and automation of work (e.g. Cruse 2008). UK Prime Ministers have repeatedly (re) defined Britishness in their political discourse to rally the nation, transforming social issues into national causes: from John Major's 'European Britishness', Tony Blair's 'cool Britannia', Gordon Brown's 'civic Britishness' and David Cameron's 'one-nation conservatism' through to Teresa May's 'burning injustices'.

EU membership has featured as a particularly contentious saga in UK political discourse; an ideological struggle between nationalist and internationalist sentiments has led to discernible constitutional challenges in every decade since UK entry to the then EEC in 1973 (Kaiser and Varsori 2012). The 2016 UK referendum on continued membership of the European Union presented the EU question to the British public in very simple terms. The British Electoral Commission, who oversees the process of elections in the UK, selected two campaigns arguing opposing perspectives in response to the question *'Should the United Kingdom remain a member of the European Union?'* The 'In Campaign' argued for continuing EU membership (some within arguing for the status quo, others for internal reform). In contrast, the 'Vote Leave' campaign argued for leaving the EU (with variable formulations of what that might mean in practice). Whilst there are many interesting and complex questions in these opposing referendum campaigns, and indeed a great deal more in continued debates in the post-referendum political landscape, for the purposes of the current chapter, suffice to say that a small majority of 52% voted in favour of the UK leaving the European Union. Following this vote, empirical studies have investigated the ways that 'Brexit' was constructed via categories, shared histories and political attitudes.

Moore and Ramsay (2017) demonstrate in their content analysis that Brexit talk dominated political discourse in over 14,000 mainstream media outlets between April and June 2016, infiltrating all other political and social issues as the quintessential political event of the UK in the twenty-first century. Recent research highlights that themes of nationhood, identity and belonging permeate Brexit discourse. Meredith and Richardson (2019) examine how 'Brexiter' and 'Remainer' categories were formulated in online responses to both Brexit-supporting and Brexit-opposing newspaper articles in 2016. They also found these terms paired together within the broader 'voters in the referendum' categorisation device. Descriptors for both terms were typically employed by the opposing group with pejorative attributions used to explain political standpoints, such as 'lack of intelligence' for Brexiters and 'scaremongers' for Remainers (pp. 46–47). Elsewhere, Goodman and Narang (2019) have argued that depictions of the 'refugee crisis' in Internet forums, which present child refugees as adults, as a 'burden' to taxpayers and as oppositional to the public's will, provide key political rhetoric and impetus for the Leave vote campaign. Krzyżanowski (2019) examines the constitution of 'Brexit-as-crisis' through conceptual mapping of past, present and future, showing how Brexit becomes signified and grounded in peril and possibility. Zappettini (2019) shows how the two campaign websites feature trade and immigration as their main argumentative schemes, producing a 'toxic' logic concerned with promoting mercantile policies and excluding 'outsiders'. Elsewhere, Maccaferri (2019) places Brexit within the question of Europe's re-narration through 'border talk' in traditional and online media, drawing on cultural and historical tropes, whilst research by Valdés-Miyares (2018) contrasts a film speech in *This Is England* with a 'victory' speech by Nigel Farage in June 2016. This research demonstrates how they both utilise mythology, symbolic allusions to war and an idealised future to advocate nationalist themes. Such works mark an emergent interest in the discursive construction of Brexit but also speak to long-standing research exploring how political communication constructs social psychological issues such as social identity, prejudice and belonging (Condor et al. 2013). In the current chapter, we seek to further these interests by undertaking a multimodal critical discursive analysis of Brexit cartoons with a specific concern to examine the place of 'rhetorical ambiguity' in Brexit discourse.

Political Communication, Discourse Analysis and Multimodality

The study of political communication is an established canon in discourse analysis, not least in traditions concerned with the maintenance and reproduction of social problems (Wooffitt 2005); this is especially so in discursive psychology (DP). DP researchers utilise a range of approaches for data collection and explore varying genres of political discourse. Previous research has examined data collected via interviews (e.g. Abell et al. 2006; Condor and Gibson 2007) and focus groups (e.g. Goodman and Burke 2010; Xenitidou and Morasso 2014) to explore everyday or lay discourses on a range of social political issues. Other work has sought to examine elite forms of public discourse such as political speeches (Capdevila and Callaghan 2008), analysis of policy documents (e.g. Popoviciu and Tileaga 2019), constituent or open letters (Barnes et al. 2004; Lynn and Lea 2003), print media articles (Kilby et al. 2013; Rosie et al. 2004) and radio/television talk (Goodman and Johnson 2013; Kilby and Horowitz 2013). This diverse body of work marks the territory in which the articulation of political attitudes, the negotiation of discrimination or prejudice and the construction of civic identities have been studied (Condor et al. 2013).

Critical discourse studies (CDS) comprises discursive work that sets out with an explicit commitment to examine areas of social inequality and seeks to reveal how relations of power and institutional structures are underpinned by discursive practices (e.g. Fairclough 1989, 2001; Fairclough and Wodak 1997; van Dijk 2001, 2015; Wodak and Meyer 2015). Historically, tensions have existed between DP and CDS with some DP proponents contending that all DP is critical, whilst some CDS scholars claim that much of DP is not critical enough (see Wooffitt 2005 for overview). Whilst acknowledging tensions between DP and CDS regarding differing intellectual ambitions and differences regarding 'what counts' as criticality, CDS scholars share much common ground with proponents of DP and there is a great deal of analytic overlap (Goodman 2017). For our own part, we see analytic benefits to synthesising the unique contributions that both DP and CDS offer, whilst upholding a critical ambition for our work.

Our concern with criticality and our DP background directly inform our analytic approach; however, our distinct focus on multimodality leads us to position our work as multimodal critical discourse analysis (see Machin 2013). Multimodal research is concerned with examining a full range of complex semiotic forms including imagery, sound, language and so on. Expanding a focus beyond the linguistic is driven by awareness across both CDS and DP that discourses are increasingly multimodal and that meaning is constructed, and derived, holistically (Iedema 2003; Kress and van Leeuwen 2001, 2006; Levine and Scollon 2004, van Leeuwen 1999, 2005). Moreover, as Machin (2013, p. 351) points out, 'different semiotic resources allow certain qualities to be glossed over and others communicated more specifically'. Thus, the key issue for multimodal analysts is to examine what differing semiotic resources can be used to do.

Political Cartoons

Since the turn of the nineteenth century, political cartoons have provided a means of societal critique, political commentary and frivolity. They 'represent an aspect of social, cultural or political life in a way that condenses reality and transforms it in a striking, original and/or humorous way' (El Refaie 2009, p. 175). They place a spotlight on situated events, simplifying complex issues and upholding some narratives whilst delegitimising others (Silaški and Đurovic 2019). Their satirical humour often parodies political figures and places them into nonsensical or extreme situations, often through metaphor. We contend that the political cartoons genre is unique in its capacity for satire and subversion. It is grounded in the potential to provoke and to convey contentious or risky discourse. Moreover, the visual mode affords a clear potential for ambiguity. These features combined give visual satire an interesting capacity for constructing ideological positions whilst avoiding explicit challenge. However, as Mazid (2008) highlights, this does not mean that 'anything goes'. When it comes to what is said and how it is received, political cartoons must rely on a shared socio-historical background as a basis for its subversion. They must also tread a delicate line of ethical and moral acceptability.

There have been relatively few MDA or MCDA (multimodal critical discourse analysis) studies of political cartoons. An early study by Gamson and Stuart (1992) explored what they interpreted as a 'symbolic contest' between universalism and nationalism in nuclear weapon cartoons. More recently, Mazid (2008) investigated a corpus of President Bush and Bin Laden cartoons, showing how contrasting features mutually invoked God and justified 'righteous' action. Notably, despite opposing representations, they were both ridiculed and delegitimised as warmongering, murderous actors. A study by Müller et al. (2009) examined depictions of the Muslim prophet Muhammad published in the Danish newspaper *Jyllands-Posten*. They investigated how aggressive imagery conflated Islam with violence, or terrorism. Despite the ambiguous potential to see cartoons like 'Bomb in the Head' as satirising fundamentalism, they can also be seen as inflammatory to those who would present Islam as a peaceful way of life. In our earlier work (Kilby and Lennon 2018), we examined the prophet Muhammad cartoon that featured on the front page of the *Charlie Hebdo* magazine following the terror attacks on the *Charlie Hebdo* offices in 2015. We demonstrated how the concepts of peace and violence were simultaneously constructed and how the ambiguity of the multi-modal form facilitated quite distinct interpretations of the same discourse dependent on the cultural and ideological context of the audience. Recently, Silaški and Đurovic (2019) studied how the 'journey' metaphor in Brexit cartoons portrays a process filled with evaluative content, such as through allusions to the ending of a marriage and its unpleasant effects ('rocky territory', 'messy divorce', etc.). Recently, Musolff (2019) investigated the fascinating history of the proverb 'having your cake and eating it' in regard to UK-EU political negotiations, landing itself to both opposition critiques of its 'absurdity' and 'bold' assertions of hope and possibility.

Our aim is to contribute to the developing body of discursive work that explores Brexit (e.g. Krzyżanowski 2019; Meredith and Richardson 2019; Moore and Ramsay 2017; Zappettini 2019) by examining how Brexit is constructed in political cartoons published between March and October 2016. Of particular interest to us is an exploration of the ways in which satirical forms of combined linguistic and visual discourse facilitate rhetorical ambiguity.

Data and Analytic Approach

Via a Google search using the phrase 'political cartoons on Brexit, UK-EU relations', time-filtered for March–October 2016 to cover an eight-month time period with the referendum vote occurring mid-way in June 2016, we source 25 individual cartoons and 2 collections of Brexit cartoons that feature in media review articles by *The Guardian* (20 March 2016) and *Politico* (25 June 2016). The inclusion criteria are that Brexit should be the focal issue of the cartoon. We ensure that the corpus reflects a range of perspectives including more distinctively 'pro' and 'anti' positions and, as befitting the satirical nature of political cartoons, cartoons that offer an ambiguous stance. Data collection took place between January and March 2019.

We review and group the initial corpus according to common tropes of nationhood. This reviewing process highlights the prominence of two metaphorical tropes that we name 'Boundedness and Isolation' and 'Uncertain Waters'. These tropes are the most common means of representing Brexit across the data. They feature in cartoons that uphold both pro- and anti-Brexit rhetoric, as well as cartoons that convey ambiguous positions. In total, 12 cartoons are categorised under these two tropes. The focal imagery involves depictions of either the nation as a bounded geographical island ('Boundedness and Isolation') or depictions of ships/boats at sea ('Uncertain Waters'). These metaphorical concepts have previously been identified in discursive analyses of nationhood and belonging (e.g. Ana 1997, 1999; Charteris-Black 2006, 2013; Musolff 2004; Silaški and Đurovic 2019). Given the prominence of these tropes in our data and the existing use of such metaphors in discourses concerned with nationhood and belonging, we selected these cartoons as the data for our analysis. The 'Boundedness and Isolation' trope comprises four cartoons, whilst the 'Uncertain Waters' trope comprises eight.

Our analysis draws upon the multimodal analytic methods of Kress and van Leeuwen (2006) and related works (Kress and van Leeuwen 2001; van Leeuwen 2005; van Leeuwen and Jewitt 2001). Characteristics including composition, colour, represented participants, perspective and textual components are examined in order to reveal multimodal rhetorical mechanisms that are used to flag nationhood. Whilst each cartoon is unique, our focus is with examining common features across the data to understand the shared ways in which nationhood, otherness and belonging are (re)produced and to assess how the multimodal qualities of these satirical cartoons interact and intersect in the construction of this complex, highly flexible form of discourse.

It is helpful at the outset to state that we are not seeking to assess the 'truth' of the messages conveyed in our data. We recognise that in the context of political discourse, and particularly with regard to Brexit, analysis of how facts are presented and, indeed, how they are distorted can be a valid endeavour. However, as Kress and van Leeuwen (2006, pp. 145–155) highlight, 'from the point of view of social semiotics, truth is a construct of semiosis, and as such the truth of a particular social group arises from the values and beliefs of the group'. In keeping with this stance, ours is not an attempt to reveal any objective truth, but to assess how multiple forms-of-knowing are realised in these Brexit cartoons through the interplay of visual and textual semiotic form. Each cartoon has been coded (C1, C2, C3, C4, etc.). Links to each of the cartoons are provided at the end of the chapter.

Analysis and Discussion

Throughout our analysis we refer to visual depictions of the British Isles, as depictions of 'the nation'. We stress that, in many cases, such depictions are only partial and often do not include Northern Ireland, the Republic of Ireland or the Channel Islands. Central to our thesis is the contention that, that in all cases, what is being constructed are arguments that foreground nationhood and national identity in a manner wholly in keeping with Billig's (1995) account of banal nationalism. As our analysis will emphasise, what is absent and what is only partial in portrayals of 'the nation' can itself reflect important rhetorical and ideological elements within these constructions of Brexit.

Trope One: Boundedness and Isolation

Composition Overview

Kress and van Leeuwen (2006) outline three inter-related elements to composition, which together cohere the representational and interactive meanings of the multimodal product: (i) information values, which result from the relative placement of each element; (ii) salience, which concerns how attention is directed to particular elements; and (iii) framing, which involves the disconnection or connection of the elements. Composition is a holistic achievement that takes into account all components of the multimodal object. In the case of cartoons, analysis thus involves an assessment of both textual and visual elements.

All four cartoons in trope one share some interesting commonality with regard to broad composition. Three cartoons (C1, C2, C4) offer a visual portrayal of 'the nation' via a simple geographic sketch outline of the landmass of Great Britain. The fourth cartoon (C3) also includes the Republic of Ireland and so the landmass portrayed is closer to the entirety of the British Isles. The relative invisibility of Ireland is something we return to later. This visual depiction of the 'nation-as-island' foregrounds a familiar portrayal of the UK, which is often engaged in discourses of nationhood (Charteris-Black 2006) and regularly deployed in debates about immigration, belonging and otherness (e.g. Gibson and Hamilton 2011; Condor 2000). In each cartoon, 'the nation' is visualised as a bounded land with no other nation at its borders. Two of the cartoons depict 'the nation' floating at sea (C1, C4), whilst another offers a simple satellite-map-style portrayal of 'the nation' upon a white background (C3). The final cartoon gives the impression of viewing the Earth from outer space with 'the nation' depicted as the only discernible land-mass (C2).

The relative placement of elements on the page is central to the production of information values. Kress and van Leeuwen (2006) outline three primary analytic considerations: (i) the value of the left and right, which relates to how visuals convey given and new information; (ii) the value of top and bottom, which concerns the construction of ideological and factual information; and (iii) the information values of centre and margin. All four cartoons locate the visual of the British Isles as central to the overall image. Moreover, each cartoon offers a relatively simple composition with little to detract from that central image. Van Leeuwen (2005) proposes that with regard to information values, centrality communicates importance, such that the more central an object is, the more important it becomes. In these cartoons, the relative lack of other elements around the central image of 'the nation' constructs the UK as, by far, the most important issue in the Brexit debate. Moreover, due to the lack of other content, in two of the four cartoons, the UK appears to be the *only* consideration (C2, C3). As our analysis develops, we will further consider this satirical construction of Brexit as a fundamentally inward-looking political debate.

In the other two cartoons (C1, C4), continental Europe/the EU is flagged in distinct ways. We use a general reference here to Europe/the EU because it is not analytically possible to discern if the intended focus is Europe itself, either as a geographic landmass or as a collective citizenry, or if the focus is the European Union as a political entity. This kind of visual ambiguity is reminiscent of the classic rhetorical linguistic act of synecdoche. Synecdoche describes 'a figure of speech from classic rhetoric in which part of a category or item is used to refer to the whole (pars pro toto) or […] the whole is used to denote only a part (totum pro parte)' (Kilby et al. 2013, p. 54). In these cartoons (C1, C4) it is not possible to know the direction of such rhetorical pointing, leaving interpretation as a flexible matter for the viewer to resolve. We suggest this is a prime example of the capacity for ambiguity inherent to forms of visual discourse. This point is underscored by Machin (2013, p. 350), who states that 'images do not have such specific denotative meaning as language and therefore it is a less easy matter to pin down precisely what meanings they convey'.

C1 flags Europe/ the EU in a small area at the bottom right of the image. Three elements are located in this bottom-right section: a black landmass, presumably Europe, disappearing from view, the EU flag flying aloft but also disappearing from view and the side profile of the faces of two onlookers. Before unpacking this further, it is worth stating that, whilst continental Europe lies geographically to the bottom right of the British Isles, the overall composition of this image could have been presented differently and still retained the same level of geographical accuracy. For example, the composition could have centred Europe in the overall frame and positioned the 'the nation' towards the top left of the frame. However, locating Europe/the EU in the bottom-right location does interesting work in terms of information values. Kress and van Leeuwen (2006) point out that information located to the left conveys what is already known and what is widely accepted, whereas information at the right is typically contestable, problematic or 'not yet agreed upon by the viewer' (p. 181). The extreme right-hand positioning is understood therefore to construct Europe/the EU in these terms. Moreover, locating Europe/ the EU at the bottom of the image conveys additional information values regarding the ideal and the real. In this particular cartoon, 'the nation' is located top and centre compared to Europe/ the EU bottom right. Relations between what is contained in the top and the bottom convey information about the ideal and the real. Whilst the top is concerned with generalised or ideological messages, the bottom typically conveys details, information and 'practical consequences' (van Leeuwen 2005, p. 205). Whilst the marginal positioning of Europe/the EU compared to the UK constructs a discourse in which the UK is the focal concern, the relative scale of the EU flag located in the bottom foreground ensures that, whilst marginal, it remains a salient element of the discourse. Salient aspects are those that attract attention, often through foreground placement (Kress and van Leeuwen 2006). Hence, whilst Europe/the EU is constructed as lacking agency and as largely secondary to the UK, the location and scale of the still visible flag ensures it is not overlooked entirely.

Colour

There is a limited colour palette across all four cartoons, with mainly muted shades of grey, brown, blue and green dominating. However, one of the cartoons to depict the EU makes use of vibrant colour (C4). Here 'the nation' is portrayed as an island-shaped plug that has been pulled from the sea causing the water to flow away. The outline of the space where the plug once nestled is retained, emphasising a nation-shaped void. Into that void flows vivid blue water, along with yellow stars that are flowing towards the void from across the bottom of the composition. Drawing on Halliday's metafunctional semiotic theory, Kress and van Leeuwen (2006) theorise that colour can fulfil ideational, interpersonal and textual metafunctions. Colour is understood to act as a signifier, providing ready associations to existing shared knowledge, and flags provide a prominent example of the ways in which colour can fulfil ideational functions (Kress and van Leeuwen 2001). In this cartoon, the water and stars are clearly indicative of the EU flag, constructing a vision of the EU rapidly disappearing without the UK to plug the void. The significance of centrality within a composition is not governed by what is, or is not, depicted in that central space. With regard to emptiness or absence, van Leeuwen (2005, p. 208) highlights that 'even when the centre is empty, it will continue to exist in absentia, as the invisible pivot around which everything else turns'. Hence, in this construction of Brexit, 'the nation' remains dominant even when it is no longer in situ. The use of vivid colour to portray the EU flag commands attention, ensuring that this depiction of the disappearance of the EU is part of the overall discourse.

The only other noticeable use of colour involves the use of red, white and blue in the depiction of the British flag, which features in two of the cartoons (C1, C2). Moreover, the only use of primary colours across all four cartoons is in the portrayal of the British flag or the EU flag. Colours are understood to carry meaning potentials linked to shared cultural history (Kress and van Leeuwen 2001); thus, when red, white and blue are depicted on the British flag in the context of UK/EU Brexit debates, British nationhood is clearly signified (cf. Annabell and Nairn 2019).

Textual Components and Represented Participants

Three of the cartoons (C1, C2, C3) include some very limited textual content. In each case, there is a notable ideological contrast or tension between the text and the image. Kress and van Leeuwen (2006) distinguish between represented participants (RPs) (people, objects and places depicted in images) and interactive participants (IPs) (producers and viewers). Before exploring textual components further, it is useful to also consider RPs in these cartoons. As previously indicated, all four cartoons in this trope (C1, C2, C3, C4) present a minimal composition with limited content; this includes strikingly few RPs. Two of the cartoons have no RPs (C3, C4), and one of the cartoons without RPs also has no textual content (C4). C4 relies solely on the visual image of the EU draining away down a plughole where 'the nation' once resided to convey the narrative. The other cartoon without participants (C3) presents a two-part title above an image that is divided into two distinct panels. Dividing the image in this way acts as a framing device. Framing devices connect or disconnect aspects of the composition (Jewitt and Oyama 2001), in this

5 A Multimodal Discourse Analysis of 'Brexit': Flagging… 129

case signifying a clear disconnection between the left and the right of the image. The left-hand panel appears directly below the first half of the title, namely 'Britain Before Brexit'. This panel portrays a simplistic satellite map of 'the nation'. The right-hand panel appears directly below the second half of the title 'Britain After Brexit'. This panel portrays the same image but the image is inverted. There is no other textual content in the left-hand panel; however, the right-hand panel depicts a word bubble emanating from somewhere in the middle of the map that contains the words 'Bugger Off.' Here again, we see how the use of the left and the right constructs the 'given' and the 'new' (Kress and van Leeuwen 2006). On the left, we see 'the nation' pre-Brexit, a known and unremarkable environment. Conversely, on the right, 'the nation' post-Brexit is constructed as an unfamiliar and confused land, it is literally upside down. As the only words in the image, the demand to 'bugger off' is highly salient. It directs attention to the right-hand panel, increasing the focus on the upside-down map, emphasising claims of an unknown future, a place where isolationism and exclusion rule.

Turning our attention to the two cartoons that contain RPs, one cartoon (C2) portrays 'the nation' as if being gazed down upon from space, appearing as the only visible nation on the planet. Depicted as standing on the map of 'the nation' is a quintessential English man in hat and umbrella; at his side is a similarly regaled woman. Above them rises a banner which reads 'Free at Last'. A speech bubble emanates from the side of the UK with the words 'Who are we going to blame for our problems now?' There is an obvious tension between the message on the banner, which suggests a welcome liberation of 'the nation', and the speech bubble, which suggests this newfound freedom might not be all it appears. As with C3, the image constructs a future outside of the EU as unknown and potentially ill conceived. It further conveys isolationism and separation.

The other cartoon (C1) includes four RPs, two standing on the map of 'the nation' and another two at the bottom right of the image. This image is the only one to make reference to differing nationalities within the UK via a stereotypical depiction of a Scottish man, wearing a kilt and walking down towards the bottom of 'the nation' with a knapsack over his shoulder. The second actor lacks the level of visual stereotyping reserved for the

Scottish character. The contrast achieved between the kilted Scottish man and the unremarkable shirt and grey trousers of the second actor suggests that this is an English man. He is closing an exaggerated, over-sized border gate to the channel wearing a somewhat harried facial expression. The gate holds a sign facing outwards across the channel with the words 'Keep Out', whilst the Scottish actor calls out 'Hold It!' clearly intending to leave before the gate closes. The other two RPs are bland profile portrayals of one man and one woman in the bottom-right corner; they are gazing across the channel from what is presumed to be Europe, looking somewhat askance.

Overall, RPs are a limited feature of the discourse, the primary job being to convey something about nationality, but little emotion or closeness is constructed. There is no use of direct gaze, therefore no direct address between the RPs and the viewer (Kress and van Leeuwen 2006). In cases where no direct contact with the viewer is made, images are understood to contain an 'offer'. They 'offer the represented participants to the viewer as items of information, the objects of contemplation, impersonally as though they were specimens for a display case' (Kress and van Leeuwen 2006, p. 119). Moreover, the size of the RPs relative to the overall image suggests a social distance between the viewer and the RPs. The smaller the participants, the greater the distance. There is the depiction of distance in both images; indeed the distance depicted in C2 as the viewer looks down upon the earth could not be greater. We contend that the lack of emphasis on people witnessed across the four cartoons minimises Brexit as a site of individual human concern, whilst the focus on 'the nation' serves to emphasise banal ideologies of nationhood (Billig 1995). C1 reflects national tensions within the UK as well as presenting 'the nation' as separate from the EU/Europe, whilst C2, C3 and C4 overlook any such internal tensions and solely construct a singular, isolated British nation.

Perspective

In each case, the visual perspective of the cartoon delivers a perpendicular, top-down angle such that the viewer is looking down upon the map of the British Isles from a high vantage point. Following Kress and van

Leeuwen (2006), this perspective presents the viewer with an objective image. An objective image does not suggest there are elements hidden from the viewer; rather it offers all there is to know. Images such as maps and diagrams are routinely understood to convey objectivity, and where a perpendicular angle is created, it provides the viewer with a privileged vantage. Kress and van Leeuwen (2006) contend that the top-down angle is 'the angle of maximum power [...] It contemplates the world from a god-like point of view, puts it at your feet rather than within reach of your hands' (p. 145). Using this perspective suggests that the viewer has the privilege of seeing the 'whole picture' and, yet, simultaneously that Brexit is happening far beyond reach.

Political cartoons enjoy a unique capacity for satire and subversion of current affairs, able to critique and disrupt political ideology from all sides. Moreover, the creative affordances of visual satire make political cartoons particularly adept at deconstructing normative arguments and opening new possibilities regarding what can be said (Mazid 2008). Satirical humour is applied across these cartoons, variously arguing that Brexit has turned the UK 'upside down' (C3), that Brexit is 'pulling the plug' on Europe (C4), that Brexit is short-sighted and isolationist (C2) and that Brexit is divisive for the UK (C1). However, it is striking that each of these cartoons relies upon a central visual representation of the British nation as a distinct, separable landmass as a basis for satirising Brexit which concentrates attention towards Brexit as a 'UK problem'. Irrespective of any given pro, anti or ambivalent stance towards leaving the EU offered by each cartoon, adopting this UK-centric approach relegates Europe to, at best, a supporting role. Moreover, little focus is given to emphasising internal UK divisions. In sum, we suggest that trope one conveys a sense of national myopia affecting all sides in the political cut and thrust of Brexit debate.

Trope Two: Uncertain Waters

Composition Overview

Eight cartoons (C5 to C12) comprise this trope. All depict either a galley-style ship or a rowing boat or lifeboat. Three are characterised by the depiction of a ship containing numerous RPs aboard choppy seas (C5, C6, C7). A fourth cartoon (C8) conveys a similar scene but the ship is only partly visible, and there is only one RP. Broadly, these four cartoons portray Brexit as chaotic and riven with political strife. RPs are busily engaged in oppositional tasks, and the vessels appear precarious, yet the RPs are largely unaware, and ideological tensions are played up via actions and speech. A further three cartoons present ships or boats on still seas (C9, C10, C11); two contain RPs. The overall composition of these three cartoons is relatively simple, constructing Brexit via variable notions of 'leaving' or 'splitting'. The final cartoon (C12) depicts a small rowing boat run aground on a dry seabed. All but one of the cartoons in trope two make use of central composition (Kress and van Leeuwen 2006) to locate the vessel, and whilst there are varying levels of detail used to depict what is happening aboard, there is little else in the overall composition. Visual placement mainly locates signifiers of the UK (i.e. British flag) to the left, thus constructing the UK as what is known (Kress and van Leeuwen 2006), whilst EU signifiers are to the right and thus the EU appears unfamiliar or contested (C5, C6, C9, C10, C12). However, C11 locates the EU to the left and the UK disappearing to the right. The focus of C11 is a critical commentary about the potential impact of leaving the EU to British commerce and business. Hence, on these issues, the EU is presented as what is known, whilst a future UK has become uncertain or problematic.

Colour

Colour and, in particular, colour contrasts serve to increase the salience of selected elements within the visual (Jewitt and Oyama 2001). As with trope one, the use of colour in trope two directs attention towards the

British flag and the EU flag. Repeatedly there is a signalling of British nationhood via portrayals of the British flag flying at full mast (C5, C6, C9, C11), whilst a fifth cartoon depicts 'Britannia'—the culturally familiar national personification of the UK—as a represented participant, regaled with a British flag-coloured shield and helmet (C12).

Coloured flags further construct opposition between the UK and the EU with four of the aforementioned cartoons also depicting the EU flag (C6, C9, C11, C12); however, on three occasions the EU flag is subverted. It is variously depicted as a plug being pulled from the ocean floor (C12); as a just-visible edge of a landmass, presumably Europe, from which the UK is sailing away from (C9); and as a sign erected on the shore of a landmass, again presumably Europe (C11). In the only cartoon to portray the EU flag as a flag (C6), we see it waving battered and torn on a ship about to crash over a ledge, whilst, in contrast, the British flag waves pristine upon a ship, sailing smoothly in the opposite direction towards a sunny horizon. The meaning potentials of colour are often related to cultural history, and national flags are a prime example of this (Kress and van Leeuwen 2001). These portrayals of the Union and EU flags in Brexit cartoons emphasise British nationhood, connecting contemporary debate to familiar histories of British Empire, whilst also conveying tensions between the UK and the EU. The preservation of the British flag *as* a flag, in contrast with the subversion of the EU flag, we suggest, serves to emphasise sovereignty and pride in British national identity (cf. Billig 1995), whilst the EU is constructed as less about identity or belonging and more about physical place. In this way, attention is directed towards geographic separation, whilst any exploration of identity as a multiple-layered concept that might simultaneously embody both Britishness and Europeanness is obscured.

Textual Components and Represented Participants

All cartoons contain some limited textual content, and all but one contain RPs. The more chaotic 'choppy seas' cartoons (C5, C6, C7, C8) offer a detailed composition of various RPs which include key political actors in Brexit—most notably, UK Prime Minister David Cameron who fought to keep the UK in the EU (C7, C8), UK politician and subsequent Prime Minister Boris Johnson who fought for the UK to leave the EU (C7) and German Chancellor and former President of the European Council Angela Merkel (C6). Stereotypical cultural portrayals of various EU nations, and one reference to Pakistan, which we read as a nod to the EU-Pakistan trade relations strategy, feature in one cartoon (C6); however, only one cartoon makes reference to differing nationalities within the UK by inclusion of a man wearing a jacket emblazoned with 'Scotland' (C5). This RP is aboard a rowboat named 'HMS Brexit' headed away from a large ship named 'Europe'. A speech bubble reads 'Nay, I'm thinking I'll swim back to the ship!'

Amongst the 'calmer seas' cartoons, two depict collections of bureaucratic featureless men dressed in grey (C10, C11), and a further cartoon constructs an iconic personification of nationhood via depiction of 'Britannia' and a 'Lion'. Both of these RPs are portrayed sitting in a boat alongside a fantastical creature (Unicorn) who has pulled an EU-styled plug from the sea (C12). The only cartoon without RPs (C9) portrays a UK-shaped boat sailing away from what appears to be the EU landmass.

As with trope one, text is used to play up ideological tensions, either through contradictions in the text itself or through contrast between text and image. Often, this is achieved through the inclusion of just a word or two. For example, in C9, the only word is the name of the ship—'Victory'. The text is very small and yet is highly salient, occupying the central position of the overall image, emblazoned on the back of a UK-shaped ship, which is sailing away from the EU into bright blue waters with a British flag flying high. In contrast, in C11 a stream of orderly British bureaucrats—each uniformly wearing a bowler hat and overcoat, carrying an umbrella and briefcase—are seen disembarking lifeboats from dark and ominous seas onto European shores. A sign above them reads 'Refugees Welcome'. In many cases uncertainty of the political position is maintained, with political actors arguing over Brexit with no clear winner (C7), or bureaucrats on a boat split in two with the British flag emblazoned on one side and 'U.E.' (*Uniunea Europeana*) on the other (C10).

Overall, as with trope one, there is lack of direct gaze used in these images, with no attempt made to create a direct connection with the viewer (cf. Kilby and Lennon 2018). Relatedly and again, as with trope one, there is a notable use of distance in the portrayal of RPs. Whilst some are recognisable through caricature of familiar features (e.g. Boris Johnson with an overly elaborate mane of foppish hair, David Cameron with an exaggerated elongated jawline), these actors are depicted using full body 'long shots', conveying significant distance from the viewer. Distance shots such as these make no 'demand' (Kress and van Leeuwen 2006) of the viewer, with little attempt to construct a close, or social, connection (Jewitt and Oyama 2001). In contrast to trope one, however, the images in trope two do reflect a substantial concern with the role of RPs, and they place a clear emphasis on contemporary political figures. Hence, whilst trope one downplays human action and emphasises Brexit as a site of abstract political ideology, trope two emphasises Brexit as a site of human endeavour. The use of distance and the lack of direct address in trope two locate the viewer as external to these events, permitting the viewer to look on at Brexit without being part of it. Regardless of any discernible 'pro' or 'anti' stance conveyed in these images, Brexit is routinely constructed as something beyond the reach of the public. In this way, any concern with Brexit as an event reflecting democratic choice, resulting from a public referendum, is downplayed, allowing the viewer to observe these events whilst not being accountable.

Perspective

In contrast to the objective perspective in trope one, cartoons in trope two engage subjective perspectives. Subjective perspectives use angles to convey a partial view of the 'whole picture'; hence the viewer is 'subjected' to a particular point of view (Kress and van Leeuwen 2006). Subjective perspective is developed via horizontal angles, utilising either a frontal or oblique positioning. These cartoons rely mainly on a horizontal frontal angle such that the viewer experiences looking directly on at the scene. This angle is understood to convey involvement between the RPs and the viewer, with frontality maximising that involvement (Kress and van Leeuwen 2006; Jewitt and Oyama 2001). Whilst there are differences across the data regarding what political point of view is upheld, subjective perspectives in these cartoons construct Brexit as a subjective issue which involves both the RPs and the viewer. As Jewitt and Oyama (2001, p. 135) point out, however, relations depicted in visual form have the capacity to 'symbolically make us relate to people who in fact have very considerable power over our lives'. Thus, the portrayal of relatability between the audience and the RPs may serve to normalise political chaos. Moreover, given the lack of direct gaze, the social distance and the wider context of these cartoons, we suggest that the elite political RPs are represented as relatable only inasmuch as they are humanised as hapless and/ or flawed and in this way confusion and uncertainty around Brexit is to be expected.

In contrast to the nation-as-island focus of trope one that emphasises boundedness and separation from Europe, trope two constructs Brexit by recourse to ideologies of 'the nation' that draw into view national history and political elites. Brexit is constructed as egoistic political theatre underpinned by competing ideologies of nationhood, with either the UK or the EU facing a perilous future, or as a 'very British' orderly separation with undertones of 'keep calm and carry on'. The satirising qualities of the genre are engaged to parody political figures (C5, C6, C7), variously constructing them as lacking direction, chaotic and ill equipped to navigate the political seascape of Brexit. Themes of British sovereignty and histories of Empire (C5, C12) embed narratives of banal nationalism (Billig 1995) into these Brexit debates, whilst the future of industry and commerce in Britain is presented as both vulnerable to isolation (C10) and at risk of leaving the UK (C11). Throughout, trope two utilises visual metaphors of troubled seas and of still waters to convey various themes of uncertainty, risk and folly. As with trope one, the capacity of visual discourse for constructing ambiguity allows the cartoons to remain open to varied interpretation, whilst ideological dilemmas (Billig et al. 1988) surrounding Brexit are revealed but left unresolved.

Discussion

Machin (2013) draws on the work of van Leeuwen and Wodak (1999) to outline how social practices can be transformed via a process of 'recontextualisation' whereby concrete people or processes are not logically or

5 A Multimodal Discourse Analysis of 'Brexit': Flagging...   137

transparently represented; instead 'a process of abstraction, addition, sub-stitution, and deletion' is deployed via a range of semiotic resources (Machin 2013, p. 352). This appears relevant to the discourse of these cartoons that simplify complex political discourse into easily consumed themes of nationhood, which benefit from ambiguity that is readily achieved when words are kept to a minimum, and satirical visuals offer multiple readings. Whilst satirical humour offers a means for critiquing and challenging the social order, we take a cautious approach to assessing how these satirical cartoons operate in the given context. In his thesis on humour and the social order, Billig (2005, p. 202) draws a distinction between disciplinary and rebellious humour, arguing 'disciplinary humour contains an intrinsic conservatism, whilst rebellious humour seems to be on the side of radicalism'. Political satire aligns comfortably with Billig's account of rebellious humour, and it is certainly the case that the cartoons in our analysis reflect the qualities of rebellious or 'contes-tive' humour that Billig describes. However, as Billig (2005) notes, decid-ing how to classify humour is rarely unambiguous and, in part, personal, ideological and ethical factors are brought to bear. Moreover, whilst rebellious humour has a long history of challenging political authority, this should not be readily assumed, particularly in the context of late capitalism where 'dutiful consumption encourages us to mock apparent authority' (Billig 2005, p. 209). Billig suggests the potential for a discon-nect between the experience and the consequence of humour such that 'what is experienced as rebellious humour possesses disciplinary func-tions' (p. 211).

In the context of our analysis, we are mindful of these possibilities. Our analysis finds that these cartoons do reflect rebellious humour—questioning the integrity and capability of political elites, emphasising uncertainty of political outcomes and highlighting isolationist ideology. However, there is much left unchallenged. Throughout trope one, irre-spective of any explicit pro-/anti-Brexit position conveyed, only scantest attention is given to divisions between Scottish and English national identity, or to Ireland or the Irish border. Moreover, Brexit is repeatedly presented as being an internal issue for the UK to settle, as opposed to a relational one between the UK and the EU. Practical issues such as trade and free movement are ignored, and the relative lack of RPs sets individual concerns and human issues aside. In trope two, again, divisions within British nationhood are left aside, along with any focus on thorny practical issues such as the Irish border question, or Scottish ambitions for independence. As trope one, despite any discernible pro/anti stance, Brexit is largely constructed as a UK issue, for the UK to settle however it sees fit.

In many ways these findings fit nearly within the context of traditional DP work. The obscuring of political opposition or ideological alternatives we have analysed is a classic concern of rhetorical psychology (Billig 1987) and interpretative repertoire-themed discursive analyses (e.g. Wetherell and Potter 1992). Such work that has since been expanded upon in contemporary arenas of civic discourse (see Condor et al. 2013) explores the construct*ive* and construct*ed* nature of discourse through the components that shape them and their interpretative implications (Edwards and Potter 1992). MCDA expands this concern, demonstrating the plethora of semiotic ways in which new social meanings can be engaged with in increasingly interconnected civic arenas, not least in political cartoons which are a long-standing feature of that discursive landscape.

As we indicated at the outset of our analysis, there is no absolute or singular lay or an analytic reading of these cartoons, and we do not attempt to speculate on the intention of the artist. In our view, these cartoons, and satirical cartoons broadly, do offer a rebellious humour, in this case, offering a critical political Brexit commentary. However, as Billig (2005) notes, the emergence of political caricature in the UK coincided with the development of democracy, and as such, satirical cartoons occupy a normative role in mainstream Western media that might, albeit unintentionally, serve to uphold rather than rebel against the social order. We align with Billig (2005) here and suggest that this potential is always available and it is very much a matter of how the audience engages with the discourse as to whether rebellious humour leads to rebellious consequences or if political satire serves as a disciplinary function.

As our analysis has demonstrated, the non-literal quality of political cartoons creates a unique capacity for engaging rhetorical ambiguity in Brexit discourse that is resistant to challenge. Sometimes ambiguity is apparent in the lack of a clear pro/anti stance on Brexit, but irrespective of any explicit political position, we suggest rhetorical ambiguity in this Brexit discourse has a far more insidious quality, both with regard to how British nationhood is constructed and concerning the capacity of the UK to enact Brexit. Billig and MacMillan (2005, p. 459) point out that 'metaphors can function as routine idioms in political discourse in ways that deaden political awareness'. In our analysis, via tropes of 'Boundedness and Isolation' and 'Uncertain Waters', Brexit is recontextualised as a through and through discourse of (partial) British national identity. Scottish, Irish and Welsh concerns are almost completely obscured and where Europe/the EU features, it is marginal, lacking agency and contestable. This portrayal of the UK not only deletes integral elements of British nationality, but along with them, practical concerns, which have since become significant stumbling blocks in resolving Brexit, prime of which being the Irish border agreement. Moreover, the overwhelming focus on the UK and relative disinterest in the EU obscures the involvement and authority of the EU in determining how the UK might leave the EU, and as such, no attention was paid towards consideration of the political realities that the UK would be subsequently left to confront after voting to leave the EU.

Cartoon Links

C1: 'Final Preparations' by Chappatte. Published in the New York Times (USA) on 21st June 2016. See https://www.nytimes.com/2016/06/21/opinion/chappatte-on-brexit-final-preparations.html?rref=collection%2Fbyline%2Fpatrick-chappatte

C2: 'FREE AT LAST' by Chappatte. Published in the New York Times (USA) on 23rd June 2016. See https://www.nytimes.com/2016/06/23/opinion/chappatte-on-brexit-free-at-last.html?rref=collection%2Fbyline%2Fpatrick-chappatte

C3: 'BRITAIN Before BREXIT' by Billy Day. First published on Caglecartoons.com (USA) on 24th June 2016. Found on https://www.politico.eu/interactive/brexit-eu-referendum-leave-david-cameron-boris-johnson-nigel-farage-ukip-cartoons/

C4: No title by Hajo de Reijger. First published on Caglecartoons.com (The Netherlands) on 24th June 2016. Found on C4 https://www.

politico.eu/interactive/brexit-eu-referendum-leave-david-cameron-boris-johnson-nigel-farage-ukip-cartoons/

C5: '"Brexit" diminishes Britain and threatens European security' by David Horsey. Published in LA Times (USA) on 28th June 2016. See https://www.latimes.com/world/la-fg-brexit-updates-horsey-brexit-diminishes-britain-and-1467127052-htmlstory.html

C6: 'Abandon Ship! Brexit, Great Britain's Escape' by Ben Garrison (UK). First published on https://grrrgraphics.wordpress.com/2016/06/11/abandon-ship-brexit-great-britains-escape-ben-garrison-cartoon/ (UK) on 11th June 2016. Found on https://www.theguardian.com/commentisfree/2016/jun/14/leave-eu-cartoon-racist-nazi-brexit-antisemitism-1945

C7: 'I THINK WE'D BE BETTER OFF STAYING IN' by Kal. Published in The Economist (UK) on 28th May 2016. Found on https://www.politico.eu/interactive/brexit-donald-trump-us-elections-brussels-terror-attacks-angela-merkel-migration-refugees-aleppo-russia-vladimir-putin-cartoons-best-of-2016/

C8: 'I've decided to step down' by Dave Granlund. First published on Politicalcartoons.com (USA), on 24th June 2016. Found on https://www.politico.eu/interactive/brexit-eu-referendum-leave-david-cameron-boris-johnson-nigel-farage-ukip-cartoons/

C9: 'Victory' by S Adams. Published in the Telegraph (UK) on 24th June 2016. See https://www.telegraph.co.uk/news/2016/06/24/what-can-we-learn-from-the-eu-referendum-results/

C10: No title by Pavel Constantin. First published on Caglecartoons.com, Romania, 22nd June 2016. See https://twitter.com/globalcartoons/status/745685181852430337. Found on https://www.politico.eu/interactive/brexit-eu-referendum-leave-david-cameron-boris-johnson-nigel-farage-ukip-cartoons/

C11: 'REFUGEES WELCOME' by Marian Kamensky. First published on Caglecartoons.com (Slovakia) on 30th June 2016. Found on https://www.politico.eu/interactive/brexit-eu-referendum-leave-david-cameron-boris-johnson-nigel-farage-ukip-cartoons/

C12: 'We could always become something like Panama' by Axel Scheffler. Published on the front page of *Süddeutsche* (Germany) on 23rd June

2016. Image of paper found on https://twitter.com/michaelsteen/status/745899134209622017/photo/1)

UK = 3 (Kal, Ben Garrison, S Adams)
USA = 5 (Dave Granlund, David Horsey, Chappatte, Billy Day)
Europe = 4 (Pavel Constantin, Axel Scheffler, Hajo de Reijger, Marian Kamensky)

References

Abell, J., Condor, S., Lowe, R., Gibson, S., & Stevenson, C. (2007). Who ate all the pride? Patriotic sentiment and English national football support. *Nations & Nationalism, 13*(1), 97–116. https://doi.org/10.1111/j.1469-8129.2007.00268.x

Abell, J., Condor, S., & Stevenson, C. (2006). "We are an island": Geographical imagery in accounts of citizenship, civil society, and national identity in Scotland and in England. *Political Psychology, 27*(2), 207–226. https://doi.org/10.1111/j.1467-9221.2006.00003.x

Ana, O. (1997). Empirical analysis of anti-immigrant metaphor in political discourse. *University of Pennsylvania Working Papers in Linguistics, 4*(1), 318–330. Retrieved from http://repository.upenn.edu/pwpl/vol4/iss1/19

Ana, O. (1999). 'Like an animal I was treated': anti-immigrant metaphor in US public discourse. *Discourse & Society, 10*(2), 191–224. https://doi.org/10.1177/0957926599010002004

Anderson, B. (2006). *Imagined communities: Reflections on the origin and spread of nationalism* (Rev. edn). Verso.

Annabell, T., & Nairn, A. (2019). Flagging a "new" New Zealand: The discursive construction of national identity in the Flag Consideration Project. *Critical Discourse Studies, 96*(1), 96–111. https://doi.org/10.1080/1740590 4.2018.1521857

Barnes, R., Auburn, T., & Lea, S. (2004). Citizenship in practice. *British Journal of Social Psychology, 43*(2), 187–206. https://doi.org/10.1348/0144666041501705

Billig, M. (1987). *Arguing and Thinking: A Rhetorical Approach to Social Psychology*. Cambridge: Cambridge University Press.

Billig, M. (1995). *Banal nationalism*. Sage Publications.

Billig, M. (2005). *Laughter and ridicule: Towards a social critique of humour*. Sage Publications.

Billig, M., Condor, S., Edwards, D., Gane, M., Radley, A., & Middleton, D. (1988). *Ideological dilemmas*. Sage Publications.

Billig, M., & MacMillan, K. (2005). Metaphor, idiom and ideology: The search for 'no smoking guns' across time. *Discourse & Society, 16*(4), 459–480. https://doi.org/10.1177/0957926505053050

Capdevila, R., & Callaghan, J. (2008). "It's not racist. It's common sense". A critical analysis of political discourse around asylum and immigration in the UK. *Journal of Community & Applied Social Psychology, 18*(1), 1–16.

Charteris-Black, J. (2006). Britain as a container: Immigration metaphors in the 2005 election campaign. *Discourse & Society, 17*(5), 563–581. https://doi.org/10.1177/0957926506066345

Charteris-Black, J. (2013). *Analysing political speeches: Rhetoric, discourse and metaphor*. Palgrave Macmillan.

Cohen, R. (1994). *Frontiers of identity: The British and the others*. London: Longman.

Colley, L. (1992). *Britons: Forging the nation 1707–1837*. Yale University Press.

Condor, S. (2000). Pride and prejudice: Identity management in English people's talk about 'this country'. *Discourse & Society, 11*(2), 175–204.

Condor, S. (2010). Devolution and national identity: The rules of English (Dis) engagement. *Nations & Nationalism, 16*(3), 525–543. https://doi.org/10.1111/j.1469-8129.2010.00441.x

Condor, S., & Gibson, S. (2007). 'Everybody's entitled to their own opinion': Ideological dilemmas of liberal individualism and active citizenship. *Journal of Community & Applied Social Psychology, 17*(2), 115–140. https://doi.org/10.1002/casp.885

Condor, S., Tileagă, C., & Billig, M. (2013). Political rhetoric. In L. Huddy, D. O. Sears, & J. S. Levy (Eds.), *Oxford handbook of political psychology* (pp. 262–300). Oxford University Press.

Cruse, I. (2008). *Library note: To call attention to the concept of Britishness in the context of the cultural, historical, constitutional and ethical tradition of the peoples of these Islands*. House of Lords Library. Retrieved from https://research-briefings.files.parliament.uk/documents/LLN-2008-015/LLN-2008-015.pdf

Edwards, D., & Potter, J. (1992). *Discursive psychology*. London: Sage Publications.

El Refaie, E. (2009). Metaphor in political cartoons: Exploring audience responses. In C. Forceville & E. Urios-Aparisi (Eds.), *Multimodal metaphor* (pp. 75–95). Mouton de Gruyter.

Fairclough, N. (1989). *Language and power*. Longman.

Fairclough, N. (2001). Critical discourse analysis as a method in social scientific research. In R. Wodak & M. Meyer (Eds.), *Methods of critical discourse analysis*. Sage.

Fairclough, N., & Wodak, R. (1997). Critical discourse analysis. In T. van Dijk (Ed.), *Discourse studies: A multidisciplinary introduction* (Vol. 2, pp. 258–284). Sage.

Gamson, W., & Stuart, D. (1992). Media discourse as a symbolic contest: The bomb in political cartoons. *Sociological Forum, 7*(1), 55–86.

Gibson, S., & Hamilton, L. (2011). The rhetorical construction of polity membership: Identity, culture and citizenship in young people's discussions of immigration in Northern England. *Journal of Community and Applied Social Psychology, 21*, 228–242. https://doi.org/10.1002/casp.1087

Goodman, S. (2017). How to conduct a psychological discourse analysis. *Critical Approaches to Discourse Analysis across Disciplines, 9*(2), 142–153.

Goodman, S., & Burke, S. (2010). "Oh you don't want asylum seekers, oh you're just racist" A discursive analysis of discussions about whether it's racist to oppose asylum seeking. *Discourse & Society, 21*(3), 325–340. https://doi.org/10.1177/0957926509360743

Goodman, S., & Johnson, A. (2013). Strategies used by the far right to counter accusations of racism. *Critical Approaches to Discourse Analysis across Disciplines, 6*(2), 97–113.

Goodman, S., & Narang, A. (2019). "Sad day for the UK": The linking of debates about settling refugee children in the UK with Brexit on an anti-immigrant news website. *European Journal of Social Psychology, 49*(6), 1161–1172. https://doi.org/10.1002/ejsp.2579

Guibernau, I., Berdún, M., & Rex, J. (2010). Introduction. In *The ethnicity reader: Nationalism, multiculturalism and migration*. Polity.

Iedema, R. (2003). Multimodality, resemiotization: Extending the analysis of discourse as multi-semiotic practice. *Visual Communication, 2*(1), 29–57. https://doi.org/10.1177/1470357203002001751

Jewitt, C., & Oyama, R. (2001). Visual meaning: A social semiotic approach. In T. In van Leeuwen & C. Jewitt (Eds.), *Handbook of visual analysis* (pp. 134–156). Sage.

Joyce, C., Stevenson, C., & Muldoon, O. (2012). Claiming and displaying national identity: Irish travellers' and students' strategic use of 'banal' and 'hot' national identity in talk. *British Journal of Social Psychology, 52*(3), 450–468. https://doi.org/10.1111/j.2044-8309.2012.02097.x

Kaiser, W., & Varsori, A. (Eds.). (2012). *European Union history: Themes and debates*. Palgrave.

Kilby, L., & Horowitz, A. (2013). Opening up terrorism talk: The sequential and categorical production of discursive power within the call openings of a talk radio broadcast. *Discourse & Society, 24*(6), 725–742. https://doi.org/10.1177/0957926513503270

Kilby, L., Horowitz, A., & Hylton, P. (2013). Diversity as victim to 'realistic liberalism': Analysis of an elite discourse of immigration, ethnicity and society. *Critical Discourse Studies, 10*(1), 47–60. https://doi.org/10.1080/17405904.2012.736398

Kilby, L., & Lennon, H. (2018). Charlie Hebdo and the Prophet Muhammad: A multimodal critical discourse analysis of peace and violence in a satirical cartoon. In S. Gibson (Ed.), *Discursive psychology perspectives: Discourse, peace, and conflict* (pp. 303–321). Springer. https://doi.org/10.1007/978-3-319-99094-1_17

Kress, G., & van Leeuwen, T. (2001). *Multimodal discourse: The modes and media of contemporary communication*. Arnold.

Kress, G., & van Leeuwen, T. (2006). *Reading images: The grammar of visual design* (2nd ed.). Routledge.

Krzyżanowski, M. (2019). Brexit and the imaginary of "crisis": a discourse-conceptual analysis of European news media. *Critical Discourse Studies, 16*(4), 465. https://doi.org/10.1080/17405904.2019.1592001

Levine, P., & Scollon, R. (Eds.). (2004). *Discourse & technology: Multimodal discourse analysis*. Georgetown University Press.

Lynn, N., & Lea, S. (2003). 'A Phantom Menace and the New Apartheid': The social construction of asylum-seekers in the United Kingdom. *Discourse & Society, 14*(4), 425–452. https://doi.org/10.1177/0957926503014004002

Maccaferri, M. (2019). Splendid isolation again? Brexit and the role of the press and online media in re-narrating the European discourse. *Critical Discourse Studies, 16*(4), 389–402. https://doi.org/10.1080/17405904.2019.1592766

Machin, D. (2013). What is multimodal critical discourse studies? *Critical Discourse Studies, 10*(4), 347–555. https://doi.org/10.1080/17405904.2013.813770

Macphee, G., & Poddar, P. (2007). Nationalism beyond the nation-state. In G. Macphee & P. Poddar (Eds.), *Empire and after: Englishness in postcolonial perspective*. Berghahn Books.

Mazid, B. (2008). Cowboy and misanthrope: A critical (discourse) analysis of Bush and bin Laden cartoons. *Discourse & Communication, 2*(4), 433–457.

Meredith, J., & Richardson, E. (2019). The use of the political categories of Brexiter and Remainer in online comments about the EU referendum. *Journal of Community and Applied Social Psychology, 29*, 43–55. https://doi.org/10.1002/casp.2384

Moore, M., & Ramsay, G., (2017, May). *UK Media Coverage of the 2016 EU Referendum campaign*. Centre for the Study of Media, Communication and Power, The Policy Institute, King's College London. Available from http://www.media-diversity.org/en/additional-files/UK-media-coverage-of-the-2016-EU-Referendum-campaign.pdf

Müller, G., Özcan, E., & Seizov, O. (2009). Dangerous depictions: A visual case study of contemporary cartoon controversies. *Popular Communication, 7*, 28–39.

Musolff, A. (2004). *Metaphor and political discourse: Analogical reasoning in debates about Europe*. Palgrave.

Musolff, A. (2019). Brexit as 'having your cake and eating it'. In V. Koller, S. Kopf, & M. Miglbauer (Eds.), *Discourses of Brexit*. Routledge. https://doi.org/10.4324/9781351041867

Parekh, B. (2000). *Rethinking multiculturalism: Cultural diversity and political theory*. Macmillan/Palgrave Press.

Politico. (2016, June 25). *Cartoonists draw Brexit*. Retrieved from https://www.politico.eu/interactive/brexit-eu-referendum-leave-david-cameron-boris-johnson-nigel-farage-ukip-cartoons/

Popoviciu, S., & Tileaga, C. (2019). Subtle forms of racism in strategy documents concerning Roma inclusion. *Journal of Community and Applied Social Psychology, 30*(1), 85–102., ISSN: 1052-9284. https://doi.org/10.1002/casp.2430

Rosie, M., MacInnes, J., Petersoo, P., Condor, S., & Kennedy, J. (2004). Nation speaking unto nation? Newspapers and national identity in the evolved UK. *The Sociological Review, 52*(4), 437–458. https://doi.org/10.1111/j.1467-954X.2004.00490.xfm

Silaški, N., & Đurovic, T. (2019). The journey metaphor in Brexit-related political cartoons. *Discourse, Context & Media, 31*, 1–10. https://doi.org/10.1016/j.dcm.2019.100318

Stevenson, C., & Abell, J. (2011). Enacting national concerns: Anglo-British accounts of the 2002 Royal Golden Jubilee. *Journal of Community and Applied Social Psychology, 21*(2), 124–137. https://doi.org/10.1002/casp.1070

The Guardian. (2016, March 20). *European Cartoonists on the EU.* Retrieved from https://www.theguardian.com/society/2016/mar/20/brexit-silly-walk-best-political-cartoons-eu-europe-referendum

Valdés-Miyares, R. (2018). The strategies of ultranationalist discourse: This is England and Brexit. *Open Cultural Studies, 2,* 50–60. https://doi.org/10.1515/culture-2018-0006

van Dijk, T. (2001). Multidisciplinary CDA. In R. Wodak & M. Meyer (Eds.), *Methods of critical discourse analysis.* Sage Publications.

van Dijk, T. A. (2015). Critical discourse studies; A sociocognitive approach. In R. Wodak & M. Meyer (Eds.), *Methods of critical discourse analysis* (3rd ed., pp. 63–85). Sage Publications.

van Leeuwen, T. (1999). *Speech, music, sound.* Macmillan Press Ltd.

van Leeuwen, T. (2005). *Introducing social semiotics.* England: Routledge.

van Leeuwen, T., & Jewitt, C. (Eds.). (2001). *Handbook of visual analysis.* Sage Publications.

van Leeuwen, T., & Wodak, R. (1999). Legitimizing immigration control: A discourse-historical analysis. *Discourse Studies, 1*(1), 83–118. https://doi.org/10.1177/1461445699001001005

Ward, P. (2009). The end of Britishness? A historical perspective. *Journal of the British Politics Society, 4*(3), 3.

Wetherell, M., & Potter, J. (1992). *Mapping the language of racism: Discourse and the legitimation of exploitation.* Harvester Wheatsheaf.

Wodak, R., & Meyer, M. (Eds.). (2015). *Methods for critical discourse analysis* (3rd ed.). Sage Publications.

Wooffitt, R. (2005). *Conversation analysis and discourse analysis: A comparative and critical introduction.* Sage Publications.

Xenitidou, M., & Morasso, S. (2014). Parental discourse and identity management in the talk of indigenous and migrant speakers. *Discourse & Society, 25*(1), 100–121. https://doi.org/10.1177/0957926513508858

Zappettini, F. (2019). The Brexit referendum: How trade and immigration in the discourses of the official campaigns have legitimised a toxic (inter)national logic. *Critical Discourse Studies, 16*(4), 403–419. https://doi.org/10.1080/17405904.2019.1593206

Part 2

Political Communication, Discourse, and New Media

6

The Discourse of Social Movements: Online Mobilising Practices for Collective Action

Petra Sneijder, Baukje Stinesen, Maartje Harmelink, and Annette Klarenbeek

Introduction

Social Movements, Discourse and Mobilisation

In this chapter, we focus on the rhetorical and the interactional features of mobilisation practices by local social movements on social media (see also Sneijder et al. 2018). Social movements have been described as repeated confrontational actions and sustained efforts by which people make collective claims on others in order to achieve changes in society (Goodwin and Jasper 2003; Tilly 2004). In recent years, social media have become an

---

P. Sneijder (✉) • B. Stinesen • A. Klarenbeek
University of Applied Sciences Utrecht, Utrecht, Netherlands
e-mail: petra.sneijder@hu.nl

M. Harmelink
Taskforce for Applied Research, The Dutch Research Council,
The Hague, Netherlands

© The Author(s), under exclusive license to Springer Nature Switzerland AG 2020   **149**
M. A. Demasi et al. (eds.), *Political Communication*, Palgrave Studies in Discursive
Psychology, https://doi.org/10.1007/978-3-030-60223-9_6

important social networking tool for collective action (Shirky 2011; Lopes 2014). They facilitate spreading the goals and frames of a movement through text and images and are becoming increasingly important in the organisation of social movements and mobilisation of their members and a broader public (Cammaerts 2015; Hwang and Kim 2015) and mobilise support for offline demonstrations (van Stekelenburg 2018).

Khamis and Vaughn (2012) underlined the role of Facebook in disseminating information and mobilising participants for protests. They describe Facebook pages and groups as safe meeting places for protesters. Social media offer opportunities for interaction (Eltantawy and Wiest 2011), such as enabling social media users to exchange information and discuss their concerns continuously (Takahashi et al. 2015). Shirky (2011) also points to the fact that social media is available to the majority of people, which increases the chance of reaching and involving even relatively uncommitted individuals.

Communication (whether offline or online) is crucial in mobilisation (Cammaerts 2015). For instance, Nicodemus (2004) identified rhetorical strategies that were used in newspapers to either stimulate or suppress the mobilisation of citizens to participate in decision making on a solid waste facility siting. Strategies to mobilise people included the construction of we-ness and the invocation of an injustice frame.

Group Identification

Group identification is described as an important factor in the prediction of collective action participation in psychological studies (van Stekelenburg and Klandermans 2007). De Weerd and Klandermans (1999), for instance, described the affective and behavioural components of group identification. The affective component corresponds with a certain identity, while the behavioural component implies membership of an organisation related to that identity. Their study showed that both components stimulated the willingness to take part in political protests, while the behavioural component increased actual participation directly. Members of organisations have access to communication networks and therefore are receptive of interpersonal control and relevant information, which increases the transformation from ideas to action (de Weerd and Klandermans 1999, p. 1092). It is important to note that these studies are predominantly concerned with predicting group identification.

In addition, as Lim (2012) points out, this type of identification is to a large extent dependent on communication between individuals. She described the relationship between social media and political change, specifically how social media played an important role in Egypt's oppositional movements in the years before the Egyptian uprising of early 2011. Social media were used to spread ideas and to stimulate the movement for democratic change. Moreover, in narratives spread on social media, complex issues were transformed to narratives closer to everyday life (Lim 2012). Important here is the notion that it is important for individuals to identify themselves with the relevant group as a precondition for participation in collective action (Wright 2011; van Stekelenburg and Klandermans 2007).

Stott and Drury (2017) argue that people's membership of a social group (Tajfel 1978) plays a role in the choice for participating in crowd events. At the same time, they argue, crowd members form a new sense of identity and new actions when they are treated as oppositional by an outgroup, such as the police or authorities. (Drury et al. 2012). The authors treat crowd events as sites for studying the relation between psychological and social change, treating social identity as changing in relation to the context as well as moderating the context in turn.

In this chapter we use Discursive Psychology to study group identification as a *communicative* rather than a *psychological* phenomenon. Rather than focusing on psychological states and underlying ideas, Discursive Psychology takes an interest in the things people actually do with language, such as legitimising participation in collective action. While the previously described psychological studies treated the language of group identification as a predictor (de Weerd and Klandermans 1999) or moderator (Drury et al. 2012; Stott and Drury 2017), we focus on how categories such as group identification are *built up and used* by people as they interact about collective action via social media.

Discursive Psychology

Discursive psychology is concerned with the way in which 'versions of reality are invoked and made available for social and psychological actions' (Wiggins 2017). In line with this perspective, this chapter describes how versions of reality are *made available for* mobilisation for collective action participation. The aim of discursive psychology is to analyse talk in terms of 'what people treat as meaningful, publicly and for each other' (Potter and Edwards 2013; p. 703). From a discursive psychological point of view, language is not neutral but builds a particular version of reality and simultaneously counters alternative versions (Edwards and Potter 1992, 2001; Potter 1996; Wiggins 2017). The discursive construction of issues is important for understanding mobilisation (Koopmans and Olzak 2004) and for explaining the role of public discourse in finding information about the actions of different groups such as authorities, opponents and sympathisers of social movements. As Bröer and Duyvendak (2009) argue, the role of language is important here. They propose discursive psychology as a useful perspective for explaining how people perform actions such as legitimising or questioning certain feelings. In this sense, public discourse can embed the right to be worried when issues are defined as legitimate social problems (Bröer and Duyvendak 2009).

In the last decades, discursive psychologists have proposed to study online discourse as a social practice in its own right (Sneijder and te Molder 2005a; Meredith and Potter 2014; Stinesen et al. 2016). Although there are many differences between face-to-face interaction and online interaction, discourse is always recipient designed. In some cases, direct recipients are available, while in other cases there are silent readers or 'overhearing recipients' (Goffman 1981; Meredith and Potter 2014). When there is no immediate interaction available, analysts may still approach discourse as 'recipient designed' and focus on the interactional business it performs (see also Lamerichs and te Molder 2003). This chapter demonstrates the value of the discursive psychological perspective for studying mobilisation, featuring recent cases from the Netherlands and elsewhere in Europe.

Data and Method

Material

We studied Facebook event pages of three local social movements: Shocking Groningen, the Free Union and the regional representatives of the Dutch Yellow Vests. The first two aim to mobilise people against the extraction of gas in the north of the Netherlands. Since 1986, the occurrences of many minor earthquakes in the northern province of Groningen in the Netherlands were ascribed to gas extraction. In 2012, a larger earthquake took place, which led to a concern among local citizens. According to an investigative report written by the State Supervision of Mines (in van der Voort and Vanclay 2015), the gas extraction was expected to lead to more and stronger earthquakes with larger impacts in the future, such as the damage to buildings and the decrease of the value of real estate. These predictions led to an increase in feelings of anxiety, distrust and anger among the Groningen population (van der Voort and Vanclay 2015).

Discussion threads from Facebook event pages were collected. Event pages are Facebook pages announcing festivals or political demonstrations. Visitors of the pages may indicate whether they are present at the announced event or comment on it or start discussion threads. Each Facebook page has its own moderator.

The first page was initiated by activist group Shocking Groningen and announces the demonstration against a visit of the minister of economic affairs, Minister Kamp, to the provincial government building of Groningen. This activist group mobilises residents of Groningen against the extraction of natural gas in Groningen. The event page mobilised people for demonstrating against a visit of Minister Kamp to the provincial government building of Groningen in January 2015. Visitors of the event page are called to be present at his arrival and to make clear that he is not welcome in Groningen. The event page contains the initial call and 17 threads that occurred until the date of the visit. Threads vary from containing 1 post to 19 posts.

The second page is initiated by the Free Union, a social movement that claims to strive for an anarchist society in which relations are based on equality. The announced event is a demonstration at the debate of the House of Representatives in February 2015. The debate involves the decision Minister Kamp made about the decrease of the extraction of natural gas in Groningen. The organisers argue that the extraction of natural gas can be toned down much further. The event page contains the initial call and 63 threads that were posted on the page until the date of the event. The number of posts within a thread varies from 1 to 27.

Thirdly, we became interested in mobilising practices of Facebook groups of the Dutch version of the 'Yellow Vests' movement that has gained terrain in several European countries. The movement started in France and was motivated by rising fuel prices and the government's tax reforms and protests by organising (violent) demonstrations. In the Netherlands, there are 129 Facebook groups affiliated with the 'Yellow Vests'.[1] One of them is the national Facebook group with over 36,000 members. Other groups are regional or local groups. Twenty-five of these groups have over 500 members, and 13 of these groups have over 1000 members. We studied calls to join these groups or events organised by these groups in 2018 and 2019 to see whether we could discern any meaningful similarities and differences between these calls and those associated with the event pages from the social movements in Groningen.

Methodological Procedure

The aim of this study is to explore how versions of reality are *made available for* mobilisation for collective action online, using the analytical principles of discursive psychology (Edwards and Potter 1992, 2001; Wiggins 2017). The analysis involves selecting materials from the larger body of interaction on the event pages and group pages in which (1) participants are invited or encouraged to participate in the planned events and/or (2) the occurrence of the event itself is supported by arguments.

---

[1] This was the case in July 2019: the number of groups or their members may have changed in the meantime. The Amsterdam and Rotterdam Yellow Vests have already altered their names to 'Resistance'.

6 The Discourse of Social Movements: Online Mobilising... 155

In this process, we applied the 'next turn proof procedure', that is, we focused on the way participants themselves treat each other's talk (Hutchby and Wooffit 2008, p. 14). We selected those contributions that were treated *as* calls to collective action by other participants, for instance by confirming their attendance. We also selected messages underlining the importance of the event. Finally, we focused on the way members of social movements presented themselves and resisted potential identity ascriptions (Widdicombe 1998). The data is originally in Dutch: fragments presented in the chapter are translated.

Ethical Considerations

There is an ongoing debate about the issue of ethical guidelines with respect to collecting online data (see Meredith and Potter 2014). The British Psychological Society (2007) states that 'When constructing research using discussion groups, requirements for consent by participants needs to be tempered by a consideration of the nature of the research, the intrusiveness and privacy implications of the data collected, analysed and reported, and possible harm caused by the research' (as cited in Meredith and Potter 2014, p. 376). This statement is in line with the General Data Protection Regulation that is applicable since May 2018 in Europe.

As both Facebook event pages and the Yellow Vests Facebook groups are publicly accessible, which means data can be retrieved using search engines such as Coosto, the authors treat these data as not requiring consent from participants. Furthermore, participants' (nick)names and the exact date were deleted from the extracts. However, it should be noted that there is an ongoing discussion on the acceptability of treating this type of data as publicly accessible in a research context. For instance, Merriman (2015) points out that publicity does not automatically entail intent. It is also important to note that traceability is not excluded which means the extracts may still lead to identification (see also Beaulieu and Estalella 2012, p. 5; Smithson 2015). See Kiyimba et al. (2019) and Tiidenberg (2018) for an elaborate discussion on the ethical considerations of using naturally occurring online data.

Analysis

Critical Citizens Rather than Victims

On both Facebook event pages related to Groningen, participants frequently refer to the role of politics in relation to gas extraction. Participants systematically construct a gap between citizens and authorities, in particular the government, by disputing the integrity of these authorities. They use two different discursive strategies to achieve this effect, that is, accusing the authorities of lying and cheating and contrasting the stake of authorities with the stake of citizens. These strategies are also used by the Yellow Vests groups to make available the invitation to become a member of the groups or to join demonstrations.

Accusing the Authorities of Lying and Cheating

When discussing the political discourse on the natural gas extractions, participants continuously construct the authorities as unreliable.

Extract 6.1 (Free Union)
```
(1 line omitted)
1 It is a lollypop that is held to us. And those guys in the
2 Hague think we believe their election talk.
```

In Extract 6.1, the writer is accusing the government of being insincere by referring to election talk, which suggests that promises will not be fulfilled. Furthermore, participants suggest that they are treated as naïve and gullible. See, for instance, line 2, in which the writer refers to the government that is located in the city of The Hague: 'those guys in the Hague think we believe their election talk' (line 2).

In Extract 6.2, the credibility of politicians is disputed:

Extract 6.2 (Free Union)
```
1 Is there still anyone who believes in politics ??? Really ???
```

The writer in Extract 6.2 uses a rhetorical question ('Is there still anyone who believes in politics? Really???' line 1). Rhetorical questions may fulfil several functions in discourse. Especially, in combination with the extreme case formulation (Pomerantz 1986) 'anyone', it allows the speaker to strengthen and commit to the position expressed (no one believes in politics anymore), as it renders affirmation or alignment to this position as the obvious or default option (Ilie 1994; Toth 2015). This implies that the speaker in Extract 6.2 does not expect an answer to the question but rather a silent confirmation of the presupposition of the speaker's point of view. This rhetorical question suggests a decrease of the credibility of politicians in this particular case but also draws on a commonly used frame or repertoire (Potter and Wetherell 1987) in public discourse on politicians.

Extract 6.3 (Free Union)

```
1 we are being cheated and deceived ... whatever that b*****d
2 Leegte announced in the train .. is brought into practice
3 by Kamp .. He plays magic tricks now with months and
4 numbers and who knows what else ..Still thinking that we
5 believe his foul lies .. I will be present on Thursday ..!!!
```

Participants use formulations that present events as routine or recurrent, so-called script formulations (Edwards 1994; Sneijder and Te Molder 2005b) to invoke the impression that certain actions of politicians are part of a pattern. Practices of authorities are constructed as recurrent malpractices and therefore illustrative of how authorities act. See, for instance, Extract 6.3: 'we are being cheated and deceived' (line 1).

Another salient feature of this formulation is the use of the pronoun 'we', referring to a collective identity that is characterised by a shared victimisation (see also Lim 2012). Note how participants use objective rather than subjective formulations in their descriptions of the deceiving practices of the authorities ('we are being cheated' rather than 'in my opinion we are being cheated'). By using factual formulations, recipients are directed to states of affairs rather than personal opinions (Edwards and Potter 2017). The suggestion that speakers' assertions are legitimate

158   P. Sneijder et al.

and not merely based on personal opinions is in line with previous research depicting objective formulations as 'persuasive' (Wiggins and Potter 2003). Furthermore, political figures (line 2: such as Leegte) are described in negative terms such as ('b*****d') and accused of intentional deceit. Mister Leegte (line 2) was a member of the Dutch House of Representatives who caused commotion by downplaying the concerns of the people in Groningen in a telephone conversation he had while travelling by train. A passenger placed this telephone call on Twitter, which caused Leegte to apologise and decline his role as a spokesperson in the domain of gas extraction.

In Extract 6.3, Minister Kamp's actions are directly related to Leegte's malpractice. Subsequently, the speaker ascribes the actions of playing magic tricks and lying (foul lies) to Minister Kamp (line 3), thereby accusing him of purposely misleading the public. Hereby, the speaker positions himself as representing 'the dispossessed', those who feel that the cheating and deceiving is a symbol of a shift in the moral order (Billig 1978, p. 296; Tileagă 2007, p. 725).

Extract 6.4 (Yellow Vests Netherlands)
```
1 The motivation to wear a yellow vest is diverse. While one
2 worries over the retirement age, the increasing power and
3 grabbing practices of Brussels, the other worries about the
4 increasing poverty in the working population, the VAT, the tax
5 increase and the unpayable care.
```

Extract 6.4 is the opening statement of the Facebook pages of the Dutch Yellow Vests (which has been copied by the local variants). The reference to 'being worried' functions as an account for wearing a yellow vest (line 1). Note that merely *wearing* the vest is mentioned here, rather than for example *being* a Yellow Vest or participating in actions of the Yellow Vests. By describing the motivation to wear a Yellow Vest as stemming from the emotion of 'being worried', this motivation is constructed as an emotional one (Edwards 1999). Edwards (1999, p. 281) notes that an important rhetorical function of using emotion words is to emphasise 'inner feelings rather than the events in the external world they are directed at', thereby constructing the issue of involvement in collective action as understandable and therefore reasonable. The emphasis on various 'worries' is used to construct 'concern' as a relevant category-bound predicate (Watson 1983) of the Yellow Vests. Note that the writer uses a construction of impersonality (while one worries about X, the other worries about Y), which detaches the worries from an agent or collective (see also Potter 1996, p. 156) and emphasises the genericity of worries as the relevant aspect.

On the other hand, 'being worried' is presented as a logical response to phenomena out there. In line 3 the 'grabbing practices of Brussels' is put forward as a potential source of worry. This can be likened to what Billig (1978) called 'the voice of the dispossessed'. By referring to 'grabbing practices', it is suggested that politics takes away something that belongs to citizens. Politician's behaviour is repeatedly constructed as violating social and moral norms (see also Tileagă 2007).

The described worries typically refer to structural inequality. The invocation of structural inequality is a repertoire (Potter and Wetherell 1987) that is often used in mobilisation by social movements. As Snow and Owens (2014, p. 657) point out, social movements are usually oriented to 'combating, constructing or sustaining actual or perceived systems of inequality'.

Contrasting the Stake of Authorities with the Stake of Citizens

The authorities are constructed as having their own stakes and interests which are in contrast to those of citizens. In this way, the government is constructed as acting against the interests of citizens. This is illustrated in Extract 6.5:

Extract 6.5 (Shocking Groningen)
```
1 Next Monday Kamp will visit Groningen once again to get the
2 "Dialie Table" on his track. As a result of the leaked report
3 by the Commission of Safety, in which we can read clearly that
4 we have been lied to, stolen from and cheated for half a
5 century, we call EVERYONE to come and greet Kamp LOUDLY at his
6 arrival around 17:30, location: Provincial Building in
7 Groningen. The event takes place from 17:00 until 19:00.
```

In Extract 6.5 (line 2), there is a reference to the 'Dialie Table', which is a sarcastic reformulation of the term 'Dialogue Table'. The 'Dialogue Table' was established to improve trust in Groningen and brings together authorities, citizens and the business community for consultation in order to reach consensus concerning gas extraction in the region (Stoker et al. 2015). By introducing the term 'Dialie' as a replacement of 'Dialogue', this group is characterised as disingenuous.

Furthermore, the writer refers to a 'leaked report' of the Commission of Safety (line 2), which suggests that the report was not intended for the public to see and further undermines the integrity of the authorities. He also uses the pronoun 'we' several times when referring to the report (line 4: 'we have been lied too'). Personal pronouns are often used in political discourse to implicitly align with collectives (for an overview, see Condor et al. 2013). Here the speaker refers to 'we' in a nonspecific way. As pointed out in research on political rhetoric, there is a strategic ambiguity in this use of 'we' suggesting alignment of interests and plural identities (Billig 1995; Wilson 1990) without explicating who exactly are included or addressed.

The leaked report is constructed as the direct cause of the demonstration against Minister Kamp (lines 1–2: 'As a result of the leaked report [...]'). The writer uses a number of rhetorical strategies to make available the action of mobilising people for this event. First, he uses the extreme case formulation 'EVERYONE' (Pomerantz 1986) in capital letters (line 5) to persuasively maximise the size of the public.

Secondly, he uses a three-part list structure (Heritage and Greatbatch 1986) 'lied to, stolen from and cheated', which emphasises the experience of injustice and constructs it as factual and real (Wiggins 2017, p. 157). By accusing the authorities of lying and cheating, participants automatically distance themselves from these authorities. One way of doing this is using specific pronouns to refer to the government as 'they' or, for instance, as 'those guys in The Hague', by which the speaker presents the group members as separated or excluded from the authorities. Furthermore, he refers to the group members by using pronouns such as 'us' and 'we', thereby increasing the construction of inclusive and exclusive identities. See, for instance, Extract 6.6 (line 2).

6 The Discourse of Social Movements: Online Mobilising...

Extract 6.6 (Free Union)
```
1 Ha! So now is the time: TURN UP THE PRESSURE!!!Let the
2 government go to pieces on the tears in our houses, our lives,
3 our faith in a good ending.
```

In Extract 6.6, again a three-part list is used: 'our houses, our lives, our faith in a good ending' (line 2). Here the list emphasises the impact of the government's lack of actions to terminate the gas extraction on the lives of the people in Groningen, ending with the general list completer 'our faith in a good ending'.

Extract 6.7 (Yellow Vests, Twente)
```
1 We organize events in the Netherlands together with our other
2 yellow vests family to show solidarity with all yellow vests
3 people's movements in the Netherlands in order to make clear
4 that we are done with the course of events in this country
5 caused by the present government.
```

The Yellow Vests recurrently construct a contrast between inclusive and exclusive identities by repeatedly using the pronoun 'we' as opposed to 'the government', like in Extract 6.7. In line 2 the Yellow Vests are presented as a family, suggesting characteristics such as solidarity and togetherness, standing up against 'the present government' (line 5).

In sum, participants use different strategies to construct the authorities as unreliable and as having their own stakes and interests which are in contrast to those of citizens. Their beliefs and interests are developed in reaction to authorities, using the pronoun 'we', and as such groups are defined in opposition to other conflicting groups (Stekelenburg et al. 2010; Stott and Reicher 2000; Stott and Drury 2017). In this way, the government is constructed as acting against citizens, and simultaneously citizens present themselves as assertive rather than merely victims. Using devices such as extreme case formulations, generalisation and script formulations, speakers construct particular events as relevant and structural problems. Moreover, the planned events are legitimised as they are constructed as urgent and as logically stemming from authorities' conduct.

Emphasising Togetherness

A dominant pattern in the event page of the Free Union is the construction of 'togetherness'. Participants in the discussions use different discursive strategies to achieve this effect. Participants talk on behalf of the group using the pronoun 'we' and underline the collective character of the event, as we saw in the previous section as well. Other participants align with this suggestion by also foregrounding the collective nature of the event:

Extract 6.8 (Free Union)
```
1 We are going to make it an assertive, yet cozy day. Shared
2 grief is half grief, shared joy is double joy :-)
3 Reply: Mass is power, power is attention, attention is
4 resilience!
```

By talking of shared grief and shared joy (Extract 6.8), collectivity is constructed and underlined. By invoking shared grief and joy rather than, say, shared goals or thoughts, the reason for gathering is constructed as an emotional one (cf. Edwards 1999) and therefore understandable and reasonable. The speaker exhorts recipients to share the emotions of grief and joy rather than dealing with these emotions by themselves. In this way, recipients are encouraged to reconstruct their private 'feelings' into public displays or expressions of emotions (cf. Edwards 1999). In their responses, participants display alignment. The respondent uses the three-part list construction, in which the power of a collective is underlined.

Especially in the Yellow Vests groups, emphasising togetherness is a dominant phenomenon. As motives for joining this movement are diffuse, collectivity is not treated as a given fact. In their statements, the Yellow Vests emphasise their nature as a citizen's movement for all people who feel disadvantaged in some way, thereby further enlarging the gap between citizens and government (see also previous section). Note again that the use of 'we' is strategically ambiguous (Billig 1995) and refrains from explicating the exact members of the group.

6 The Discourse of Social Movements: Online Mobilising...

Extract 6.9 (Yellow Vests Netherlands)
```
1 In this group we don't want to emphasise the personal
2 motivation, but we want to call everyone who feels limited,
3 financially exhausted and silenced.
```

In Extract 6.9 the relevance of personal motivations is undermined while a common cause is underlined (lines 1–3). In this way, the Yellow Vests invoke the suggestion that the collective is characterised by the experience of structural inequality in society.

Managing the Fine Line Between Commitment and Activism

In the discussions on the event page of the Free Union and in the Yellow Vests groups, participants use strategies for constructing commitment. We also see how participants carefully manage the balance between commitment and activism: they display a concern for not coming across as activists, to minimise the impression they merely address activists, a category that potentially is associated with violent actions.

Extract 6.10 (Free Union)
```
1 This dossier was closed completely. That time is over. It has
2 now been broken. By the Groningers Themselves. NAM/Shell do no
3 longer have the power. Kamp balances in between two fires now.
4 Our fire is bigger. We are going to show that on Thursday. Make
5 sure you are heard!
```

In Extract 6.10, the speaker who is the organiser of the event (demonstration at debate) constructs the event as a future success by using several rhetorical devices (Potter 1996) such as contrasts (line 1: 'This dossier was closed completely. That time is over'), factual language and generalising formulations (line 4: 'We are going to show that on Thursday'). In line 3, he uses an imperative suggesting the urgency of being heard (line 4). These exhortations emphasise the speaker's commitment to the cause and stress empowerment and involvement (Milewa et al. 1999).

164   P. Sneijder et al.

Extract 6.11 (Free Union)
```
1 I really don't like protesting, but I'm going this time.
```

In Extract 6.11, the speaker uses a disclaimer (Potter and Wetherell 1987). By first indicating that he or she does not like protesting, the potential critique that the speaker would be a typical activist, and therefore has a stake in going to the protest, is countered (Potter 1996, p. 111). The speaker in Extract 6.11 thus heads off the suggestion that his participation in the protest stems from his identity as a typical 'protester'. By indicating that he is going this time, despite his dislike of protesting, he suggests genuine commitment in the Groningen case. This 'genuineness' is a recurrent concern also in the Yellow Vests groups.

Extract 6.12 (Yellow Vests Netherlands)
```
1 The Yellow Vests are normal, hardworking, peaceful citizens,
2 who come together to give way to discontent among the
3 population, and we distance ourselves from groups who do not
4 adhere to this. Although some of our opinions agree with
5 various political parties we are not a party, nor are we
6 connected to any party. We want to be seen and heard, and we do
7 this by getting together at agreed times and places. In that
8 way we stand out and start the conversation. So we do not seek
9 confrontations with the police or other movements!
```

In Extract 6.12, the Yellow Vests present themselves as 'normal, hardworking, peaceful citizens…' (lines 1–4). As demonstrated in other research, people may resist identity ascriptions by invoking alternative identities. For instance, this was the case in interviews with youngsters whose appearance suggested they could be member of a particular subcultural category (Widdicombe 1998) and in discussions in forums on veganism (Sneijder and te Molder 2009). The Yellow Vests recurrently emphasise that they are peaceful and not searching for any kind of trouble (see lines 8–9), and as such they undermine potential associations with violent demonstrations that took place in France. Furthermore, they resist the ascription of a connection to a particular political party (lines 4–6). Case in point, there are nine Yellow Vests Facebook groups who actually call themselves 'the Peaceful Yellow Vests'.

6 The Discourse of Social Movements: Online Mobilising... 165

Addressing (a Lack of) Commitment

Commitment is also regularly at stake in the discussions. On the event page of Shocking Groningen for instance, participants regularly address a lack of commitment in relation to the demonstration. For instance, the number of visitors as is visible on the Facebook page is treated as a sign of 'weakness' ('62 people go [...] bit of a weak number [...] too bad'). Another way of addressing a potential lack of commitment is contrasting the number of visitors with the turn-out at other events. The organisation of the event treats this type of messages as an implicit accusation of not being committed by accounting for their efforts (for instance, 'But we also sent an e-mail and a press release. Not everyone has Facebook').

The event page of the Free Union rather shows an active construction of commitment. When participants cannot be present at the demonstration, they account for this by describing alternative actions ('I'm not able to be there, have to work, but I have signed in the meanwhile [...]').

Extract 6.13 (Free Union)
```
1 Cannot be there, have to work, but have signed in the
2 meanwhile, and wish you good luck on the 12th of February!
3 Groningen people, make some noise!!!!
```

In Extract 6.13, the speaker announces that she cannot be there but also provides several accounts and thereby treats cancelling as an accountable action. Furthermore, she shows that she has made other efforts such as signing the petition, by which she manages to maintain an image of being committed. In addition, she shows support to the people who live in Groningen (line 2: Groningen people) by suggesting that they should make some noise. The same thing happens in posts in which Yellow Vests members cancel their participation:

Extract 6.14 (Yellow Vests Zoetermeer)
```
1 I'm going to be honest, but I think I speak for many. Yesterday I
2 was convinced that I, I live in Zoetermeer, was going to the
3 Hague. Woke up early, my wife and I went to IKEA for a short
4 while. We were back at half past twelve, so enough time to travel
5 to the Hague. We have one car, so I would drive to the Hague. Then
6 my wife says: I have to do groceries, is that possible after you
```

```
7  get back? Don't know, no idea how long it will take. Groceries
8  tomorrow? No, tomorrow we have to do something else and Monday
9  we're going to work. Conclusion, no the Hague. Sorry, that's how
10 things go. Setting priorities, sorry. Respect to those who went.
```

In Extract 6.14, the speaker elaborately accounts for his cancellation and makes it seem inevitable due to circumstances. He practices 'stake inoculation' by using devices that defend against claims that he might have a stake in the cancellation (Potter 1996). First of all, the speaker starts with what Edwards and Fasulo (2006) call an 'honesty phrase', a way of asserting sincerity. Honesty phrases are optional members' ways of asserting sincerity and independence as underlying their statements when the opposite is to be expected (line 1). Then in line 2, the speaker refers to his previous conviction that he would attend the protest, underlining the unexpectedness of his cancellation. In the account that follows (lines 3–9), the reason for cancellation is constructed as a report of events leading up to the cancellation (cf. Potter 1996, p. 165). By reporting rather than evaluating facts, recipients are directed to minimise the speaker's personal accountability for the events and invited to draw their inferences (see also Sneijder 2006). Finally, the account is constructed as 'scripted'; the events are formulated as if they would happen to any person in the same situation (Edwards 1994).

In Extract 6.15, it is suggested that there is no reason for not joining the event.

Extract 6.15 (Free Union)
```
1 If you think the problem is big enough, you will find a way. If
2 you are not capable of going physically, that's another
3 story. Otherwise it's a choice.
```

By implicating a logical connection between 'thinking the problem is big enough' and 'finding a way to come', using an if-then formulation (Sneijder and Te Molder 2005a), the speaker implicitly attributes responsibility for joining the event to the recipient and appeals to his moral accountability (line 1). The suggestion is that if one does not attend the event, he or she does not show commitment to the issue or does not care enough about it.

As we saw, participants build commitment and constructed a lack of commitment as an accountable matter. By constructing commitment as a relevant and preferred characteristic, participants are encouraged to actively participate in gatherings. Creating commitment implicitly invites others to show their commitment as well. At the same time, organisers of these groups carefully protect the distinction between commitment and activism and undermine any suggestions that they would be seeking 'trouble'.

Discussion

This chapter explored how versions of reality are *made available for* mobilisation for collective action by Dutch social movements. The chapter shows that particular discursive activities are depicted as relevant for mobilisation, such as legitimising the cause (in this case by disputing the integrity of authorities), the construction of genuine commitment rather than activism and the construction of togetherness.

We explored the ways in which speakers managed their exhortations for collective participation in events. Members of social movements calling for collective participation resisted identity descriptions (Widdicombe 1998); in particular they displayed a concern for not coming across as mere victims or as (violent) activists. In this way, they constructed genuine commitment to their particular goals and presented themselves as reasonable people. This seems especially important in the Yellow Vests groups, who are faced with the challenge to undermine potential associations with violent manifestations as they occurred elsewhere in Europe. This resembles findings in studies of political communication where people making political arguments need to be seen as reasonable (e.g. Goodman and Johnson 2013). The Yellow Vests typically present themselves as a peaceful group. Within the Yellow Vests groups, emphasis lies on the collective rather than diffuse nature of the Yellow Vests movement by reference to the shared experience of 'being worried'. As such, the Yellow Vests demonstrate anticipating a potential critical stance towards the diffuse motivations people may have for becoming a member of this movement.

We found that calls for participation invoked a divide between members of the social movements and the authorities as a shared reason for joining. This shows how group identification is constructed in opposition to other relevant groups. Perceived structural inequalities are constructed as legitimate social problems and make relevant emotion talk that indexes one's right to show concern (Broër and Duyvendak 2009). As Snow and Owens point out, constructing actual or perceived systems of inequality is part of social movements' conduct (2014).

In line with this, it was also demonstrated that social movements emphasise the emotional grounds (being worried) for participating in collective action. People are invited to transform their inner feelings into actions (see Edwards 1999). The invocation of 'worries' makes the investment in collective action understandable and therefore reasonable. Furthermore, 'commitment' is constructed as an important feature of calls for collective action and vice versa invites recipients to demonstrate the same commitment. Cancelling participation is treated as an accountable action.

With this chapter we have shown the merits of the discursive psychology as an innovative perspective to the study of mobilisation and depicted how psychological categories such as 'emotion' and 'identity' are invoked for making available mobilisation for collective action participation.

References

Beaulieu, A., & Estalella, A. (2012). Rethinking research ethics for mediated settings. *Information, Communication & Society, 15*(1), 23–42.

Billig, M. (1978). *Fascists: A social psychological view of the national front.* Academic Press.

Billig, M. (1995). *Banal nationalism.* Sage Publications.

British Psychological Society. (2007). *Report of the working party on conducting research on the internet: Guidelines for ethical practice in psychological research online* (No. 62/06.2007). British Psychological Society.

Bröer, C., & Duyvendak, J. W. (2009). Discursive opportunities, feeling rules and the rise of protests against aircraft noise. *Mobilization, 14*(3), 337–356.

Cammaerts, B. (2015). Social media and activism. In R. Mansell & P. Hwa (Eds.), *The international Encyclopedia of digital communication and society* (pp. 1027–1034). Wiley-Blackwell.

Condor, S., Tileagă, C., & Billig, M. (2013). Political rhetoric. In L. Huddy, D. O. Sears, & J. S. Levy (Eds.), *Oxford handbook of political psychology* (pp. 262–300). Oxford University Press, Chapter 9.

de Weerd, M., & Klandermans, P. G. (1999). Group identification and social protest: Farmers' protest in the Netherlands. *European Journal of Social Psychology, 29*, 1073–1095.

Drury, J., Reicher, S., & Stott, C. (2012). The psychology of collective action: Crowds and change. In B. Wagoner, E. Jensen, & J. A. Oldmeadow (Eds.), *Culture and social change: Transforming society through the power of ideas. Advances in cultural psychology* (pp. 19–38). Information Age Publishing.

Edwards, D. (1994). Script formulations: A study of event descriptions in conversation. *Journal of Language and Social Psychology, 13*, 211–247.

Edwards, D. (1999). Emotion discourse. *Culture & Psychology, 5*(3), 271–291.

Edwards, D., & Fasulo, A. (2006). 'To be honest': Sequential uses of honesty phrases in talk-in-interaction. *Research on Language and Social Interaction, 30*(4), 343–376.

Edwards, D., & Potter, J. (1992). *Discursive psychology*. Sage Publications.

Edwards, D., & Potter, J. (2001). Discursive psychology. In A. McHoul & M. Rapley (Eds.), *How to analyse talk in institutional settings. A casebook of methods* (pp. 12–14). Continuum International Publishing Group.

Edwards, D., & Potter, J. (2017). Some uses of subject-side assessments. *Discourse Studies, 19*(5), 497–514.

Eltantawy, N., & Wiest, J. B. (2011). The Arab spring| Social media in the Egyptian revolution: reconsidering resource mobilization theory. *International Journal of Communication, 5*, 1207–1224.

Goffman, E. (1981). *Forms of talk*. Basil Blackwell.

Goodman, S., & Johnson, A. J. (2013). Strategies used by the far right to counter accusations of racism. *Critical Approaches to Discourse Analysis Across Disciplines, 6*, 97–113.

Goodwin, J., & Jasper, J. (2003). *The social movements reader: Cases and concepts*. Blackwell Publishing.

Heritage, J., & Greatbatch, D. (1986). Generating applause: A study of rhetoric and response at party political conferences. *American Journal of Sociology, 92*(1), 110–157.

Hutchby, I., & Wooffit, R. (2008). *Conversation analysis*. Polity Press.

Hwang, H., & Kim, K. (2015). Social media as a tool for social movements: The effect of social media use and social capital on intention to participate in social movements. *International Journal of Consumer Studies, 39*(5), 478–488.

Ilie, C. (1994). *What Else Can I Tell You? A pragmatic study of English rhetorical questions as discursive and argumentative acts.* Almqvist & Wiksell International.

Khamis, S., & Vaughn, K. (2012). We Are All Khaled Said': The potentials and limitations of cyberactivism in triggering public mobilization and promoting political change. *Journal of Arab & Muslim Media Research, 4*(2–3), 145–163.

Kiyimba, N., Lester, J. N., & O'Reilly, M. (2019). Engaging with ethical principles in collecting naturally occurring data. In *Using naturally occurring data in qualitative health research.* Springer.

Koopmans, R., & Olzak, S. (2004). Discursive opportunities and the evolution of right-wing violence in Germany. *American Journal of Sociology, 110*(1), 198–230.

Lamerichs, J., & Te Molder, H. F. M. (2003). Computer-mediated communication: From a cognitive to a discursive model. *New Media and Society, 5*(4), 451–473.

Lim, M. (2012). Clicks, cabs, and coffee houses: Social media and oppositional movements in Egypt, 2004–2011. *Journal of Communication, 62*, 231–248.

Lopes, A. R. (2014). *The impact of social media on social movements: The new opportunity and mobilizing structure* (p. 23). Creighton University.

Meredith, J. & Potter, J. (2014). Conversation analysis and electronic interactions: methodological, analytic and technological considerations. In Lim, H.L. & Sudweeks, F. (Eds). Innovative Methods and Technologies for Electronic Discourse Analysis. IGI Global, Hershey, PA, pp. 370–393.

Merriman, B. (2015). Ethical issues in the employment of user-generated content as experimental stimulus: Defining the interests of creators. *Research Ethics, 10*(4), 196–207.

Milewa, T., Valentine, J., & Calnan, M. (1999). Community participation and citizenship in British health care planning: Narratives of power and involvement in the changing welfare state. *Sociology of Health & Illness, 21*(4), 445–465.

Nicodemus, D. (2004). Mobilizing information: Local news and the formation of a viable political community. *Political Communication, 21*, 161–176.

Pomerantz, A. (1986). Extreme case formulations: A way of legitimizing claims. *Human Studies, 9*(2–3), 219–229.

Potter, J. (1996). *Representing reality. Discourse, rhetoric and social construction.* Sage Publications.

6 The Discourse of Social Movements: Online Mobilising... 171

Potter, J., & Edwards, D. (2013). Conversation analysis and psychology. In T. Stivers & J. Sidnell (Eds.), *The handbook of conversation analysis* (pp. 701–725). Routledge.

Potter, J., & Wetherell, M. (1987). *Discourse and social psychology: Beyond attitudes and behaviour*. Sage Publications.

Shirky, C. (2011). The political power of social media: Technology, the public sphere, and political change. *Foreign Affairs, 90*, 28–41.

Smithson, J. (2015). Using discourse analysis to study online forums for young people who self-harm. In J. N. Lester & M. O'Reilly (Eds.), *The Palgrave handbook of child mental health. Discourse and conversation studies*. Palgrave Macmillan.

Sneijder, P. (2006). *Food for talk: Discursive identities, food choice and eating practices*. Thesis,Wageningen University.

Sneijder, P., Stinesen, B., Harmelink, M., & Klarenbeek, A. (2018). Monitoring mobilization: A discursive psychological analysis of online mobilizing practices. *Journal of Communication Management, 22*(1), 14–27.

Sneijder, P., & te Molder, H. F. M. (2005a). Moral logic and logical morality: Attributions of responsibility and blame in online discourse on veganism. *Discourse and Society, 16*, 675–696.

Sneijder, P., & te Molder, H. (2005b). Moral logic or logical morality: Attributions of responsibility and blame in online discourse on veganism. *Discourse and Society, 16*(5), 675–696.

Sneijder, P., & te Molder, H. (2009). Normalizing ideological food choice and eating practices.: Identity work in online discussions on veganism. *Appetite, 52*(3), 621–630.

Snow, D., & Owens, P. (2014). Social movements and social inequality: Toward a more balanced assessment of the relationship. In J. McLeod, E. Lawler, & M. Schwalbe (Eds.), *Handbook of the social psychology of inequality. Handbooks of sociology and social research*. Springer.

Stinesen, B., Sneijder, P., & Klarenbeek, A. (2016). Rumour construction on social media: A discursive psychological analysis of tweets concerning a missing case. *Tijdschrift voor Communicatiewetenschap (Dutch Journal of Communication Science), 44*(4), 316–335.

Stoker, J., Winter, H., Akerboom, C., & Geertsema, B. (2015). *Dialoogtafel: woorden en daden*. Groningen University.

Stott, C., & Drury, J. (2017). Contemporary understanding of riots: Classical crowd psychology, ideology and the social identity approach. *Public Understanding of Science, 26*(1), 2–14.

Stott, C., & Reicher, S. (2000). Collective action and psychological change: The emergence of new social identities. *British Journal of Social Psychology, 39,* 579–604.

Tajfel, H. (1978). *Differentiation between social groups: Studies in the social psychology of intergroup relations.* Associated Press.

Takahashi, B., Tandoc, E. C., & Carmichael, C. (2015). Communicating on twitter during a disaster: an analysis of tweets during Typhoon Haiyan in the Philippines. *Computers in Human Behavior, 50,* 392–398.

Tiidenberg, K. (2018). Ethics in digital research. In U. Flick (Ed.), (2017) *SAGE handbook of qualitative data collection.* SAGE Publications.

Tileagă, C. (2007). Ideologies of moral exclusion: A critical discursive reframing of depersonalization, delegitimization and dehumanization. *British Journal of Social Psychology, 46*(4), 717–737.

Tilly, C. (2004). *Social movements, 1768–2004.* Paradigm Publishers.

Toth, C. (2015). Do children need religious education? Discursive construction of children in talk shows by means of rhetorical questions. *Journal of Comparative Research in Anthropology and Sociology, 6,* 67–89.

van der Voort, N., & Vanclay, F. (2015). Social impacts of earthquakes caused by gas extraction in the Province of Groningen, the Netherlands. *Environmental Impact Assessment Review, 50,* 1–15.

van Stekelenburg, J. (2018). *How does protesting work in the age of social media?* Retrieved June 5, 2020, fromhttps://www.chathamhouse.org/event/chatham-house-forum-how-does-protesting-work-age-social-media

van Stekelenburg, J., & Klandermans, P. (2007). Individuals in movements: A social psychology of contention. In P. G. Klandermans & C. M. Roggeband (Eds.), *The handbook of social movements across disciplines* (pp. 157–204). Kluwer.

van Stekelenburg, J., Oegema, D., & Klandermans, P. G. (2010). No radicalization without identification: How ethnic Dutch and Dutch Muslim web forums radicalize over time. In A. Azzi, X. Chryssochoou, B. Klandermans, & B. Simon (Eds.), *Identity and participation in culturally diverse societies. A multidisciplinary perspective* (pp. 256–274). Blackwell Wiley.

Watson, R. (1983). The presentation of "victim" and "motive" in discourse: The case of police interrogations and interviews. *Victimology, 8*(1/2), 31–52.

Widdicombe, S. (1998). 'But you don't class yourself': The interactional management of category membership and non-membership. In C. Antaki & S. Widdicombe (Eds.), *Identities in talk* (pp. 52–70). London: Sage Publication.

Wiggins, S. (2017). *Discursive psychology: Theory, method and applications.* Sage Publications.

Wiggins, S., & Potter, J. (2003). Attitudes and evaluative practices: Category vs. item and subjective vs. objective constructions in everyday food assessments. *British Journal of Social Psychology, 42,* 513–531.

Wilson, J. (1990). *Politically speaking.* Blackwell.

Wright, R. (2011). *Rock the Casbah: Rage and rebellion across the Islamic World.* Simon & Schuster.

7

Analysing Multimodal Communication and Persuasion in Populist Radical Right Political Blogs

Katarina Pettersson and Inari Sakki

Introduction

Political rhetoric has for long been a central area of interest among discursive and political psychologists. This line of research, notably the work of Michael Billig and colleagues (e.g. Billig 1987; Condor et al. 2013) and that of Stephen Reicher and Nick Hopkins (e.g. 2001), has developed social psychological theorising and methodology concerning how issues of ideology, the two-sidedness and dilemmatic character of human argumentation, categorisation and attitudes and identity constructions of speaker and audience are implicated in political rhetoric and persuasion. Traditionally, discursive work on political discourse has focused on its forms in contexts such as parliamentary debates and political speeches

---

K. Pettersson (✉)
University of Helsinki, Helsinki, Finland
e-mail: katarina.pettersson@helsinki.fi

I. Sakki
University of Eastern Finland, Kuopio, Finland

© The Author(s), under exclusive license to Springer Nature Switzerland AG 2020
M. A. Demasi et al. (eds.), *Political Communication*, Palgrave Studies in Discursive
Psychology, https://doi.org/10.1007/978-3-030-60223-9_7

(e.g. Billig and Marinho 2017; Every and Auguoustinos 2007; Tileagă 2008; Verkuyten and Nooitgedagt 2018) as well as news articles and interviews in so-called traditional media (e.g. Verkuyten 2003).

However, the era of the Internet and social media has posed new methodological challenges for researchers in the field. Thus, during the past decade, scholars have begun to show interest in the ways in which the social media have enabled and accelerated the successes of populist, radical right and nationalist parties across Europe, as well as, for instance, in the US and Australia, and, conversely, how these parties have managed to efficiently exploit these media for their political purposes (e.g. Burke 2018; Pajnik and Sauer 2017; Sori and Ivanova 2017). This new stream of research has increasingly acknowledged the analytical challenges that the multimodal, including visual, forms that political communication in the social media may take. This has led to initiatives for developing qualitative research approaches that reflexively acknowledge, for instance, the power relations involved in online environments and relationships, and that thus may challenge existing power structures (e.g. Giles et al. 2015; Jowett 2015; Morison et al. 2015; Pajnik and Sauer 2017). There remains, however, a shortage of discursive research focusing on political blogs as a medium for populist radical right and nationalist communication and how they through their specific features—such as the lack of the mediating role played by journalists and the possibility for readers to communicate with the blogging politician within the blog space—allow politicians to interact with, engage and mobilise their voters (e.g. Baumer et al. 2011; Nilsson and Carlsson 2014; Pettersson 2017).

With our research on populist radical right political blogs (e.g. Pettersson and Sakki 2017; Sakki and Pettersson 2016), we have strived to fill this gap in discursive research, highlighting the peculiar features of political blog communication and how these may be analytically approached from a critical discursive psychological (CDP) perspective (Edley 2001; Edley and Wetherell 1997; Wetherell 1998). Building upon this research project (2014–2017) that investigated blogs of members of the populist radical right Finns Party (Fin: *Perussuomalaiset*) and the Sweden Democrats (Swe: *Sverigedemokraterna*) from a critical discursive psychological perspective, the present chapter aims to contribute to the discursive paradigm's analytical toolkit for studying the forms, contents and mediums of contemporary nationalist(ic) political communication. Specifically, the chapter will propose a methodological approach through which the politicians' use of the audio-visual, communicative and digital affordances (Chadwick and Stromer-Galley 2016) that the blog environment provides can be studied. The approach maintains CDP as its methodological core, yet it includes analytical tools from visual rhetorical analysis (Kress and van Leeuwen 2006) and also pays analytic attention to the use of digital affordances in communication in political blogs (e.g. Chadwick and Stromer-Galley 2016). Since it considers the immediate discursive micro-context (i.e. the particular affordances of the blog space) as well as the wider social and political environment (Edley 2001; Wetherell 1998), we argue that CDP is a particularly useful approach for studying how political blog messages are constructed and what implications the messages may have on a broader societal level.

As such, Finland constitutes a highly interesting context for studying populist radical right political blogs. Being a small fringe party only a decade ago, the Finns Party has since then become one of Finland's largest parties in terms of voter support (2011 and 2019) and entered the national government (2015). The party's success has been largely due to its efficient use of the social media, specifically political blogs, when reaching out to the electorate with its strong views against immigration, multiculturalism and the EU (e.g. Hatakka 2017; Horsti 2015; Kamenova and Pingoud 2017; Keskinen 2013; Mäkinen 2016; Pettersson 2017; Sori and Ivanova 2017). In 2017, the Finns Party elected Jussi Halla-aho as the successor of the long-term party leader Timo Soini. Halla-aho, a famous blogger and front figure of the Finnish anti-immigration movement, became prosecuted in 2012 for incitement to racial hatred and breach of the sanctity of religion because of his blog entry in which he had labelled Islam a 'paedophilic religion' and claimed that stealing and abusing welfare benefits is a national and even genetic powerful than verbal communication. Blair (2004). Following the election of Halla-aho, the party's more 'moderate' faction left in protest and formed a new party called Blue Future (Fin: *Sininen Tulevaisuus*), remaining in government, whereas Halla-aho's devotees in the Finns Party found themselves in political opposition. In the subsequent national parliamentary elections in 2019, however, the Finns Party enjoyed success, ending up with the second biggest share of votes, 17.5 per cent, whereas Blue Future yielded one per cent of the votes and, accordingly, lost its seats in parliament (Finnish Ministry of Justice—Information and Result Service 2019).

In the present chapter, we introduce and argue for our integrative, discursive approach to studying political blogs through presenting in detail the steps we take when analysing one single blog entry. As we have argued elsewhere (Pettersson and Sakki 2017) and unlike some work, for instance, within conversation analysis that applies large sets of material (e.g. Stokoe 2012), using a case-study approach is particularly useful for the detailed demonstration of an analytical approach (Tileagă 2005). To this end, we have chosen a blog entry entitled 'Population changes that we are not allowed to speak of' (Fin: '*Väestönmuutokset, joista ei saa puhua*') written by Riikka Purra of the Finns Party on 3 January 2019. The blog entry serves as an illustrative example of the multifaceted verbal and visual conglomerate that discourse in political blogs may take and thus enables us thoroughly to present to the reader our analytical approach. As a recently elected MP and vice president of the Finns Party, Purra holds a prominent position as ideological influencer and spokesperson for the party and often appears next to its leader Jussi Halla-aho in public appearances.

This chapter is structured as follows. First, we outline some existing discursive and other relevant work on online populist and radical right political communication, discussing the current state of the field and the methodological challenges that require attention. Second, we introduce our methodological approach and how it may contribute to tackling these challenges. Third, we present the chosen blog entry and our detailed analyses of its discursive, visual and digital content, form and functions. Finally, we conclude by discussing remaining challenges for discursive research into contemporary populist radical right political communication and persuasion.

Previous Research on (Populist Radical Right[1]) Political Discourse in the Social Media

Research on the rise of nationalist and populist radical right parties has demonstrated that active use of and visibility in the media has been a crucial factor behind the electoral successes of the radical right (Aalberg and de Vreese 2017; Pajnik and Sauer 2017). This pertains especially to the 'new' forms of web-based, social media, where the parties may circumvent the journalists as intermediaries in order to engage in direct communication with the public—the presumptive voters—about typically sensitive issues such as immigration and asylum-seeking (e.g. Pettersson and Sakki 2017; Sauer et al. 2017). Populist radical right communication is characterised by criticising the 'political correctness' of mainstream media and 'political elites', drawing upon and constructing collective emotions of fear and threat (e.g. Wodak 2015) and creating antagonistic divisions between 'us' (the people) and 'them' (political antagonists, mainstream media and immigrants) (e.g. Sakki and Pettersson 2016). In their discourse, populist radical right politicians often claim to be the sole protectors of the right to freedom of speech (Pettersson 2019; Sori and Ivanova 2017) and have proven successful in conveying powerful political messages, not only through catchy verbal slogans that appeal to 'common sense' or emotions but also through innovative use of visual communication (Pettersson and Sakki 2017; Sauer et al. 2017). As research indicates (e.g. Pettersson and Sakki 2017; Stanyer et al. 2017) and as we shall see in detail in this chapter, the social media enable such forms of political communication, as they allow for the co-creation of antagonistic views and sentiments by the populist radical right politicians and their supporters, without the involvement of third parties such as journalists or ideological opponents.

---

[1] In the social and political scientific literature, various labels, such as 'right-wing populist', 'far right' and 'extreme right' are sometimes used to describe these parties. Following, for example, Jungar and Jupskås (2014) and Mudde (2007), we here apply the term 'populist radical right' to describe the Finns Party. The term essentially entails that the party holds an authoritarian stance on socio-cultural issues (e.g. promoting traditional family values, opposing multiculturalism) and a less clear stance on socio-economic ones (e.g. welfare services). See also Jungar and Jupskås (2014) and Pettersson (2017) for a discussion of these issues.

A recent cross-country research project compared the communication strategies on the Internet of European (populist radical right) political parties and movements (Pajnik and Sauer 2017). In deploying both large-scale quantitative and critical frame analysis of the online communication of populist radical right parties and movements, the research shed light on the innovative ways in which the online sphere has been utilised by these actors, thus enabling the rise and spread of their ideologies. The research demonstrated between-country variations in the use of the Internet among the actors, for instance how the sophistication and extent of the utilisation depended on the country's restrictions on Internet use, or in terms of how gender issues were framed depending on the level of gender equality in the country. Thus, albeit contextual factors remaining important, the researchers concluded that the use of online communication tools has become increasingly important for political actors and especially for right-wing populist ones.

During the past few years, also discursive (e.g. Burke 2017, 2018) and other qualitative (e.g. Giles et al. 2015; Jowett 2015; Morison et al. 2015) researchers have begun to show interest in political communication within the online sphere. This line of research has deepened our understanding of the discursive tools and strategies involved in radical right movements' use of the social media, such as Facebook, in their discursive othering of ethnic and religious minorities and in their mobilisation of voters (e.g. Burke 2018; Sakki and Pettersson 2016). Indeed, discursive approaches have much to offer to the study of political discourse, as they specifically focus on exploring discourse *in situ*, that is, they take into account the ways in which rhetorical strategies differ depending on the immediate discursive context (e.g. Burke and Demasi 2019). Yet, as this bulk of research—including our own—concludes, there is still much to be done in terms of developing our tools for studying the particularities of online political communication through qualitative, discursive methods. Accordingly, our present aim is to show how such discourse, and in particular, populist radical right political blog discourse, may be explored from a critical discursive psychological perspective. The critical element in this approach entails investigating the discursive functions of discourse, that is, unmasking the seemingly 'neutral' contents of discourse by exploring the cultural meanings they embed, and analysing how the discourse may serve to promote and sustain certain ideological positions or power relations (cf. Edley 2001; Tileagă and Stokoe 2015). To illustrate our approach and to allow the reader to follow the analytical procedure systematically, we will provide a screenshot of a populist radical right blog entry, followed by our detailed analyses. First, however, we will present our analytical approach.

Methodological Approach: Combining Critical Discursive and Visual Rhetorical Analyses

The core of our analytical approach relies on work in critical discursive psychology (CDP) (Edley 2001; Edley and Wetherell 1997; Wetherell 1998). CDP is a broad methodology that stems from the social constructionist paradigm and combines ontological as well as epistemological assumptions from critical discourse analysis and post-structuralism (Wetherell 1998). Further, it shares the focus of discursive psychology (e.g. Edwards and Potter 1992) on the action orientation of discourse and incorporates insights from Michael Billig's (1987) rhetorical social psychology, which highlights the argumentative nature of discourse. The main thrust of CDP—and what, in our view, makes it particularly useful for studying political discourse—is that it takes into account not only the immediate social setting of the discourse but also its broader, societal, historical and political context.

We have previously developed our three-step analytic procedure based on CDP to explore the content, form and function of political discourse (Pettersson and Sakki 2017; Sakki and Pettersson 2016). In the first step, we thoroughly familiarise ourselves with the content of the blog entry we have chosen for analysis. At this stage, our aim is to identify the patterns, that is, the consistency and variability in the discourse (e.g. Potter and Wetherell 1987). We do this through a data-driven, explorative perspective with a focus on the contents of the discourse, in order to identify the major topics that the blogger brings up in the blog entry and, for instance, how in- and out-groups are constructed and what labels are attached to these groups (cf. Sakki and Pettersson 2016). Second, we investigate the form, or rhetorical organisation, of the blog entry by identifying the rhetorical devices, for example, consensus warranting, active voicing (Potter 1996), footing (Goffman 1979) and resources, such as rhetorical commonplaces and liberal principles (Potter 2012; Wetherell and Potter 1992), that the blogger uses in order to build the claim and enhance his or her credibility as a speaker. At this stage, we also focus upon the ways in which the bloggers exploit the digital features (such as hyperlinks) of blogs as rhetorical devices. Third, following Billig (1987) and Edley (2001), in order to elaborate on the broader discursive functions of the messages, we examine the blog entry as part of its argumentative, that is, its immediate and broader social and political context.

To date, despite the possibilities this approach offers, the application of CDP to visual discourse has been insufficient, as, for instance, Burke (2017) notes. Consequently and as political communication in social media takes multimodal forms, in this chapter we take one step further in our three-step model and explicate how CDP and visual rhetorical analysis (VRA) can be combined in the analysis of online political discourse.

Traditionally, the study of rhetoric has focused on verbal language, but since the 1970s its scope expanded into visual images (Foss 2005), and today, the growth of visually mediated communication, for example in the social media, has made visual images a timely topic in the social sciences (Danesi 2017). However, as Sonja Foss (2005, p. 150) reminds us:

Not every visual object is visual rhetoric. What turns a visual object into a communicative artefact – a symbol that communicates and can be studied as rhetoric – is the presence of three characteristics. The image must be symbolic, involve human intervention, and be presented to an audience for the purpose of communicating with that audience.

The focus of VRA is thus on the content, structure and social, political and ideological functions of images (Danesi 2017); in other words, it shares CDP's focus on the action orientation and functionality of discourse (cf. Edley 2001; Penn 2010).

Visual communication is often considered rhetorically more powerful than verbal communication. Blair (2004) argues that the particular qualities of visual images—their immediacy, vividness and concreteness—make them more persuasive than verbal rhetoric. In political communication the visual works through emotional pathways: it has potential to appeal to readers' emotions in ways words cannot (e.g. Blair 2004). As Wodak and colleagues (Wodak and Forchtner 2014; Richardson and Wodak 2009) point out, simple fallacies and unreasonable argumentation in conjunction with pragmatic devices, such as irony and sarcasm, seem to form an intentional and integral part of populist radical right visual rhetoric. The study by Richardson and Wodak (2009) of political leaflets of right-wing parties illustrates, however, that verbal and visual elements should be read together in order to fully uncover their racist and anti-Semitist message, as the messages of the verbal and visual support and complement each other.

Similar to our three-step analysis of (verbal) discourse described above, our analysis of images involves moving beyond the analysis of contents (the 'what' question) and focuses on the performative and ideological aspects of the visual (the 'how' and 'why' questions). Thus, our approach leans on Kress and van Leeuwen's (2006) framework for the semiotic analysis of visual communication that is based on three meta-semiotic tasks of images: the representational, compositional and interpersonal metafunctions. The people, places and objects within an image construct the content, the representational metafunction, and answers the question, 'What is the image about?' By contrast, the performative functions are investigated by focusing on interpersonal and compositional characteristics of an image. The analysis of the interpersonal metafunction entails considering the actions of all the participants involved in the production and viewing of an image (the creator, the characters in an image and the audience), and it predominantly answers the question, 'How does the picture engage the audience?' Thus, this kind of analysis pays attention to the choices related to gaze, perspective (e.g. horizontal and vertical angle) and degrees of social distance and intimacy. The analysis of compositional features, on the other hand, requires the investigation of the aspects related to the layout of the webpage and involves the study of the visual components in relation to each other through the main principles of composition, that is, the distribution of the information value or visual salience, such as size, colour, lighting, focus and visual framing

(Kress and van Leeuwen 2006). These three aspects are dynamically related and together they construct the meaning and ideological function of the visual image.

Following Kress and van Leeuwen's (2006) framework, Hook and Glăveanu (2013) have further elaborated the ways of approaching the 'how' question and suggest identifying four kinds of compositional elements of images: (1) sensory elements (such as colour, lighting and texture), (2) structural elements (such as vectoriality and perspective), (3) dynamic elements (such as gaze and position of figures) and (4) emerging elements (such as focal point and directionality). For example, colours can be used to draw attention to certain aspects of an image, to prioritise some contents or to build relations or associations between different objects. In our previous work (Pettersson and Sakki 2017), we have demonstrated how blue-white colours (as in the Finnish flag) work in Finnish nationalist rhetoric as 'colours of grammar', that is, their meaning is so deeply anchored in the collective mind of the Finnish people that they have become automatically associated with Finnishness and national identity, thus constituting an example of what Michael Billig (1995) calls 'banal nationalism'.

Additionally, structural elements can be used to imply multiple meanings: different sizes of the objects may indicate different social relations; close-ups indicate an intimate or personal relationship between the characters of an image and the viewer, while medium shots indicate social and long shots impersonal relationships (Kress and van Leeuwen 2006). The focus on dynamic elements can reveal different social relations between the image and its viewer; for example, a direct gaze can be considered as an indicator of engagement, while a person portrayed in profile may imply greater detachment and that the person is 'one of them and not of us' (Kress and van Leeuwen 2006). In addition, one should consider the way different compositional elements act together and propose reading the image in a particular way. For example, it may matter whether the main character is depicted high or low on the page (indicating ideal/real), in the centre or in the margin (central/marginal) or on the left-hand side or the right (given/new).

At the third level of analysis, we combine the analyses of content and form, analysing the images in their immediate and broader argumentative context, which means considering also the verbal communication of the blog entry. As the desirable meaning of an image is often strengthened with a verbal explanation (Barthes 1977; Blair 2004), we pay special attention also to the text surrounding the blog images, as well as to the blog entry's broader context of social and political events. This third level of analysis answers the question of what the particular function of a given image may be in the context of populist radical right communication and persuasion.

It is important to note that the meaning of an image is not in the visual elements themselves, but becomes constructed by the audience based on a cultural matrix of meanings (Kress and van Leeuwen 2006). Besides the culturally preferred ways of interpreting, different people may and do perceive and interpret the same verbal or visual elements in different ways due to their varying motivations, goals, knowledge and prior experiences. The researcher is acting on the text and image just as the text and image act on the researcher, meaning, among other things, that the active position of the researcher as interpreter should be acknowledged in this type of research. The same pertains to the application of CDP: it is important that the researcher reflects on his or her own position in relation to the subject of research and how this may affect the interpretations. As we have expressed elsewhere (Sakki and Pettersson 2016), as women holding higher university degrees in the social sciences and one of us belonging to the Swedish-speaking minority in Finland whose rights the Finns Partys overtly opposes, we represent groups that are often constructed as ideological antagonists in the party's rhetoric. Although our position thus cannot be regarded as 'neutral'—which indeed the researcher's position never is—our strive for maximum transparency in the research process and our strict abidance by the methodological principles outlined by CDP and VRA allow us to make, we hope, a useful contribution to research on political communication (Fig. 7.1).

Fig. 7.1 *Population changes that we are not allowed to speak of.* Source: https://riikkapurra.net/2019/01/03/vaestonmuutokset-joista-ei-saa-puhua/

Analysis

Population changes that we are not allowed to speak of[2]
1 Swedes born with Swedish parents today constitute only
2 approx. 68.5% of the population.
3 Syrians have surpassed Finns as the biggest group of
4 foreigners – other runners up include Somalis, Turks,
5 Afghans and Eritreans.
6 Finland follows closely behind, but many either simply do
7 not believe or know about this. Our media reports scarcely,
8 and talking about the entire theme is demonised. As if it
9 would be propaganda to report about statistics and
10 predictions.
11 Mass-immigration from developing countries is slowly
12 changing large European cities in the same way – this of
13 course first becomes apparent in the suburbs. What there is
14 then Sweden, France or Finland? Street names and
15 architecture?
16 Because of leftist and other identity politicians, bringing
17 up the topic always ends up in questions about definitions
18 – what is Finnishness, is he or she Finnish, and what if
19 he or she did not eat sausages or go to the sauna and
20 ski!
21 Last time I brought up the matter, I first became the
22 target of an enormous Twitter-attack, and then ended up in
23 <u>NYT-liite</u>, where I was presented as a nonsense-spreading
24 populist.
25 I am not at all surprised that many do not dare to say
26 anything about the matter. Or about immigration in general.
27 Finns just discreetly investigate the immigrant percentages
28 of residential areas when looking for housing, compare

---

[2] We have translated the blog entry, originally written in Finnish, into English and added line numbers in order for the readers to be able to follow the analyses.

29 schools and quietly share information amongst each other
30 whilst otherwise keeping up a tolerant poker face. That is
31 how we Finns often are – kind, unsuspecting and sensitive.
32 Still, I am sure that the average Finnish (or Swedish)
33 person does not want his or her country to become
34 unrecognisable Many surely do not agree with the
35 assistant professor who told me last summer that Finland
36 would still be Finland even with a 100 percent foreign-born
37 population.
38 Naturally that would not even be financially possible – the
39 money will be spent much earlier – but for now I want to
40 focus on other things than the economy.
41 ((Fund for Peace map))
42 I am often cynical, but I also have hopes.
43 Firstly, I hope that Finns would dare to look truth in the
44 eyes. Secondly, I hope that they would demand acts from the
45 decision-makers. Thirdly, that they would vote based upon
46 facts. Fourthly, that the Finnish media would seize its
47 responsibility to report to the citizens on these matters.
48 Because than it [the population] would straighten – that does
49 not require miracles.
50 The other option is to succumb to the gloomy scenario given
51 in the <u>comments-section of my blog</u> by the blogger
52 <u>Vasarahammer</u>:
53 *Not a single Western European country has
been able to stop*
54 *mass-immigration after it has begun.*
55 *Explanations* [for the need for mass-immigration] *are*
56 *invented when they are needed. This has happened in every*
57 *European country that has become the target
of mass-*
58 immigration *Explanations vary from lack of
labour force to*
59 *enrichment of the culture. When no other
explanation is*

60 *enough, suddenly multiculturalism is inevi-*
table, some kind
61 *of natural force.*

Description of the Blog

When taking a glance at Riikka Purra's blog above, one is first greeted by a picture banner at the very top, in which we to the left see the blogger herself, smiling and looking straight into the camera. On the right-hand side of the banner is the Finns Party logo and slogan 'Some limit' (Fin: '*Jotain rajaa*'), which has been used in various contexts and, particularly, in debates and campaigns about immigration. Below the banner, one can choose between the categories of the 2019 Finnish parliamentary elections, the label 'Riikka' with information about the politician and the blog itself. Scrolling down, one may notice the multiple modes of interaction that the blog provides: there are links to the politician's other social media accounts, such as Facebook and Twitter; one can share her blog entries in the social media; and it is possible to comment on the entries in the blog itself. On the right-hand side of the main text, the blogger has organised earlier posts into various categories. One can see that the categories 'immigration', 'illegal immigration', 'politics', 'liberalism', 'media', 'society', 'feminism' and 'islam' are among the largest and thus the most used categories.

Content

The present blog entry was posted during the election campaign for the Finnish parliamentary elections in 2019, during which immigration and the consequences of the 2015 'refugee crisis' were still among the major concerns. The topic of the blog entry 'Population changes that we are not allowed to speak of' deals with a classic topic in populist radical right political blogging: the claim that the native Finnish population is under threat and diminishing because of the influx of foreigners and especially people from Muslim countries (e.g. Otova and Puurunen 2017; Pettersson and Sakki 2017). The blogger refers to Sweden in order to demonstrate a proximate context where this process has already gone too far and predicts that Finland will follow suit if nothing is done. Despite the alleged severity of the issue, and as the title already suggests, Purra claims that the entire topic is silenced by left-wing politicians and mainstream media. She maintains that she has been the target of a hostile Twitter storm and publicly ridiculed as a consequence of daring to talk about the issue. She links to an article in the paper *NYT-liite* (a magazine belonging to the largest Finnish daily newspaper *Helsingin Sanomat*), where her claims about the population change had been considered populist exaggerations. She concludes that it is no wonder that the Finns—a 'kind, unsuspecting, sensitive people'—do not dare to speak of the issue, as one easily becomes demonised, and left-wingers immediately twist the debate into oversimplified definitions of Finnishness.

Purra expresses her assumption that no Finn (or Swede) would like their country to turn into unrecognisability, nor agree with an academic who has claimed that Finland would remain Finland even with a 100 per cent foreign population. This, the blogger withholds, would not even be financially possible in the first place. Although she often feels cynical, she continues, she has four hopes for a brighter future: that the Finnish people would dare to face the truth, to demand action from the decisionmakers and to base their votes upon facts and that the Finnish media would seize its responsibility to report to the citizens about 'these matters'. If this fails, the blogger provides the alternative scenario, quoting the anti-immigration blogger and activist 'Vasarahammer' ('*Vasara*' means hammer in Finnish), whose grim prediction is that the processes of mass-immigration and multiculturalism will go on as if they were natural, since new excuses are always invented for their continuation. We return to analyse the rhetorical functions of these formulations at our third and final analytical stage below.

The blog entry contains two images: the first one precedes the text and depicts a huge pile of dark metal faces that seem to cry or scream. No source or title is provided for the image. Scrolling down, one arrives at a world map of 'fragile states', with the colours from green ('sustainable') to dark red ('alert') indicating the fragility of the globe's countries. The source 'Fund for Peace (2014)' is placed below the map.

Form

The blog entry at hand is replete with what Potter (1996) terms rhetorical devices for the speaker to enhance both her own credibility and the factual impression of the claims that she is presenting. In order to establish her position as a trustworthy, knowledgeable and unbiased speaker, the blogger deploys the strategy of consensus warranting (Potter 1996), for example, through presenting her claims as representing the opinion of the 'average' Finn (line 32). By contrast, the blogger constructs her left-wing, 'pro-immigration' political antagonists and the Finnish media as both hostile (lines 7–10, 21–24) and irrational (lines 16–20), as they allegedly attack anyone who dares to speak of the 'facts' and twist the debate in their own favour. Linking to the article in which the blogger's views had been criticised increases the credibility of the blogger's message (Silva 2016): her position is that of a target of public persecution and humiliation, a victim, merely because she dares to speak the truth (cf. Pettersson 2019).

The blogger furthermore makes use of rhetorical questions (lines 13–15), which serve to engage the readers, allowing them to draw their own conclusions and thus participate in the construction of the politician's message without her needing to provide explicit—and potentially questionable—statements (Pettersson and Sakki 2017). The blog milieu provides a similar reader-engaging function through the possibility for the readers to comment upon the blog entry, enabling an implicit dialogue and a creation of mutual understanding between the politician and her readership. The reference to the assumed will of the Finns to protect Finland from becoming 'unrecognisable' (lines 32–34) is an example of Goffmanian (1979) footing: through simply reporting what certain unspecified persons might say, Purra distances herself from the claim that is being made, rendering it the *volonté générale* of the people, rather than her own, subjective opinion. Through consensus warranting, rhetorical questions and footing, the blogger manages to dodge potential accusations of prejudice or irrationality and instead come across as informed, rational and brave, in stark contrast to her political antagonists and the Finnish media.

In terms of constructing her claim, the blogger makes use of the language of quantification through presenting the relevant population figures of the Swedish context (lines 1–2) in order to make her claim seem grounded in facts (e.g. Potter et al. 1991; Rapley 1998; Verkuyten 2013). The three-part lists (lines 14, 18–20, 31) add rhetorical, persuasive force to the blogger's argument. Another tool she exploits is that of reported speech or active voicing (Potter 1996): the apocalyptic scenario for Finland if 'mass-immigration' is allowed to proceed is not delivered in the blogger's own words, but through the direct citing as well as linking to another blogger who shares her views (lines 50–61). The person behind the name 'Vasarahammer' is Marko Parkkola, an activist and active debater in nationalist and anti-immigration circles, who is a member of the nationalist organisations the Finnish Defence League and *Suomen Sisu* (Uusi Suomi 2019). Thus, he is likely to be known and appreciated by the vast majority of Purra's readers. Further, the use of voicing, or digital voicing, as we have called this strategy of linking within political blogs (Pettersson and Sakki 2017), serves to increase the air of consensus around the blogger's message: it is not merely her concern—others share it as well. As his texts circulate widely in Finnish anti-immigration online communities, Vasarahammer here appears as an external authority and expert on the matter at hand; thus, in quoting him, Purra ascribes a category entitlement (Potter 1996) to him.

Turning now to the analysis of the visual components, the dark colour dominating the first picture builds associations to the 'non-white' Other, particularly given the verbal message of the sentence that follows immediately upon the picture. The composition of the picture—the endless pile of metal faces—seems to symbolise the masses in which the Other arrives and the endless threat this entails. The point of tension in the image—the face with the open, crying mouth in the front—constructs emotional appeals of sadness, threat and danger.

The symbolic value of the colour-world of the second picture, the world map, is perhaps even more evident: green symbolises safety, whereas red stands for threat, thus making Finland's position as small and safe, yet vulnerable to the intrusion of people from the threatening states. The focal point is upon the predominantly red, large African countries in the middle, with the small, green Finland vertically right above. In contrast to the previous, emotion-evoking picture, this one adds a scientific tone to the blog entry through providing seemingly objective, research-based knowledge from a trustworthy source, Fund for Peace.

The picture banner on top of the blog is a further important visual element. As Kress and van Leeuwen (2006) argue, the left-hand side of an image depicts the 'given', whereas the right contains the 'new'; the upper aspects form the 'ideal', and the lower the 'actual'. The 'given' element is thus constituted by Purra herself, whose inviting smile, gaze into the camera and pose indicate kindness, informality and openness. Her open hair draws associations to youth and informality, whereas her jewels and clothes add a pinch of conservativeness and official air to her appearance (Berggren et al. 2017; Carpinella and Johnson 2013; Huddy and Terkildsen 1993; Lee 2013; Todorov et al. 2005; Wagner and Wodak 2006). The medium shot (cutting the figure from the waist) denotes a social relationship with the readers, she belongs to 'us', not to 'them' (Kress and van Leeuwen 2006), and combined with the direct gaze it indicates engagement: it is a demand picture, meaning that the figure in the picture looks at us and symbolically demands something from us (Kress and van Leeuwen 2006; cf. Edley 2001). On the right-hand side of the banner, attention is drawn to the highlighted colours of the Finns Party logo, which keeps the viewer reminded of the blogger's party and ideological home. In other words, the horizontal frontal angle (Purra presented frontally in relation to the viewer) and the medium vertical angle (Purra looking horizontally) between the viewer and Purra together imply that she is 'one of us' and thus promote intense involvement with Purra and by association with the Finns Party (Kress and van Leeuwen 2006).

Function

As we have discussed above, the blog entry follows a storyline in which the self—the blogger together with her party, speaking on behalf of 'the people'—is constructed as trustworthy, rational and courageous. Through continuously depicting herself as concerned about the survival of the Finnish nation and people, the blogger implicitly positions herself within this extended in-group category of the 'Finnish people', whose true (good) nature and concerns she comprehends and whom she seeks to protect (lines 25–34). The 'out-group', the blogger's political antagonists and mainstream media, who try to silence the opponents of 'mass-immigration' (lines 7–10, 16–20), on the other hand, becomes constructed as 'evil', as it specifically counteracts the interests of the nation and the people. Indeed, this rhetoric is a typical feature of Finnish radical right and anti-immigration discourse, where the 'societal elite', that is, leftist politicians, allegedly conspire and control mainstream media in order to implement their 'elitist plan' of allowing mass-immigration (e.g. Sakki and Pettersson 2016; Ylä-Anttila 2018). As we can see throughout the blog entry, the blogger repeatedly seeks to justify her arguments against immigration and multiculturalism and protect herself from potential accusations of ideological radicalism. This resonates with Billig's (1987) view of the argumentative nature of discourse and how an argument is always constructed in relation to (implicitly) available counterarguments. These argumentative aspects of the blog entry become especially important in its broader discursive context: the aftermath of the European 'refugee crisis' and the ongoing Finnish parliamentary election campaign, in which the entry promotes the Finns Party's campaign promising to limit immigration and asylum-seeking to Finland. Purra's blog entry illustrates the harsh tone of Finnish populist radical right politicians' online rhetoric ever since the 2015 'refugee crisis', when Purra's party colleague Olli Immonen wrote his infamous Facebook entry in which he summoned the Finnish people to join him in a war against multiculturalism (cf. Nortio et al. 2020).

Moving on to the third step of the visual analysis, images are here interpreted in their immediate argumentative context by considering the verbal discourse and particularities of the blog context, as well as the blog entry's broader socio-political context. The text following the first picture states 'Swedes born with Swedish parents'. This allows us to interpret the endless dark metal faces as children, which are used as a rhetorical resource in the construction of a dark future. Later in the blog entry (lines 32–34) another textual explanation for the picture is given in the blogger's statement 'I am sure that the average Finnish (or Swedish) person does not want his or her country to become unrecognisable', emphasising the idea of a faceless, unfamiliar threat. In a similar vein, the truth value of the second picture of the blog entry is strengthened with the verbal cues referring to mass-immigration from developing countries (lines 3–5, 11–15) and describing mass-immigration and multiculturalism as natural forces (lines 59–61). Thus, the real danger, according to the blogger, is that the influx of foreigners entails that the 'true' Finland will become unrecognisable and ultimately lost. Such arguing resonates with Billig's (1995) discussion on how the nation-state, despite being a social and political construction, is often depicted as an inevitable and 'natural' entity in lay as well as (nationalist) political discourse.

The two images of the blog entry, the first one appealing to emotions and the second one to 'facts', are both used to enhance the truthfulness and rationality of the conclusion: Finland is under real threat and can only be saved through supporting the Finns Party. The eye-catching slogan and logo in the picture banner provide additional support to this message. Research on the use of political slogans has demonstrated their potential to mobilise voters, as was the case, for instance, with Barack Obama's 2008 presidential election campaign slogan 'Yes we can', which resonated with an array of different constituencies and gained meaning in the discursive context of the campaign promises of hope, optimism and the power of citizens who unite for a common cause (Kephart and Rafferty 2009). In our present example, the ongoing 2019 parliamentary election campaign, where the Finns Party stood out as the party promoting closed borders and an end to 'unlimited immigration', provides the broader discursive meaning for the function of the images and slogan.

Through our analyses of the verbal, visual and digital components of the blog entry, we have seen the creative ways in which the politician makes use of the specific affordances that the blog environment provides, such as the possibility for readers to comment on the blog entry and for the blogger to direct her message specifically at the readers of the blog without the involvement of journalists. Through rhetorical questions and through constructing for herself and her readers the common in-group of the 'Finnish people', she manages to produce her message in mutual understanding with the readers, which functions to create an important sense of connectedness: of 'us' against 'them'. Importantly, the use of consensus warranting, and, especially, of digital voicing—giving up partial control of the immigration-hostile message through speaking through the voice of others (Silva 2016)—allows the blogger to protect herself from accusations of possessing biased or extreme views. These features are particular affordances of the social media, where, for instance, hyperlinking to external sources and engaging in a dialogue with the readership provide politicians with unique ways of transmitting and mobilising support for their (nationalist) messages. In sum, the blog entry above is a prime example of how a political message becomes rhetorically convincing through the mixing of verbal, visual, digital and reader-engaging features that the blogosphere provides.

Concluding Remarks

This chapter has shown the multifaceted and complex forms that populist radical right and anti-immigration communication in political blogs can take. It has discussed the challenges that the verbal, visual and digital construction of a political message entails for discursive analysis and suggested how these challenges may be tackled through an integrative methodological approach. This approach, relying on analytical tools from critical discursive psychology and visual rhetorical analysis, allows the researchers to go beyond the mere textual content of blog entries. In the case of populist radical right political discourse, the approach enables the researcher to 'read between the lines', that is, to demonstrate how the use of visual, digital and interactive communication allows the politician to convey nationalist, immigration-hostile and even discriminatory political messages without coming across as bigoted. The specific benefit of this integrative approach is that it both unpacks the intricate rhetorical work and considers the social and political context of the blog message, thus shedding light on the consequences that the blog discourse of influential politicians can have for its targets.

This chapter has aimed to contribute to the efforts of the discursive research paradigm to develop effective tools for analysing political communication in the digital era. As we noted in the beginning of this chapter, the authors have spent several years studying discourse contained namely in political blogs, which were of paramount importance for the triumphal marches of the (Nordic) populist radical right parties in the twenty-first century. During the course of this research endeavour, however, we have noticed that the blogging activity among these politicians has faded, especially among the Swedish politicians, and some have stopped blogging completely. Instead, social media platforms such as Twitter and Instagram, which enable more intense and high-speed communication than blogs, have gained in popularity as channels for conveying forceful, immediate and engaging political messages, as the cross-country research project discussed above confirms (cf. Pajnik and Meret 2017). These media share features with political blogs, yet they also profoundly differ in terms of the immediacy and briefness they demand and enable for discursive formulations and for the use of digital components and audio-visual elements. The constant transformations of the social media and its various evolving platforms, and the changing ways in which politicians exploit them, entail that keeping our 'online' methodological toolkit up to date remains an ongoing challenge for discursive researchers with an interest in the contemporary forms of populist, radical right and nationalist political communication. It also speaks for developing an interdisciplinary agenda when it comes to studying the complexities of online political communication and hate speech, where social psychological approaches would incorporate theoretical and methodological insights, for instance, from media and communications studies, as argued by Tileagă (2019).

Nevertheless, blogs do remain an important channel for politicians when they wish to construct contemplated, elaborate political messages. Specifically, through blogs, politicians—with or without the help of visual and digital tools—may express personalised messages whilst circumventing the interrogating and interpreting role played by journalists. The blogs of influential political figures become widely cited by news media, shared in other social media and discussed in online political fora (e.g. Baumer et al. 2011; Farrell and Drezner 2008; Nortio et al. 2020; Pettersson and Sakki 2017; Sori and Ivanova 2017). This is a central way in which populist radical right parties have been able to set the discursive agenda on issues such as immigration and asylum—to 'mainstream' their politics (e.g. Mudde 2007; Pettersson 2017; Sakki and Pettersson 2018; Sauer et al. 2017), with worrying consequences for political decision-making and the protection of liberal democracies. In this sense, studying political blog messages and their travels in the hybrid media system remains a pertinent challenge for discursive researchers into political communication and persuasion. Finally, as has been the case, for instance, in Finland and Sweden (cf. Pettersson 2017), we should remain conscious of the importance of blogs as an opinion-forming, voter-mobilising channel for fringe nationalist, populist and radical right political parties who strive, slowly but certainly, to approach a nation's main political stage from the margins. It is, in fact, at this stage that they tend to get considerable attention from mainstream media (Mazzoleni 2008). Thus, as scholars of political discourse, privileged to be able to contribute to the maintenance of democratic, pluralistic societies with research-based knowledge, we should be cautious not to leave this particular niche within the online sphere without analytical attention in the future.

Acknowledgement This research was funded by the Academy of Finland (grant 295923 and grant 33219).

References

Aalberg, T., & de Vreese, C. H. (2017). Introduction: Comprehending populist political communication. In T. Aalberg, F. Esser, C. Reinemann, J. Stromback, & C. H. de Vreese (Eds.), *Populist political communication in Europe* (pp. 3–11). Routledge.

Barthes, R. (1977). *Image-Music-Text*. Fontana.

Baumer, E., Sueyoshi, M., & Tomlinson, B. (2011). Bloggers and readers blogging together: Collaborative co-creation of political blogs. *Computer Supported Cooperative Work, 20*, 1–36.

Berggren, N., Jordahl, H., & Poutvaara, P. (2017). The right look: Conservative politicians look better and voters reward it. *Journal of Public Economics, 146*, 79–86.

Billig, M. (1987). *Arguing and thinking. A rhetorical approach to social psychology.* Cambridge University Press.

Billig, M. (1995). *Banal nationalism.* Sage Publications.

Billig, M., & Marinho, C. (2017). *The politics and rhetoric of commemoration: How the Portuguese parliament celebrates the 1974 revolution.* London: Bloomsbury Academic.

Blair, J. A. (2004). The rhetoric of visual arguments. In C. A. Hill & M. Helmers (Eds.), *Defining visual rhetorics* (pp. 41–62). London: Erlbaum Associates.

Burke, S. (2017). *Anti-semitic and islamophobic discourse of the British far-right on Facebook.* Unpublished Thesis. Loughborough University.

Burke, S. (2018). The discursive "othering" of Jews and Muslims in the Britain first solidarity patrol. *Journal of Community and Applied Social Psychology, 28*(5), 365–377.

Burke, S., & Demasi, M. (2019). Applying discursive psychology to 'fact' construction in political discourse. *Social and Personality Psychology Compass*, 1–9.

Carpinella, C. M., & Johnson, K. L. (2013). Appearance-based politics: Sex-typed facial cues communicate political party affiliation. *Journal of Experimental Social Psychology, 49*, 156–160.

Chadwick, A., & Stromer-Galley, J. (2016). Digital media, power, and democracy in parties and election campaigns: Party decline or party renewal? *The International Journal of Press/Politics, 21*(3), 283–293.

Condor, S., Tileagă, C., & Billig, M. (2013). Political rhetoric. In L. Huddy, D. O. Sears, & J. S. Levy (Eds.), *The Oxford handbook of political psychology* (pp. 262–297). Oxford University Press.

Danesi, M. (2017). Visual rhetoric and semiotic. In *Oxford research Encyclopedia of communication*. Oxford University Press.

Edley, N. (2001). Analysing masculinity: Interpretative repertoires, ideological dilemmas and subject positions. In M. Wetherell, S. Taylor, & S. J. Yates (Eds.), *Discourse as data: A guide for analysis* (pp. 189–228). Sage.

Edley, N., & Wetherell, M. (1997). Jockeying for position: The construction of masculine identities. *Discourse and Society, 8*, 203–217.

Edwards, D., & Potter, J. (1992). *Discursive psychology*. London: Sage Publications.

Every, D., & Auguoustinos, M. (2007). Constructions of racism in the Australian parliamentary debates on asylum seekers. *Discourse & Society, 18*, 411–414.

Farrell, H., & Drezner, D. W. (2008). The power and politics of blogs. *Public Choice, 134*, 15–30.

Finnish Ministry of Justice - Information and Result Service.(2019). *Parliamentary Elections 2019 / Results / Whole country.* Retrieved April 24, 2019, from https://tulospalvelu.vaalit.fi/EKV-2019/en/tulos_kokomaa.html

Foss, S. K. (2005). Theory of visual rhetoric. In K. Smith, S. Moriarty, G. Barbatsis, & K. Kenney (Eds.), *Handbook of visual communication: Theory, methods, and media* (pp. 141–152). Lawrence Erlbaum.

Giles, D., Stommel, W., Paulus, T., Lester, J., & Reed, D. (2015). Microanalysis of online data: The methodological development of "Digital CA". *Discourse, Context, and Media, 7*, 45–51.

Goffman, E. (1979). Footing. *Semiotica, 25,* 1–29.

Hatakka, N. (2017). When logics of party politics and online activism collide: The populist finns party's identity under negotiation. *New Media & Society, 19,* 2022–2038.

Hook, D., & Glăveanu, V. P. (2013). Image analysis: An interactive approach to compositional elements. *Qualitative Research in Psychology, 10*(4), 355–368.

Horsti, K. (2015). Techno-cultural opportunities: Anti-immigration movement in the Finnish media environment. *Patterns of Prejudice, 49,* 343–366.

Huddy, L., & Terkildsen, N. (1993). Gender stereotypes and the perception of male and female candidates. *American Journal of Political Science, 37*(1), 119–147.

Jowett, A. (2015). A case for using online discussion forums in critical psychological research. *Qualitative Research in Psychology, 12*(3), 287–297.

Jungar, A. C., & Ravik-Jupskås, A. (2014). Populist Radical Right Parties in the Nordic Region: A New and Distinct Party Family? *Scandinavian Political Studies, 37,* 215–238.

Kamenova, D., & Pingoud, E. (2017). Anti-migration and Islamophobia: Web populism and targeting the "Easiest Other". In M. Pajnik & B. Sauer (Eds.), *Populism and the web communicative practices of parties and movements in Europe* (pp. 108–121). Routledge.

Kephart, J., & Rafferty, S. (2009). "Yes we can": Rhizomic rhetorical agency in hyper-modern campaign ecologies. *Argumentation and Advocacy, 46,* 6–20.

Keskinen, S. (2013). Antifeminism and white identity politics: Political antagonisms in radical right-wing populist and anti-immigration rhetoric in Finland. *Nordic Journal of Migration Research, 3,* 225–232.

Kress, G., & van Leeuwen, T. (2006). *Reading images: The grammar of visual design* (2nd ed.). London: Routledge.

Lee, J. (2013). You know how tough I am? Discourse analysis of U. S. Midwestern congresswomen's self-presentation. *Discourse & Communication, 7,* 299–317.

Mäkinen, K. (2016). Uneasy laughter: Encountering the anti-immigration debate. *Qualitative Research, 16,* 541–556.

Mazzoleni, G. (2008). Media populism. In D. Albertazzi & D. McDonnell (Eds.), *Twenty-first century populism: The spectre of Western European Democracy* (pp. 49–64). Palgrave Macmillan.

Morison, T., Gibson, A., Wigginton, B., & Crabb, S. (2015). Online research methods in psychology: Methodological opportunities for critical qualitative research. *Qualitative Research in Psychology, 12*(3), 223–232.

Mudde, C. (2007). *Populist radical right parties in Europe.* Cambridge University Press.

Nilsson, B., & Carlsson, E. (2014). Swedish politicians and new media: Democracy, identity and populism in a digital discourse. *New Media & Society, 16,* 655–671.

Nortio, E., Niska, M., Renvik, T. A., & Jasinskaja-Lahti, I. (2020).The nightmare of multiculturalism. In *Interpreting, deploying and challenging anti-immigration rhetoric in social media.* https://doi.org/10.1177/1461444819899624

Otova, I., & Puurunen, H. (2017). From Anti-Europeanism to welfare nationalism: Populist strategies on the web. In M. Pajnik & B. Sauer (Eds.), *Populism and the web: Communicative practices of parties and movements in Europe* (pp. 90–107). Routledge.

Pajnik, M., & Meret, S. (2017). Populist political communication in mediatized society. In M. Pajnik & B. Sauer (Eds.), *Populism and the web: Communicative practices of parties and movements in Europe* (pp. 36–54). Routledge.

Pajnik, M., & Sauer, B. (2017). Populism and the web: An introduction to the book. In M. Pajnik & B. Sauer (Eds.), *Populism and the web: Communicative practices of parties and movements in Europe* (pp. 1–13). Routledge.

Penn, G. (2010). Semiotic analysis of still images. In M. Bauer & G. Gaskell (Eds.), *Qualitative researching with text, image and sound* (pp. 227–245). Sage Publications.

Pettersson, K. (2017). *Save the Nation! A social psychological study of political blogs as a medium for nationalist communication and persuasion.* Doctoral dissertation. Helsinki: Unigrafia.

Pettersson, K. (2019). Freedom of speech requires actions.' Exploring the discourse of politicians convicted of hate-speech against Muslims. *European Journal of Social Psychology, 49*(5), 938–952.

Pettersson, K., & Sakki, I. (2017). 'Pray for the Fatherland!' Discursive and digital strategies at play in nationalist political blogging. *Qualitative Research in Psychology, 14*(3), 315–349.

Potter, J. (1996). *Representing reality. Discourse, rhetoric and social construction.* Sage Publications.

Potter, J. (2012). Discourse analysis and discursive psychology. In H. Cooper (Ed.), *APA handbook of research methods in psychology: vol. 2. Quantitative, qualitative, neuropsychological, and biological* (pp. 111–130). American Psychological Association Press.

Potter, J., & Wetherell, M. (1987). *Discourse and Social Psychology – Beyond Attitudes and Behaviour*. London: Sage Publications.

Potter, J., Wetherell, M., & Chitty, A. (1991). Quantification rhetoric—cancer on television. *Discourse & Society, 2*(3), 333–365.

Rapley, M. (1998). 'Just an Ordinary Australian': Self-categorization and the discursive construction of facticity in 'new racist' political rhetoric. *British Journal of Social Psychology, 37*, 325–344.

Richardson, J., & Wodak, R. (2009). The impact of visual racism: Visual arguments in political leaflets of Austrian and British Far-right parties. *Controversia, 6*(2), 45–77.

Sakki, I., & Pettersson, K. (2016). Discursive constructions of otherness in populist radical right political blogs. *European Journal of Social Psychology, 46*(2), 156–170.

Sakki, I., & Pettersson, K. (2018). Managing stake and accountability in Prime Ministers' accounts of the 'Refugee Crisis': A longitudinal analysis. *Journal of Community and Applied Social Psychology, 28*(6), 406–429.

Sauer, B., Krasteva, A., & Saarinen, A. (2017). Post-democracy, party politics and right-wing populist communication. In M. Pajnik & B. Sauer (Eds.), *Populism and the web: Communicative practices of parties and movements in Europe* (pp. 14–35). Routledge.

Silva, C. E. (2016). Beyond links: Understanding meaning and control in political blogs. *New Media & Society, 18*(1), 82–98.

Sori, I., & Ivanova, V. (2017). Right-wing populist convergences and Spillovers in hybrid media systems. In M. Pajnik & B. Sauer (Eds.), *Populism and the web: Communicative practices of parties and movements in Europe* (pp. 55–71). Routledge.

Stanyer, J., Salgado, S., & Strömbäck, J. (2017). Populist actors as communicators or political actors as populist communicators: Cross-national findings and perspectives. In T. Aalberg, F. Esser, C. Reinemann, J. Strömbäck, & C. H. De Vreese (Eds.), *Populist political communication in Europe* (pp. 353–364). Routledge.

Stokoe, E. (2012). Moving forward with membership categorization analysis: Methods for systematic analysis. *Discourse Studies, 14*(3), 277–303.

Sundqvist, V. (2012). The Supreme Court sharpened Halla-aho's Sentence (Fin: *KKO kovensi Halla-ahontuomiota.) Finnish Broadcasting Company YLE, 8.6.2012.* Retrieved November 7, 2019, from https://yle.fi/uutiset/3-6171365

Tileagă, C. (2005). Accounting for extreme prejudice and legitimating blame in talk about the romanies. *Discourse and Society, 16*(5), 603–624.

Tileagă, C. (2008). What is a 'Revolution'?: National commemoration, collective memory and managing authenticity in the representation of a political event. *Discourse & Society, 19*(3), 359–382.

Tileagă, C. (2019). Communicating misogyny: An interdisciplinary research Agenda for social psychology. *Social and Personality Psychology Compass, 13*(7). https://doi.org/10.1111/spc3.12491

Tileagă, C., & Stokoe, E. (Eds.). (2015). *Discursive psychology: Classic and contemporary issues*. Routledge.

Todorov, A., Mandisodza, A., Goren, A., & Hall, C. (2005). Inferences of competence from faces predict election outcomes. *Science, 308*, 1623–1626.

Uusi Suomi. (2019). *Marko Mjlnir Parkkola*. Marko Parkkola's Column. Retrieved August 30, 2019, from http://markomjlnirparkkola.puheenvuoro.uusisuomi.fi/kayttaja/markomjlnirparkkola

Verkuyten, M. (2003). Discourses about ethnic group (De-)essentialism: Oppressive and progressive aspects. *British Journal of Social Psychology, 42*, 371–393.

Verkuyten, M. (2013). Justifying discrimination of Muslim immigrants: Outgroup ideology and the five-step social identity model. *British Journal of Social Psychology, 52*, 345–360.

Verkuyten, M., & Nooitgedagt, W. (2018). Parliamentary identity and the management of the far-right: A discursive analysis of dutch parliamentary debates. *British Journal of Social Psychology, 58*, 495–514.

Wagner, I., & Wodak, R. (2006). Performing success: Identifying strategies of self-presentation in women's biographical narratives. *Discourse & Society, 17*(3), 385–411.

Wetherell, M. (1998). Positioning and interpretative repertoires: Conversation analysis and poststructuralism in dialogue. *Discourse and Society, 9*(3), 387–412.

Wetherell, M., & Potter, J. (1992). *Mapping the language of racism. Discourse and the legitimation of exploitation*. Harvester Wheatsheaf.

Wodak, R. (2015). *the politics of fear: What right-wing populist discourses mean*. Sage Publications.

Wodak, R., & Forchtner, B. (2014). Embattled Vienna 1683/2010: Right wing populism, collective memory and the fictionalization of politics. *Visual Communication, 13*(2), 231–255.

Ylä-Anttila, T. (2018). Populist knowledge: 'Post-truth' repertoires of contesting epistemic authorities. *European Journal of Cultural and Political Sociology, 5*(4), 356–388.

8

"This Country Will Be Big Racist One Day": Extreme Prejudice as Reasoned Discourse in Face-to-Face Interactions

Shani Burke and Mirko A. Demasi

Introduction

Traditional approaches in social psychology, such as social cognition studies, have granted a great deal of attention to issues such as prejudice (e.g. Adorno et al. 1950; Tajfel 1981). However, various arguments exist that such approaches may, implicitly or not, take the actual existence of racial categories for granted (e.g. Condor 1988). Quantitatively informed methods in general and social cognitive approaches in particular encourage a largely psychological view of racism, which in turn runs the risk of ignoring issues such as implicit reification:

S. Burke (✉)
Psychology Department, Teesside University, Middlesbrough, UK
e-mail: s.burke@tees.ac.uk

M. A. Demasi
Psychology Department, York St John University, York, UK

© The Author(s), under exclusive license to Springer Nature Switzerland AG 2020
M. A. Demasi et al. (eds.), *Political Communication*, Palgrave Studies in Discursive
Psychology, https://doi.org/10.1007/978-3-030-60223-9_8

205

> It is suggested that, by portraying 'race' stereotypes and categories as cognitive phenomena which can be traced to an external 'reality' of racial distinction, some social cognition texts may, themselves, adopt elements of 'race thinking'. (Condor 1988, p. 69)

Treating racial categories as "real", residing within the minds of individuals and reflective of an external reality—rather than recognise their interactional, common-sensical origin (Durrheim 2016)—results in overlooking the social nature of prejudice. Treating racial categories as "real" discourages the questioning of how they have come about in the first instance. Discursive psychology, on the other hand, has a long history of studying racism and prejudice from a different angle. Prejudice has long been a central concept for scholars who have come to influence what we now call discursive psychology (henceforth DP) (e.g. Billig 1978, 1991; Billig et al. 1988; Tileagă 2005, 2007, 2016; Wetherell and Potter 1992). We will forego a detailed overview of the issues to do with approaches that conceptualise prejudice as primarily a problem of faulty cognition and instead opt to talk about how DP conventionally engages with the concept of prejudice as a form of social action. These overviews and their issues can be found elsewhere (e.g. Condor 1988; Potter and Wetherell 1987; Tileagă 2016; Wetherell and Potter 1992).

DP's starting point, on the other hand, is to look at prejudice as an interpretive concept (cf. Tileagă 2016) and a practical concern (Augoustinos and Every 2007). That is, a phenomenon and a problem that is a matter for members of society to decide upon (Edwards 2003; Durrheim et al. 2016). Crucially, hearably prejudiced talk is an accountable matter for those producing it and for those who resist it. Viewing prejudice as such, as opposed to a faulty cognition, enables one to study it as a flexible, occasioned and rhetorically oriented resource. We are interested, in particular, in exploring and describing the rhetorical complexity of extreme prejudiced discourse.

It is usually believed that extreme forms of prejudice are a thing of the past. However, the work of Michael Billig has contributed significantly to understanding the rhetorical complexity of prejudice. He has highlighted how expressions of prejudice, usually couched in the innocuous language of opinions, are largely hedged even when there are no reasonable voices present to challenge said prejudice (e.g. Billig 1991). Billig (1978) showed how far-right parties such as the National Front in the UK partially concealed their nationalist ideologies in order to appeal to a mass audience despite an underlying anti-Semitic position, in order to avoid direct accusations of anti-Semitism. Indeed, Billig noted that there tends to be a norm against being viewed as prejudiced, something echoed in other research (e.g. van Dijk 1992), meaning that expressions of views that can be heard as prejudiced are rarely presented without some rhetorical move towards mitigating this as a potential interpretation. This focus on the so-called old-fashioned racism, especially when viewed as something caused by faulty cognition, largely overlooks the more subtle forms of racism—where expressions of prejudice become complex, occasioned and rhetorically designed to come across as non-prejudiced as possible (Durrheim et al. 2016). This is not to say that these complex forms of racism did not exist before, or that the old-fashioned forms of racism are a thing of the past (Leach 2005).

One of the strengths of DP is its empirical approach to capture this more subtle, occasionally elusive, form. DP focuses on everyday discursive strategies used by speakers to present hostile views towards outgroups as reasonable and, thus, not prejudiced (Augoustinos and Every 2007; Goodman and Johnson 2013; Tileagă 2006). Prejudice is no longer conceptualised as a purely mental construct, an error of otherwise normal cognitive processes of categorisation (Ashmore and Del Boca 1981), but is, instead, viewed as a social action expressed in the way people speak. The social actions and the words of prejudice are not indicative of a bigoted mind: "those actions and words were, in the most literal sense, pure hatred" (Billig 2002, p. 179). Importantly, this concept of prejudice moves away from treating it as a natural cognitive process— avoiding the risk of going too close to excusing it (ibid.) and, in its place, treats it as an accountable matter for those involved in speaking or resisting prejudiced views. The issue of being perceived as "racist" or "bigot" becomes one that needs to be rhetorically managed (Durrheim et al. 2016). Prejudice discourse is "discourse that denies, rationalizes and excuses the dehumanization and marginalization of, and discrimination against, minority out-groups" (Every and Augoustinos 2007, p. 412). This shift to viewing prejudice as a form of behaviour reorients the focus of the problem of racism from faulty cognition of the perpetrator to racism as a social problem and behaviourally accountable.

Wetherell and Potter (1992) identified variation and competing discourses about culture in Pākehā[1] peoples' talk about Māori and Polynesian populations in New Zealand. Māori people were simultaneously constructed as a group to be protected but also a group to be marginalised. This study paved the way for researching attitudes around racism as a flexible construct (Tileagă 2013), as well as challenging the assumption that racist discourse should be analysed in terms of how "truthful" claims are. In treating racism as a flexible, rhetorical tool, DP has been able to explore and identify the complexities of prejudice discourse. Augoustinos et al. (1999) identified various discursive strategies—such as the use of neoliberal discourse or invoking inclusive nationhood—in ways that held the Aboriginal people of Australia as accountable for their own suffering. Byford (2006) demonstrated how accusations of anti-Semitism are managed, denied and often turned around on those claiming the presence of anti-Semitism,[2] at an institutional level. According to Tileagă (2007), the invocations of moral boundaries and placing Romanies outside of this allowed for the existence of prejudiced discourse without necessarily opting for openly bigoted language. Likewise, he has since argued that prejudice, in its "modern" forms, can sometimes operate through a denial of personal and collective dignity rather than as an attitudinal expression of outright antipathy (Tileagă 2016). In summary, these examples of the substantial body of DP research into prejudice indicate that modern language of prejudice is no longer the language of open bigotry.

As we have shown, DP has a large body of research that deals with the nature of contemporary prejudice. However, we argue that what seems to be lacking from this body of research, even in the case of hostile expressions of prejudice (e.g. Billig 2001), is a focus on public, naturally occurring manifestations of extreme prejudice. Billig et al. (1988) argued that the discourse of the extreme bigot can be "freed from the dilemmas of 'reasonableness'" (p. 118), indicating the lack of a need to moderate their

---

[1] A white New Zealander, as opposed to a Māori.
[2] This in itself is indicative of a "norm" against accusations of prejudice (see Goodman 2010, 2014).

statements. We show that cases of extreme prejudice that, at a glance, seem to ignore the norm against the overt expression of prejudice still contain rhetorical moves towards justifying such extreme language.

Hostile Expressions of Prejudice

Whereas research into hostile expressions of prejudice does not appear to receive the same level of attention in the literature as analyses of indirect expressions of prejudice, work that has been carried out is nonetheless significant. We now turn to discuss some key examples of this work, highlighting that, despite their seminal contributions, the particular context of face-to-face racism remains understudied. Billig (2001) showed how public, extreme forms of racism described as "just a joke" are easier to defend. Billig's (2001) analysis of Ku Klux Klan support websites showed that strategic use of humour allowed the boundaries around racist discourse to be broken. Categories depicting ethnic groups as certain stereotypes were defended as merely to be used through enjoyment between people. Rooting such categories in humour protects speakers from being challenged. The discourse was constructed as purportedly being intended for entertainment, rather than reflecting hatred.

Another way that extreme racism can be communicated is through online discourse (Burke and Goodman 2012), where the lack of physical presence in interaction can make hostile language easier to communicate (McGuire et al. 1987). Social media can be used to disseminate explicit racism (e.g. Faulkner and Bliuc 2016), as well as Islamophobia and the "othering" of Muslims (Burke 2018; Wood and Finlay 2008). However, Burke and Goodman (2012) identified individuals on Facebook displaying the norm against prejudice by protesting that they were being victimised for their anti-asylum views, suggesting that discourse can still be managed with caution online.

So, there is a body of research that looks at extreme forms of prejudice but not always in everyday, mundane settings. We are using an ethnomethodological approach, in that we analyse a case of spontaneous talk rather than collect data by, say, interviewing participants or analysing posts on social media. Edwards (2003) advocates this as a particularly fruitful way of unpacking matters of prejudice and race in discourse. This type of approach enables us to study extreme prejudice on its own terms, as made relevant by people featured in the data (e.g. Durrheim et al. 2016). What is of particular analytic relevance is that one can make sense of prejudiced discourse as prejudiced by analysing the mundane, everyday conversational features that people deploy:

> To the extent that 'attitudinal' talk involves a play-off between mind and world, it shares that with mundane and institutional talk of all kinds, not just in recognised sites of prejudicial discourse, and it involves the same kinds of devices and rhetoric found virtually anywhere else we may look. (Edwards 2003, p. 46)

This is where we contribute to the existing discursive literature on prejudice in general and on the study of mundane prejudice in particular. We focus on two instances of face-to-face allegedly racist encounters caught on camera and uploaded online, where the victims of prejudice are in direct physical presence of their abusers. Conventionally, this type of condition would be rare in an everyday encounter considering the norm against prejudice (Billig 1978)—the expression and defence of extreme views would be different (though no lesser in its extremity). Considering the rise of hate crime by 10% in 2018/2019 since 2017/2018 (e.g. Home Office 2018; Quinn 2019) and the difficulty of systematically capturing this (European Union Agency for Fundamental Rights 2018), understanding how face-to-face extreme prejudice unfolds is of increasing social importance. What we show is that it is not always the case that the bigot is freed from all dilemmas of reasonableness (Billig et al. 1988), even in seemingly unabashed expressions of bigotry; even when the extreme bigot is facing their victim, there may be traces of "reasonableness" in their bigotry. In the presence of extreme hatred, one can observe some attempt at legitimising the bigot's views by way of rationalising markers. What is discursively complex is the management of extreme bigotry, as unpopular views are likely to elicit stronger challenges (Billig 1991), in a way that they can be heard but not challenged.

Data and Method

Due to the relative novelty of these kinds of encounters being used as data, we use a case study approach, a common occurrence when studying new or rare interactional phenomena (e.g. Carr et al. 2019; Jackson 2011; Schegloff 1988/1989). A case study approach also allows us to go into depth when demonstrating the discursive strategies being used in mundane settings. We chose these recordings in particular due to them having made news headlines in their respective countries. More on our data below.

The first video, filmed in 2015, shows a Finnish woman racially abusing a Kenyan woman in Finland and was recorded by the victim of the abuse. The interaction took place in English, and the Finnish woman can be heard telling the victim that she is "not human" and that Finland will become a "racist country" "because you are black". The clip is 0:57 long. The video was uploaded to the Finnish news website Iltalehti with the caption *Unimaginable eruption recorded on video: "Our country is like this because you are black"*[3] (Taponen 2015). We will show this extract in its entirety due to its relative shortness. This video is filmed in the midst of what was termed the refugee "crisis", when Finland received a significant increase in the number of asylum seekers in 2015, a total number of 32,476 arrivals (European Migration Network 2017; Wahlbeck 2019) which sparked strong anti-foreign reactions among some Finns.

The second case is of a video filmed by a passenger on a bus in London, of a British woman racially abusing Muslim women. The video lasts 5 minutes and 15 seconds.[4] The perpetrator can be seen racially abusing the women, referring to them as "sand rats" and "ISIS bitches". She also threatens to kick one of the women, who is pregnant, in the stomach. The video was uploaded to YouTube, shared on various news websites and subsequently reported to the police. The perpetrator pleaded guilty to causing racially aggravated distress and received a suspended sentence ("Simone Joseph admits viral racist bus rant", 2015). The context behind the attack is a rise in Islamophobia following ISIS terrorist attacks such as the Charlie Hebdo shooting in Paris in January 2015. Muslims continue

---

[3] See Extract 8.1 title for the original Finnish caption.
[4] Video has since been removed by the uploader, as of August 2019.

to be targeted as victims of religiously motivated hate crime, and in 2017/2018 52% of religious hate crimes were targeted against Muslims (Home Office 2018).

The two encounters were analysed using discursive psychology, an approach that, as argued earlier, focuses on what people *do* with their talk. The language of these encounters is analysed for the social actions being accomplished (Tileagă 2013). Discursive approaches tend to work with naturalistic data (e.g. Potter 2010; Wiggins and Potter 2008). Wiggins and Potter (2008) argue that looking at naturalistic data comes with significant benefits to research: (1) it avoids the influence of the researcher's assumptions on the data; (2) it avoids separating people from the complex social situations in which everyday social life takes place; (3) there is no need to apply findings from one context to another because phenomenon is studied *in situ*; (4) there is room to take the analysis to new avenues of research if the data dictates this; (5) "it captures life as it happens" (p. 79). This fits with our approach because we look at naturalistic data rather than material that is "researcher provoked" (Augoustinos et al. 2005, p. 321) This means that prejudice was analysed *in situ* as a social accomplishment (Wiggins and Potter 2008). In the analysis, we will be focusing on how speakers use language that is construed as explicitly racist, whilst also framing such talk as in some way justifiable.

Analysis

The Finnish case is presented in its entirety here (Extract 8.1). Our analysis will focus on three areas. First, we discuss the dehumanising aspect of the prejudiced discourse. Second, we analyse the rationalising aspects of the prejudiced discourse. Finally, we discuss the function of threats in racist discourse. In our case it is managing a public norm against being seen as prejudiced while producing unambiguously prejudiced views. In Extract 8.1, speaker A is the Finnish woman who is producing the extreme racist talk in English and speaker B is the victim.

8 "This Country Will Be Big Racist One Day"... 213

Extract 8.1 "Maamme on tällainen koska olet musta" ("Our country is like this because you are black")

```
 1 A: little bits respect please.
 2 B: I am a nurse
 3 A: I am Finnish [wo]man
 4 B:             [I-]
 5 B: so [what if]
 6 A:    [you are] FUCKing African woman
 7 B: [[↑so    what↓    ]
 8 A: [[(don't)   meani]ng nothing you are zero
 9    (.3)
10 A: you are not (human/humane) in my eyes.
11    (.4)
12 A: ↑you know what happened in our country↓
13    (.5)
14 A: <↑why: ↓all come rape our country> (.2) ↑we are in trouble↓ cos
15    black peoples yes it's reality
16    (.6)
17 A: and be ready this country will be big racist one day
18    (.5)
19 A: also I'm not before but I become racist °.h° what I see (.2) no
20    respect no anything .h ↑just try to (.6) live good↓ (.2) here
21    (.6) work (.7) don't use our social please
22 B: I am a nurse
23    (0.4)
24 B: by profession I ↑treat peop[le↓]
25 A:                            [go ]
26 B: in the hospital
27    (.2)
28 A: then [go:            back] to work
29 B:      [why are you attacking me]
30    (.7)
31 B: so ↑why are you attacking me↓
32    (.8)
33 B: wha[t did I do to you]
34 A:    [    why        ] cause you are black
35    (.5)
36 B: because [°I'm black°.]
37 A:         [    this    ] country will be like (this) because you
38    are black
39    (1.0)
40 B: [thank you]
41 A: [   and   ] I'm white
42    (.2)
43 B: tha:nk you
44    (.3)
45 A: you are welcome (.2) but not in my country
46    (.2)
47 B: o:kay
48    (.4)
49 A: yes
```

Dehumanisation

In lines 2–10 of Extract 8.1, we can see both speakers producing different categories for person B. A refers to herself as a "Finnish woman" (3) and B as "fucking African woman" (6), "zero" (8) and "not human" (10). B resists by categorising herself as a nurse (2) and twice challenging the relevance of A's categories (5, 7). There are subject positions used to accomplish category entitlement (Potter 1996)—I am a nurse (2), and I am a Finnish woman (3). The subject position of nurse is reformulated to "fucking African woman" by A; the addition of "fucking" (6) contrasts with Finnish woman to orient to this being a lesser category and has the function of intensifying the insult (Culpeper et al. 2017). Furthermore, as Stokoe and Edwards (2007) argue, what marks racist talk as *racist* (as opposed to a personal insult) in many instances is its two-word formulation where one of the words is an expletive—in this instance, "fucking African" as opposed to "African". The categorising of B as outside of "being human" draws a moral boundary (Tileagă 2007) between A and B where the latter is firmly based in the moral transgressor category.

Early on in Extract 8.1, A positioned herself as a "Finnish woman" in relation to B, excluding B from the same category, and so is positioning herself as entitled to express this view. This instance may initially come across as striking due to the apparent lack of "delicacy" with which hearable prejudiced discourse usually presents itself (e.g. Augoustinos et al. 1999; Billig 1991; Billig et al. 1988; Goodman and Burke 2010; Goodman and Johnson 2013). The interaction ends with the most palpable manner of a racist claim: A directs her bigotry at B because B is black (34, 37–38).

Aside above, another practice of exclusion-by-categorisation in the case of Extract 8.1: both speakers are talking in English. B has stated that she is a nurse, which by implication means that she works with Finnish speakers and would be required to have at least a basic functional grasp of Finnish. Yet, A speaks in English. As to the reason why B complies, this is not clear. A's accent is clear enough to mark her as a native Finnish speaker, so B could, feasibly, speak Finnish to her. In any case, the very choice of language here is indicative of treating B as an outsider. It may not feature the extreme hatred of the words, but the persistent use of English over Finnish is an unambiguous categorising of B as an outsider to Finland. In this manner, this interaction is a signal to B that she is treated by A as a member of an out-group.

To return to excluding categorisation work, in the second case study, this dehumanisation is done through the derogatory term "sand rat",[5] as well as references to the victims being dirty.

Extract 8.2

```
1 S:dirty whore you could be sharing a husband is it have you both got the
2   same husband have you are you still sleeping with the same man is that
3   how it works are you sleeping with her husband are you sleeping with
4   the same >husband< >do you all< do all your kids live in the same house
5   is that how you run a::h you don't like it now though that's your
6   fuckin lifestyle di:rty people di:rty talkin=about um all of that livin
7   together all of that twenty thousand wives that's nasty that's
8   disgusting you lot are the first ones to talk about haram (.) yeah
9   {livin in the most disgustin (way to survive)
```

Here we see derogatory categorisations and the use of extreme case formulations (Pomerantz 1984). The association of Muslims with "dirt" (6–7) and sexual immorality (references to "dirty whore" and polygamy) again allows them to be categorised in a dehumanising manner. Tileagă (2007) argues that the association of certain ethnic groups with "dirt" paves the way to categorising them in a depersonalised and dehumanised manner. Referring to "Haram" in line 9 (forbidden by Islamic law) also presents Muslims as intolerant, a common strategy used in justifying hostility towards minority groups (van Dijk 1992). The use of "insider" language of "Haram" positions her as knowledgeable of the religion, rather than displaying prejudice based on ignorance.

In this section we have considered how in extreme face-to-face racist discourse speakers dehumanise their victims by the categorising work that they do. We demonstrated how the categorising is unambiguously

---

[5] Not featured in the extracts of this chapter, but a frequent insult used by S in the full clip.

216 S. Burke and M. A. Demasi

racist, and this lack of ambiguity plays a large role in what marks these racist instances as particularly extreme and aggressive. Next, we discuss how one can trace some rationalising work present in the data.

Rationalising

We have discussed the dehumanising element of extreme prejudiced discourse, particularly in the form of categorising the victims as outside of conventional moral boundaries because of their racial background or religion. We now highlight the practices of rationalising within these cases. Even in cases of extreme prejudice one can observe some rhetorical work being performed in an attempt to portray the bigots as having "justified" views.

While the dehumanising element of A's claims is present, she treats the epistemological orientation of her description (Potter 1996)[6] and, in consequence, her own position as a matter of perspective. The addition of "in my eyes" locates the position as one of opinion, which is less amenable to a factual challenge as the argument is based on one's view. This reduced certainty turns the assessment from an object-side to a subject-side assessment. A switch from an object-side to subject-side, Edwards and Potter (2017) argue, serves to manage interactional trouble and disagreement. In this sense, one can observe an orientation to interactional norms that seek to avoid conflict or giving offence. However, to stop here would be to miss the larger part of what is going on. While in interactional terms this may be something that softens the claims, it is by no means ambiguous in its hostility. Instead one can view these practices as something designed to rationalise and rhetorically bolster the position of the bigot, a move which makes sense considering the negotiable nature of prejudice[7] (Durrheim et al. 2016). If subject-sides are used to manage trouble,

---

[6] What Potter (1996) means with this is how a particular description is designed to come across as "mere" description. This orientation is paired with the action orientation of accounts. Thus, accounts are designed to perform actions and to come across as a simple reflection of how things "really" are. Edwards (2003) makes a similar point in relation to racism.

[7] That is, "prejudice" is not a given but has to be rhetorically worked up or rhetorically undermined—whether something or someone is prejudiced is subject to debate and a number of rhetorical moves (e.g. Billig 1985; Durrheim et al. 2016).

then their deployment in the extreme case of A in Extract 8.1 can be viewed as an attempt to resist any upcoming critique or resistance from B, in that it puts B in a difficult position to claim what A does or does not think. A is managing a rhetorically delicate balance here. On the one hand, she is offering her extreme position as a matter of opinion. On the other hand, by using the visual metaphor "in my eyes", it implies that this position comes from a simple reflection on the reality of things. Thus, A is putting forward a prejudiced case while all the same rhetorically moving away from being seen as prejudiced: "offering a report of something on the basis that it was not really in one's mind to start with, but was accidentally observed, can counter the category of being, in a general sense, prejudiced" (Edwards 2003, p. 35).

After having downgraded her position as one of her views, A then goes on to produce "evidence" for her prejudiced stance. In lines 12–15 of Extract 8.1, A claims the state of Finland as evidence readily accessible to B as evidence for A's position. A presents little evidence or what could be treated as a fact aside from the extreme case formulation (Pomerantz 1986) of everyone coming to rape Finland (14)—of course, with "everyone" one can argue that this is a reference to the non-Finnish population that have moved into the country.[8] Crucially, though, A's evidence is formulated as common knowledge (Edwards and Potter 1992) and something, by being common knowledge, that B has a moral obligation to be aware of. This way B is treated as the transgressor to and the cause of the problem of racism, not A. Later on, in line 19, A bases her view as coming from evidence rather than personal disposition. A presents racism as a comparatively new problem (Goodman and Burke 2010), further implying that it is the presence of people who are neither Finnish nor white that is causing this problem of racism. This portrayal of having come to a conclusion locates A's claim as something to do with the "real" state of affairs as opposed to a personal disposition: "people will often make a dubious version or conclusion factually robust by formulating it as reluctantly arrived at" (Edwards 2005, p. 265). Rationalising Islamophobic views can also be seen in the UK case study.

---

[8] This raises the interesting question of how the seemingly inclusive category of "everyone" can be used for excluding purposes. That is, however, beyond the scope of our chapter.

Extract 8.3

```
1 S: you talk your fucking language↑ HA HA HA HA fucking ISIS
2    bitches carry on laughin: carry on laughin with your fucking
3    bombs hidden underneath your fucking clothes >you see< that's
4    why people don't fucking like you people cos you're fucking
5    rude you come to England and you have no fucking manners go
6    back to your fucking country: (.) where their bombin: (.) every
7    day and go there ↑don't come here↓where we're free↑ and try to
8    bring your (fuckery) do you understand me
```

The account begins with an orientation to the recipients speaking a non-English language, along with laughter. This is then mocked by S, emphasised through the increase in volume of her laughter in line 1. Here another extreme case formulation is utilised: "twenty thousand wives". In a similar way to the Finnish case study, generalisations are made about particular groups. However, S then switches to construct her complaint about "not liking" (4) the passengers based on the passengers seemingly having no manners, thus something more plausible. These formulations are constructed to emphasise cultural differences between English people and Muslims (Verkuyten 2013). Previous research has seen people legitimise Islamophobia through presenting Muslims as a threat or intolerable (Verkuyten 2013; Wood and Finlay 2008). Public prejudice is usually something done collaboratively (Condor 2006); however, here, this woman is acting alone. She carefully manages her position ("people don't like you") by constructing distaste towards a particular group not as a matter of personal prejudice but a feature of the world "out there" (Edwards 2003). By framing the source of the prejudice as a feature of the world rather than the mind, one can construe dislike as a matter of public concern rather than individual psychology (Tileagă 2005, 2016).

S displays footing (Goffman 1979) and an orientation to the wider political climate of hostility towards Muslims "people don't like you" (4) and complaining on other peoples' behalf (Drew and Walker 2009). The victims are presented as threatening the British way of life—Muslims who want to come to "free" countries is also seen in discourse of far-right politicians such as Geert Wilders (Verkuyten 2013) as a way of seeming "understanding" as to why people come to other countries, as well as making hostility towards out-groups seem reasonable and non-racist.

These strategies work to present the majority as requiring protection from the threat of cultural diversity (Di Masso et al. 2014; Wood and Finlay 2008).

Veiled Threats, Challenges and Racist Discourse

In this section we consider the function of veiled threats in racist discourse. In the case of our data, veiled threats constituted a pervasive feature of talk where the perpetrator of racist abuse continues to negotiate the tension of categorising their victims as morally abject, worthy of violence, while presenting this type of prejudice as "reasonable" and "justified".

In Extract 8.1, A initially produces a veiled threat in telling B to "be ready this country will be big racist one day" (17). The actual threat is not fully spelled out, but the threat itself is unambiguous. B provides no response to this (18), possibly indicating silent resistance (Pomerantz 1984). This absence of uptake from B then results in A giving advice to B (19–21). The tension that follows from this is that her "reasonableness" is based on advice given on "living good and working" (20–21) rather than not being black, whilst simultaneously threatening B on account of her being black. The attempt at resolving the tension is to move from racist to "benefit scrounger" discourse (Goodman and Carr 2017). A's attack is based on the assumption that B comes to Finland to claim social support, a form of positive self-presentation and negative other presentation (van Dijk 1992; see also "differentiating the self", Lynn and Lea 2003). After B states that she is a nurse, A shuts down the interaction with the directive "then go back to work" (28)—effectively an attempt at neutralising B's challenge. Nonetheless, at the neutralisation of moral culpability of being someone who abuses the social support system (by stating what she does for a living), B returns to question A on why she has been attacked, which she does three times (29, 31, 33). B is taking A to task in demanding accountability for her views, while A is trying to manage the rhetorically dilemmatic position of producing racist and reasonableness discourse at the same time. A's position is particularly tricky, as racist discourse that

220 S. Burke and M. A. Demasi

tries to adhere to Enlightenment values of reasonableness is generally more ambivalent[9] (Billig et al. 1988).

In the previous section, on rationalising, we observed how A tries to externalise the source of her prejudice and thus excuse her prejudice (Edwards 2003). A does this by claiming that it is the rape of Finland (14) and lack of respect (19–20) she sees that accounts for her racism. However, the extremity of A's claims enables B to challenge A while side-stepping A's attempts at rationalising. Three times A is held to account by B for her attack, without B conceding to A's rationalising attempts to blame B for A's racism. As a result of B's holding A to account that A concedes that her attack is because B is black (34, 37–38). In this instance, A's attempt at managing the original threat has failed. A has been rhetorically outmanoeuvred because the normative assumptions of her telling B what to do (20–21) are countered by B as being factually incorrect (lines 22, 24, 26). In this case, what becomes salient is not only A's racial prejudice but also her assumption of B's social role. This makes A normatively challengeable (see Reynolds 2015), as well as observably dispositionally prejudiced, which affords B the rhetorical space to challenge A's prejudice further. Put simply, if A can be wrong about B's social role, then it affords the rhetorical freedom for B to question A's other, racist, claim. B does this by pushing A to go "on the record" as basing her bigotry on racial grounds—giving B A's own speech as a "matter of record" that is particularly difficult to challenge (Antaki and Leudar 2001). In this, A's prejudice becomes fully exposed: she is a bigot because she is recognisably talking and behaving like a bigot.

Although B's challenge of A has not stopped A's racism, and this may be little comfort to the victim of racist abuse, in this instance one can see a rhetorically effective strategy when challenging extreme bigotry. Initially it may seem odd that B does not challenge A on the grounds that racism is, simply, unacceptable. However, in the face of such extreme prejudice, there is little ground to hope that this would be an effective strategy. Instead, the challenging of the rationalising of the racism has forced the bigot to speak with a directness that is usually not presented seriously

---

[9] See Billig et al. (1988) for an overview of the complex relationship between Enlightenment values and prejudice.

(Billig 2001; Billig et al. 1988). Stopping racism may not be an option in a situation like this, but forcing it out of its ambiguous terrain—and, thus, out of its veneer of rationality—gives the bigot less rhetorical manoeuvrability by pushing their claims beyond acceptable Enlightenment values. B has, at the very least, exposed the "deadly seriousness… [which] tends towards a violence which is only too real" (Billig et al. 1988, p. 118). It is this exposure, then, that begins to close the interaction, with A walking away.

In the final extract, S uses disturbingly violent discourse whilst also explaining why there are no physical violent actions.

Extract 8.4

```
 1 S: you're so lucky shut up you lucky you got a child >cos I was-<
 2    I was about to kick you in the stomach {I will pull back this
 3    long leg and <kick you in your stomach> keep talking to each
 4    other⌐ fuckin sick bitches (.) fuckin} ISIS {so angry haven't
 5    started ( ) (uterus) ( ) (kick in the uterus) ( ) lucky I have
 6    my baby I'm not gonna go to jail for no ISIS bitch for you're
 7    lucky I don't kick you in the uterus} you never have a kid
 8    again stupid bitch I take back this long leg and donkey kick
 9    you it's the first time I've ever got to fuckin violence
10    somebody in public NO
```

The speaker here accounts for why she is not harming another passenger and uses threats of being "lucky" (1) that this passenger is X, so she will not do Y. We see the use of two-word category constructions "sick bitches" (4) and "ISIS bitch" (6). Guimarães (2003, p. 137) argues that emphasising a group name alongside "despicable characteristics" is how racial insults are brought about (see also Stokoe and Edwards 2007). S is portraying herself as one with high moral standards by not harming someone who has a child (something taken as common knowledge to be wrong), suggesting that the passenger is worthy of being subjected to violence otherwise. She later switches this to being about avoiding jail. Finally, she holds the passenger accountable for this violence, by showing that this is her first time of displaying violence, so has "reduced" her to resort to violence. The account is done in a way that explicitly holds the victim to blame. Hepburn and Potter (2010) demonstrate that threats can take the grammatical form of an if-then formulation: if you do not do X, then Y will happen. In our case, we see a variant of this. Because the victim has a child, S will not enact the violence she claims the victim to be deserving of. This, in a way, turns the threat construction shown by Hepburn and Potter (2010) on its head but retains the nature of the threat. To this end, S is required to offer some form of justification as to why she has not behaved as she stated she would: because her target is pregnant, because S does not want to go to jail and so forth. S reverts to a moral order of civility to avoid the legal implications of violent behaviour, but this moral order that stops the violence excludes the victims. This type of violence, furthermore, is not limited to racism. It is part of a broader category of violence that humiliates and denies the dignity of its victims (e.g. Tileagă 2019).

Conclusion

In this chapter, we have shown how speakers who are expressing explicitly hostile, racist, views also frame this talk as justifiable. Dehumanising and depersonalising categorisations coexist with displays of reasonableness. These findings show that extreme forms of prejudiced discourse are not without the need for rhetorical management, and this applies to instances of face-to-face bigotry too. These enable the use of thinly veiled threats, of a violence that denies the dignity (Tileagă 2016, 2019) of the victim and is all too real (see Lemke n.d.).

These rhetorical practices are seen in everyday discourse. For example, in the case where Edwards and Potter (2017) focus on instances where the interactants are on good terms with each other, the analysis need not go further there. However, in the case of our data, the context is confrontational; to observe normal standards of interaction does more than that. We argue that in our data this switch, while also superficially "rational" in its politeness, also enables the dehumanising claim to be heard in the first instance. Thus, normal, everyday, discursive practices can play a part in extreme prejudiced discourse.

These findings highlight that we need to find ways to combat face-to-face racism, which research suggests is easier to do online (Fozdar and Pederson 2013; Guerin 2003) as challenging face-to-face racism is difficult and can affect social relationships (Condor 2006; Every and Augoustinos 2007). In the UK case, no one intervenes, and the altercation does not appear to cause any disturbance, other than from an unknown speaker who displays offence at being late rather than the altercation itself, although the offence has been displayed through being filmed and exposed online. In the Finnish case, the victim argues back. Prejudiced claims and threats are by no measure non-challengeable, and a more extreme claim can be challenged. As Billig (1991) suggests, people are not impassive and helpless "receivers" of ideology (in this case, that of hatred)—we can, and often do, argue back, challenge and negate. This does not mean to enter into dialogue with bigotry, but, when faced with extreme prejudice, there is the possibility to expose the unreasonableness of the perpetrator.

There is widespread scholarly recognition, both within and without psychology, of the subtle forms of racism, but an implicit assumption that the overt forms are by and large a thing of the past. Thanks to smartphones and social media, we can see that this type of racism is still, sadly, present. We argue that this overt form of racism has previously not been analysed with the same detail and finesse as the subtle, "modern" racism, yet to treat extreme prejudice as an obvious matter would leave the bigots without a potential challenge. Tileagă (2019) argues that social psychology has much to learn from the field of media and communications in understanding contemporary misogyny as a form of extreme racism; we reiterate this point for the study of social media as enabler of extreme prejudice.

This type of discourse has perhaps been overlooked in discursive research due to its obviousness, but, as we have shown, the same strategies used by speakers to disguise racist discourse is also utilised in this explicit discourse to make such talk justifiable. There are forms of reasoning in the data taken as acceptable by the antagonists involved. To seek to understand this is not the same as trying to identify with the offender, something which Billig (2002) warns against as being close to excusing the prejudice, but, rather, a way to resist extreme prejudice. Focusing on the strategies used to construct this talk as "reasonable" may be a solution to combating this type of talk—by constructing counterarguments to these tropes of reasoning. By using a case study approach, we have shown in detail how such discourse can be rationalised and, in one case, how such discourse can be combated. The incidences featured here are not isolated events, and future research that analyses the prevalence and effects of such discourse on a wider scale would be beneficial. This is a step towards investigating and, hopefully, developing discursive strategies that can help combat hate speech.

References

Adorno, T. W., Frenkel-Brunswick, E., Levinson, D. J., & Sanford, R. N. (1950). *The authoritarian personality*. Harper and Row.

Antaki, C., & Leudar, I. (2001). Recruiting the record: Using opponents' exact words in parliamentary argumentation. *Text, 21*(4), 467–488.

Ashmore, R., & DelBoca, F. (1981). Conceptual approaches to stereotypes and stereotyping. In D. Hamilton (Ed.), *Cognitive processes in stereotyping and intergroup behaviour* (pp. 1–36). Erlbaum.

Augoustinos, M., & Every, D. (2007). The language of 'race' and prejudice: A discourse of denial, reason, and liberal-practical politics. *Journal of Language and Social Psychology, 26*(2), 123–141. https://doi.org/10.117 7/0261927X07300075

Augoustinos, M., Tuffin, K., & Every, D. (2005). New racism, meritocracy and individualism: Constraining affirmative action in education. *Discourse and Society, 16*(3), 315–340. https://doi.org/10.1177/0957926505051168

Augoustinos, M., Tuffin, K., & Rapley, M. (1999). Genocide or failure to gel? Racism, history and nationalism in Australian talk. *Discourse and Society, 10*(3), 351–378.

Billig, M. (1978). *Fascists: A social psychological view of the national front.* Academic Press.

Billig, M. (1985). Prejudice, categorization and particularization: From a perceptual to a rhetorical approach. *European Journal of Social Psychology, 15*(1), 79–103.

Billig, M. (1991). *Ideology and opinions – studies in rhetorical psychology*. Sage Publications.

Billig, M. (2001). Humour and hatred: The racist jokes of the Ku Klux Klan. *Discourse and Society, 12*(3), 267–289. https://doi.org/10.1177/0957926 501012003001

Billig, M. (2002). Henri Tajfel's 'cognitive aspects of prejudice' and the psychology of bigotry. *British Journal of Social Psychology, 41*(2), 171–188. https://doi.org/10.1348/014466602760060165

Billig, M., Condor, S., Edwards, D., Gane, M., Middleton, D., & Radley, A. (1988). *Ideological Dilemmas: A social psychology of everyday thinking*. Sage Publications.

Burke, S. (2018). The 'othering' of Jews and Muslims in the Britain first solidarity patrol. *Journal of Community and Applied Social Psychology, 28*(5), 365–377.

Burke, S., & Goodman, S. (2012). "Bring Back Hitler's Gas Chambers": Asylum seeking, Nazis and Facebook: A discursive analysis. *Discourse and Society, 23*(1), 19–33. https://doi.org/10.1177/0957926511431036

Byford, J. (2006). 'Serbs never hated the Jews': The Denial of Antisemitism in Serbian Orthodox Christian culture. *Patterns of Prejudice, 40*(02), 159–180.

Carr, P., Goodman, S., & Jowett, A. (2019). 'I don't think there is any moral basis for taking money away from people': Using discursive psychology to explore the complexity of talk about tax. *Critical Discourse Studies, 16*(1), 84–95.

Condor, S. (1988). 'Race stereotypes' and racist discourse. *Text – Interdisciplinary Journal for the Study of Discourse, 8*(1–2), 69–90.

Condor, S. (2006). Public prejudice as collaborative accomplishment: Towards a dialogic social psychology of racism. *Journal of Community and Applied Social Psychology, 16*(1), 1–18. https://doi.org/10.1002/casp.845

Culpeper, J., Iganski, P., & Sweiry, A. (2017). Linguistic impoliteness and religiously aggravated hate crime in England and wales. *Journal of Language Aggression and Conflict, 5*(1), 1–29.

Di Masso, A., Castrechini, A., & Valera, S. (2014). Displacing xeno-racism: The discursive legitimation of native supremacy through everyday accounts of 'urban insecurity'. *Discourse and Society, 25*(3), 341–361.

Drew, P., & Walker, T. (2009). Going too far: Complaining, escalating and disaffiliation. *Journal of Pragmatics, 41*(12), 2400–2414. https://doi.org/10.1016/j.pragma.2008.09.046

Durrheim, K. (2016). 'Race stereotypes' and 'racist' discourse. In C. Tileagă & E. Stokoe (Eds.), *Discursive psychology – Classic and contemporary issues* (pp. 257–270). Routledge.

Durrheim, K., Quayle, M., & Dixon, J. (2016). The struggle for the nature of "prejudice": "prejudice" expressions as identity performance. *Political Psychology, 37*(1), 17–35.

Edwards, D. (2003). Analyzing racial discourse: The discursive psychology of mind-world relationships. In H. van den Berg, M. Wetherell, & H. Houtkoop-Steenstra (Eds.), *Analyzing race talk* (pp. 31–48). Cambridge University Press.

Edwards, D. (2005). *Discursive Psychology*. In K. L. Fitch and R. E. Sanders (Eds.) Handbook of Language and Social Interaction (pp. 257–273). New Jersey: Erlbaum.

Edwards, D., & Potter, J. (1992). *Discursive Psychology*. London: Sage Publications.

Edwards, D., & Potter, J. (2017). Some uses of subject-side assessments. *Discourse Studies, 19*(5), 497–514.

European Migration Network. (2017). *Annual report on migration and asylum policy – Finland 2016*. European Migration Network.

European Union Agency for Fundamental Rights. (2018). *Hate crime recording and data collection practice across the EU*. Retrieved from fra.europa.eu. [17th June 2019].

Every, D., & Augoustinos, M. (2007). Constructions of Racism in the Australian Parliamentary Debates. *Discourse and Society, 18*(4), 411–436. https://doi.org/10.1177/0957926507077427

Faulkner, N., & Bliuc, A. (2016). 'It's okay to be racist': Moral disengagement in online discussions of racist incidents in Australia. *Ethnic and Racial Studies, 39*(14), 2545–2563. https://doi.org/10.1080/01419870.2016.1171370

Fozdar, F., & Pederson, A. (2013). Diablogging about asylum seekers: Building a counter-hegemonic discourse. *Discourse and Communication, 7*(4), 371–388. https://doi.org/10.1177/1750481313494497

Goffman, E. (1979). Footing. *Semiotica, 25*, 1–29.

Goodman, S. (2010). "It's not racist to impose limits on immigration": Constructing the boundaries of racism in the asylum and immigration debate. *Critical Approaches to Discourse Analysis Across Disciplines, 4*(1), 1–17.

Goodman, S. (2014). Developing an understanding of race talk. *Social and Personality Psychology Compass, 8*(4), 147–155.

Goodman, S., & Burke, S. (2010). 'Oh you don't want asylum seekers, oh you're just racist': A discursive analysis of discussions about whether it's racist to oppose asylum seeking. *Discourse and Society, 21*(3), 325–340.

Goodman, S., & Carr, P. (2017). The just world hypothesis as an argumentative resource in debates about unemployment benefits. *Journal of Community and Applied Social Psychology, 27*(4), 312–323.

Goodman, S., & Johnson, A. J. (2013). Strategies used by the far right to counter accusations of racism. *Critical Approaches to Discourse Analysis across Disciplines, 6*(2), 97–113.

Guerin, B. (2003). Combating prejudice and racism: New interventions from a functional analysis of racist language. *Journal of Community and Applied Social Psychology, 13*(1), 29–45. https://doi.org/10.1002/casp.699

Guimarães, A. S. A. (2003). Racial insult in Brazil. *Discourse and Society, 14*(2), 133–151.

Hepburn, A., & Potter, J. (2010). Threats: Power, family mealtimes, and social influence. *British Journal of Social Psychology, 50*(1), 99–120.

Home Office. (2018). Hate crime, England and wales, 2017/18. Available at: https://assets.publishing.service.gov.uk/government/uploads/system/uploads/attachment_data/file/748598/hate-crime-1718-hosb2018.pdf. [15th July 2019].

Jackson, C. (2011). *Interaction, gender, identity: A conversation analytic examination of person reference.* PhD thesis, University of York.

Leach, C. W. (2005). Against the notion of a 'new racism'. *Journal of Community and Applied Social Psychology, 15*(6), 432–445.

Lemke, J. L. (n.d.). *Violence and language: The signs that hurt.* Retrieved April 26, 2020, from http://www.columbia.edu/cu/21stC/issue-1.2/Language.htm

Lynn, N., & Lea, S. (2003). 'A phantom menace and the new apartheid': The social construction of asylum-seekers in the United Kingdom. *Discourse and Society, 14*(4), 425–452. https://doi.org/10.1177/0957926503014004002

McGuire, T., Kielser, S., & Siegel, J. (1987). Group and computer mediated discussion effects in risk decision making. *Journal of Personality and Social Psychology, 52*(5), 917–930.

Pomerantz, A. (1984). Agreeing and disagreeing with assessments: Some features of preferred/dispreferred turn shapes. In M. Atkinson & J. Heritage (Eds.), *Structures of social action: Studies in conversation analysis* (pp. 57–101). Cambridge University Press.

Pomerantz, A. (1986). Extreme case formulations: A way of legitimizing claims. *Human Studies, 9*, 219–229.

Potter, J. (1996). *Representing reality – discourse, rhetoric and social construction.* Sage Publications.

Potter, J., & Wetherell, M. (1987). *Discourse and social psychology.* Sage Publications.

Quinn, B. (2019, October 15). Hate crimes double in five years in England and wales. *The Guardian.* Retrieved from https://www.theguardian.com/uk. [16th October 2019].

Reynolds, E. (2015). How participants in arguments challenge the normative position of an opponent. *Discourse Studies, 17*(3), 299–316.

Schegloff, E. A. (1988/1989). From interview to confrontation: Observations on the bush/rather encounter. *Research on Language and Social Interaction, 22*, 215–240.

Simone Joseph Admits Viral Racist Bus Rant. (2015, 19th of October). Retrieved from https://www.bbc.co.uk/news/uk-england-london-34571284. [31st October 2015].

Stokoe, E., & Edwards, D. (2007). 'Black this, black that': Racial insults and reported speech in neighbour complaints and police interrogations. *Discourse and Society, 18*(3), 337–372.

Tajfel, H. (1981). *Human groups and social categories: Studies in social psychology.* Cambridge University Press.

Taponen, T. (2015, 24th of October). Käsittämätönpurkaustallentuivideolle: "Maamme on tällainen, koskaoletmusta". *Iltalehti.* Retrieved from https://www.iltalehti.fi/uutiset/a/2015102420553621. [8th August 2016].

Tileagă, C. (2005). Accounting for extreme prejudice and legitimating blame in talk about the Romanies. *Discourse and Society, 16*(5), 603–624. https://doi.org/10.1177/0957926505054938

Tileagă, C. (2006). Representing the 'other': A discursive analysis of prejudice and moral exclusion in talk about Romanies. *Journal of Community and Applied Social Psychology, 16*(1), 19–41.

Tileagă, C. (2007). Ideologies of moral exclusion: A critical discursive reframing of depersonalization, delegitimization and dehumanization. *British Journal of Social Psychology, 46*(4), 717–737.

Tileagă, C. (2013). *Political Psychology.* United Kingdom: Cambridge University Press.

Tileagă, C. (2016). *The nature of prejudice – society, discrimination and moral exclusion.* Routledge.

Tileagă, C. (2019). Communicating misogyny: An interdisciplinary research agenda for social psychology. *Social and Personality Psychology Compass, 13*(7), e12491.

van Dijk, T. A. (1992). Discourse and the Denial of Racism. *Discourse and Society, 3*, 87–118. https://doi.org/10.1177/0957926592003001005

Verkuyten, M. (2013). Justifying discrimination against Muslim immigrants: Out-group ideology and the five-step social identity model. *British Journal of Social Psychology, 52*(2), 345–360. https://doi.org/10.1111/j.2044-8309.2011.02081.x.

Wahlbeck, Ö. (2019). To share or not to share responsibility? Finnish refugee policy and the hesitant support for a common European asylum system. *Journal of Immigrant and Refugee Studies, 17*(3), 299–316. https://doi.org/10.1080/15562948.2018.1468048

Wetherell, M., & Potter, J. (1992). *Mapping the language of racism: Discourse and the legitimation of exploitation.* Harvester Wheatsheaf.

Wiggins, S., & Potter, J. (2008). Discursive psychology. In C. Willig & W. S. Rogers (Eds.), *The SAGE handbook of qualitative research in psychology* (pp. 73–90). Sage Publications.

Wood, C., & Finlay, W. M. L. (2008). British national party representations of muslims in the month after the London bombings: Homogeneity, threat, and the conspiracy tradition. *British Journal of Social Psychology, 47*(4), 707–726. https://doi.org/10.1348/014466607X264103

Part 3

Discursive Psychology, Discourse, and Social Problems

9

Presenting Support for Refugees as Naivety: Responses to Positive Media Reports About Refugees

Lise Marie Børlie and Simon Goodman

Introduction

The civil war in Syria continues to cause mass civil migration internally, across the Middle East and further afield including into Europe (Ostrand 2015). Over 5 million individuals have fled Syria since 2011, and it is considered the largest humanitarian crisis in modern times (OCHA 2019; UNHCR 2016). The resulting "refugee crisis" is also considered an emergency within Europe, as many refugees fled, and continue to flee, to European countries. In 2015 alone, more than one million Syrian refugees travelled to Europe by boat, and over 30,000 travelled by land (BBC 2016a, b). However, Europe's response to receiving refugees during this period has been mixed, with much opposition. Berry et al. (2015) suggest

---

L. M. Børlie
Nottingham Trent University, Nottingham, UK

S. Goodman (✉)
De Montfort University, Leicester, UK
e-mail: simon.goodman@dmu.ac.uk

© The Author(s), under exclusive license to Springer Nature Switzerland AG 2020   **233**
M. A. Demasi et al. (eds.), *Political Communication*, Palgrave Studies in Discursive Psychology, https://doi.org/10.1007/978-3-030-60223-9_9

that a key reason for EU leaders' unwillingness to adopt a decisive and coherent approach occurs due to the increasing levels of public opposition regarding refugees and asylum seekers across Europe. This increasing negativity has been attributed to the negative portrayal of all aspects of migration in the media (Saeed 2007; Van Dijk 1995). This is in a wider context of anti-migration sentiment, where "globalisation" and multiculturalism have been criticised. This anti-migration sentiment is part of the phenomenon of a wider global movement towards anti-globalisation "populist", right-wing governments all around the world, where one of the features of this politics is staunchly anti-migrant policies (e.g. Jay et al. 2019).

Media representations of the "crisis" have varied across Europe. Berry et al. (2015) compared coverage in Sweden, Spain, Italy and the UK. They found that media in Germany and Sweden frequently utilised the word "refugee" or "asylum seeker", while the UK and Italy more commonly used the word "migrant" or "immigrant". The British, Spanish and German press were less likely to address humanitarian themes in comparison to Italian coverage, and themes that implied threat (i.e. towards culture or welfare system) were significantly more widespread in the UK, Spain and Italy. Overall, the Swedish press was the most positive towards refugees and migrants during the "refugee crisis", while the UK was the most negative and polarised, although British coverage varied across the "crisis" (Goodman et al. 2017). Crawley et al. (2016) demonstrated the negativity of the UK's press towards refugees, indicating that the approach towards asylum seekers in the UK is narrow. Refugees' voices were largely missing in these representations, so instead they were framed either within a humanitarian concept, in which they needed saving, or more commonly as "villains" who challenged people's jobs and security. This demonstrates that despite the serious plight of refugees, media representations are generally negative and can be damaging; this appears to be mirroring the shift to the right in global politics (Jay et al. 2019).

Discursive Psychology and Representations of the "Refugee Crisis"

There is now a growing discursive literature on representations of the "refugee crisis", addressing the ways in which talk and writing is used to perform social action (Edwards and Potter 1992; Tileagă and Stokoe 2015; Wiggins 2016), such as arguing for or against an inclusionary approach to refugees (e.g. Kirkwood et al. 2016). Goodman et al. (2017) show that the way in which the crisis was presented changed over time, shifting from a "migrant" and "refugee" crisis following the circulation of photographs of the drowned three-year-old refugee, Alan Kurdi. They show that these different terms change the way that those affected by the crisis are viewed, with "refugees" eliciting a more sympathetic approach. Goodman and Kirkwood (2019) show how arguments about integrating refugees can be used to argue both for and against supporting refugees concluding that support for refugees is contingent on them behaving in particular ways. A key event in the "refugee crisis" was the image of the drowned three-year-old refugee, Alan Kurdi. Goodman et al. (2017) demonstrated how it was the prominence of this image that temporarily changed the "migrant" crisis into a "refugee" one. Parker et al. (2018) showed how this led to a more positive representation of refugees across Australia, Norway and the UK, adding that Norway already had a more positive portrayal of refugees than the UK did before the photographs were seen.

Prejudice Towards Refugees in Online Settings

Communication does not only take place in physical human interaction, however, with much interaction now taking place online. There is therefore now a growing body of work looking at anti-refugee prejudice in online settings. Burke and Goodman (2012) explored how supporters and opponents of asylum seeking talk about Nazis and racism in Internet discussion forums. Three strategies were identified: (1) people supporting asylum seeking accused the opponents of being racist by referring to Nazis;

(2) opponents of asylum seeking handled these accusations by arguing that the debate is suppressed because of the references to Nazis; (3) the opponents of asylum seekers drew upon extreme ideas associated with the Nazis and Hitler to support their anti-asylum position. As a result, the authors suggested using arguments that cannot be presented as merely a tool that suppresses the debate to support refugees. This involves increasing the focus on the persecution and harsh treatment these individuals undergo, while also avoiding the use of extreme accusations against the opponents.

The use of prejudicial language online has been demonstrated through various discursive analyses (e.g. Burke and Goodman 2012). However, there has been a limited focus on responses to positive representations of refugees, which is necessary given that representations of refugees have been shown to be largely negative and prejudicial. The exceptions to this are Nightingale et al. (2017) and Kirkwood (2017) who focused on these more humanitarian approaches that did feature in the debate, concluding that even these more sympathetic approaches to refugees are not always enough to challenge dominant arguments against supporting refugees, as supposedly practical considerations like economic costs win out. The current research study explores online discussion forums from two European countries, the UK and Norway, which have both been destinations for refugees during the "refugee crisis" and which both restrict the entry of refugees (Salbi 2015; Roberts 2016). Norway is considered a wealthy country with a relatively small population compared to its geographical size, and the main language is Norwegian (Facts About Norway, 2020). This is in contrast to the UK, which is arguably considered to be a country that is more densely populated, which exacerbates the competition for space and resources (Nordic Cooperation 2020). Norwegian media has been shown to be more positive towards refugees than in the UK (Parker et al. 2018). The aim of the current research project is to explore the diverse ways prejudicial language is used across different languages, with a particular focus on how positive representations are responded to. A secondary aim is to investigate whether similar discourse is used across national borders within Europe. The study therefore provides insight into the arguments that are used by opponents of migration against pro-refugee stances, in order to locate potential counter-arguments. The research question is therefore "How do opponents of migration in the UK and Norway respond to positive representations of refugees?"

Procedure

The study applies discourse analysis to explore the comments in British and Norwegian online discussion forums regarding the Syrian refugee crisis. The analytic focus is therefore on understanding the ways in which arguments against supporters of refugees are made. The analysis uses naturalistic data (e.g. Potter 2004); however, the discussion forums are moderated on these news platforms which means that the data available may exclude other posts that the (unknown) moderators removed.[1] Using online discussion forums to extract data is a highly useful source in order to gain relatively unguarded information (Thorseth 2003; Meredith 2016).

The chosen sources were as follows:

1. A discussion forum on the website of The Independent, following an article with the headline "Macedonian police fire tear gas and rubber bullets at refugees trying to break through Greek border", posted on 10 April 2016.[2]
2. A discussion forum on Facebook, following an article posted by BBC, which contained the headline "Migrants met with tear gas at Greek border with Macedonia", posted on 10 April 2016.[3]
3. A discussion forum obtained from VG, following an article with the (translated) headline "Used Teargas against Refugee-revolts – at least 260 injured", posted on 10 April.[4]

---

[1] For example, see the BBC discussion forum guidelines here: https://www.bbc.co.uk/social/moderation.

[2] http://www.independent.co.uk/news/world/europe/idomeni-macedonia-police-tear-gas-refugee-border-greece-a6977141.html

[3] https://www.facebook.com/pg/bbcnews/posts/?ref=page_internal

[4] http://www.vg.no/nyheter/utenriks/flyktningkrisen-i-europa/brukte-taaregass-mot-flyktning-opproer-minst-260-skadet/a/23656272/

4. The fourth comment section was abstracted from Dagbladet, following an article with the (translated) headline "The Lie of the welfare state's demise", published on 26 August 2016.[5]

While the news platform VG still held an open Facebook discussion forum on their website, the discussion forums of the BBC and Dagbladet had to be extracted directly from the news platforms' Facebook site, as they had closed the discussion forum on their own website. The first three news articles were chosen as they focused on the same event while representing different editorial policies and political alignments, as it gives basis for a valuable comparison of the arguments found across the discussion forums, which allows for some comparison of the different ways that the same topic is discussed in the different contexts. The fourth article, by Dagbladet, was chosen as it challenges the general prejudicial notion of disallowing the refugees' entrance to Norway, which offered the opportunity to identify how controversial, pro-refugee arguments are responded to. All four news platforms are mainstream, despite being different, sources. Line numbers have been added to the data. The comments are presented with the number of "likes" or upvotes each comment received from other readers, which is written in parenthesis after each individual comment using the arrow symbol directing upwards (↑). This feature was available on all four sources and may provide an idea of whether the arguments hold support within the discussion forum. The comment sections from The Independent further include the feature of "downvoting", and this is therefore marked with an arrow symbol directing downwards (↓).

The posts from the British news articles used in this analysis are replicated as found, including errors and grammar mistakes. The Norwegian posts are translated by the first author, which means that errors written in these comments may not be as evident as within the British comments despite the attempt of replicating the intention and nature of the posts as much as possible. Attention was given to the rhetorical strategies and discursive features of the constructed language in the comments. As this discourse analysis also uses a comparative element, through the use of two different countries' news sites, the discussion forums were compared

---

[5] http://www.dagbladet.no/kultur/lognen-om-velferdsstatens-endelikt/60675783

collectively in order to identify potential similarities and distinctions. These patterns were then further analysed to determine the potential functions of these linguistic strategies.

The level of anonymity available to people contributing to discussion forums varies by platform. In the British news website The Independent, it is also possible to use anonymous nicknames when writing comments, which may contribute to less considerate language due to the increased anonymity this provides (Bomberger 2004). Within the news platforms BBC, VG and Dagbladet, however, the option to be anonymous has been removed by linking the discussion forums to the social media platform Facebook. As the individuals commenting on these three websites were unable to comment anonymously, the names used below were replaced in order to ensure full anonymity. The data collection occurred between April and August 2016, where two discussion forums from each country were chosen as they contained interaction and a variety of viewpoints and opinions that were appropriate for the discourse analysis.

Analysis

The analysis demonstrates how responses to any positive representations of refugees were frequently incorporated with criticisms directed towards other groups of individuals and public institutions within the European society. The first strategy identified features criticism of the mainstream media, due to its (alleged) frequent portrayal of Syrian refugees as victims of the failing European management of the "refugee crisis". The second strategy identified relates to the negative portrayal of "liberal" individuals, who were frequently portrayed as "naïve", "politically correct" or "controlled by emotions", while also receiving blame for what are deemed to be problems stemming from the "refugee crisis". Both strategies will be analysed and discussed in turn.

Criticism of the Media for Positive Representations of Refugees

In Extract 9.1 the commenters portray the BBC as dishonest, deceiving and biased, in contrast with the commenters who present themselves as holding knowledge regarding the true and factual occurrences.

Extract 9.1, BBC, Kevin, Christoph and James, 11 April 2016

Kevin
1 Media needs to stop sugar coating. These are not refugees. They are criminal invaders and
2 need to be shot on sight or imprisoned! (↑5)

Christoph
3 Title should read: border guards met with violent crowd throwing stones
4 Come on already BBC - stop the one sided sensationalism!(↑2)

James
5 Well, it looks like 100% of the people commenting on here have had enough of this "poor
6 refugee" rhetoric being shoved down their throats by the bbc and cnn. Guessing those two
7 news organizations have lost a lot of respect from their presumed audience. Quit lying to
8 people, we're not as dumb as you think we are. ...(0)

This extract consists of three comments posted on a BBC article that was shared on Facebook, which depict the various ways media, and the BBC specifically, is portrayed as deceptive and responsible for spreading dishonest information. The first comment, written by "Kevin", commences by demanding that the media stop "sugar coating" (1), which suggests that the media intentionally chooses an angle to ensure that refugees appear in a more positive light. Kevin continues by rejecting the term "refugees" (1) as a descriptive noun in this news article and claims that they are in fact "criminal invaders" (1). Through this argument, Kevin shifts the categorisation of the refugees from victims, as suggested

9 Presenting Support for Refugees as Naivety: Responses... 241

by the BBC article, to aggressive perpetrators who generate the conflict (Goodman and Speer 2007). By portraying the refugees as criminals (e.g. Leudar et al. 2008), it legitimises punitive and hostile treatment of refugees, justified on the grounds of protecting "us" from the "threat", the refugees (Kirkwood 2017).

The second comment, written by "Christoph", utilises an argument that is similar to Kevin's, however through a less direct approach. By suggesting a contrasting, alternative title for BBC's news article (3), the author obliquely claims that the refugees are violent perpetrators, while the border guards are the victims of the situation. The comment continues through a statement directed towards the BBC, where the author demands that they "stop the one sided sensationalism" (4). Through this argument, the commenter suggests that the media intentionally portray the situation in a fashion that increases their circulation, which implies that they are attempting to sway public opinion, rather than sharing objective news with the public.

The third commenter, named "James", implies that the audience is aware of the deceitfulness of the media and that the BBC is losing credibility as a result, so as to add to the criticism. He introduces his argument through reference to his observation of the other comments in the discussion forum. By claiming that "100%" of the individuals commenting are tired of the "poor refugee" rhetoric (5–6), an extreme case formulation (Pomerantz 1986), the author implies that the other commenters are aware of the BBC's methods of intentionally victimising the refugees, consecutively initiating sympathy in the readers. Through this footing, the speaker claims to speak on behalf of everyone (Goffman 1981) which has the effect of generalising the comments and removing the possibility of any opposition to this idea. "James" further claims that BBC's "rhetoric [is] shoved down the commenters' throats by the bbc and cnn" (6), which suggests a forcefulness where the audience is the victim. The comment also implies that the BBC is part of a wider problem, by referring to the American news channel, CNN. It is also an example of lay discourse analysis, whereby the commenter is conducting his own version of discourse analysis of news reporting. The next sentence suggests the results of this supposed deceitfulness ("have lost a lot of respect from their presumed audience" (7)). The author finishes his comment by writing a

242   L. M. Børlie and S. Goodman

sentence directed towards the BBC, ("quit lying to people" (7–8)). This upgrades the severity of the criticism of the BBC, by demanding an end to "lies". By further claiming that "we're not as dumb as you think we are" (8), the author depicts an "us versus them" situation consisting of the media and the general public, where the notion of the BBC's falsehood is presented as a shared perception within the audience. This also does important identity work around the public "we" who are positioned as being patronised by news organisations, which builds an "elite"/public distinction.

The commenters in the forum following the BBC article frequently imply that BBC reporting is intentionally deceitful, through suggesting that its reporting favours refugees. According to the commenters, this is done through "sugar coating", "one sided sensationalism" and "poor refugee rhetoric". A similar finding was also detected in the Norwegian comment sections, where the media was implied to be spreading propaganda and intentionally altering information. In Extract 9.2 from the Norwegian news platform Dagbladet, the comments aim attention at the supposed emotional manipulation of the media and the media as spreading propaganda in order to increase newspaper sales.

> Extract 9.2, Dagbladet. Johan and Daniel, 21 August 2016 (translated)
> Johan
> Venstre propaganda fraDagbladet. 2000 flyktninger tar ikkeknekken-påvelferdsstaten men nårallehar mega store familiersomfårblipåfamilieg-jenforeningog 90 prosentaldrikommerijobbsåerdetikke bra. Bedre å hjelpefolkene der di er.Såsantdetikkeerkrig
>
> Daniel
> Ogdetbør man gjøreitryggestenærområde. For dethjelperihvertfallikke-dissemenneskene at man formidleretnaivt signal tilverdensomifjorog man fårmassivikke-vestliginnvandring. For husk påfølgende: Selvom media tåkeladettesåvardetikkeflertallavsyrieresomkom Europa. Ogselvom media ideresføleripropagandaklistretopp store rundetårefyltebrunebarneøynepåallebaugerogkantersåvardetnokflestvoksnemennsomkom. Men skjeggedevoksnemennselgerikke like godtsom propaganda som Alan ellerOmran

9 Presenting Support for Refugees as Naivety: Responses...   243

Johan

1 Leftist propaganda by Dagbladet. 2000 refugees don't ruin the welfare system but when they all

2 have massive families who are accepted in family reunion and 90 per cent never work, it is not

3 good. Better to help people where they are. Unless there's war (↑24)

Daniel

4 And this should be done in safe close area. It doesn't help these people to send a naïve signal to

5 the world like last year where we get massive non-western immigration. Remember the

6 following: Even though media blurred this, there weren't mostly Syrians who

7 arrived in Europe. And even though the media with their emotional propaganda used big teary

8 children's eyes at any given opportunity, there were mostly adult men arriving. But bearded

9 adult men don't sell as well as propaganda like Alan or Omran (↑11)

The first comment in this extract, written by Johan, is introduced by claiming that Dagbladet is delivering "leftist propaganda" (1). By terming it propaganda, the news organisation can be accused of intentionally providing distorted news stories. The commenter concedes a point (Antaki and Wetherell 1999) in the article that "2000 refugees won't ruin the welfare system" (1); however, he continues by claiming long-term issues as a result of the admittance of refugees.

The second comment in this extract is written as a response to a previous comment where it was claimed that it is Europe's duty to help the refugees. The current commenter, Daniel, states in response that the media uses propaganda and deception, so as to increase sales for the news corporation. By writing that the media blurred the "fact" that there are not mostly Syrians arriving in Europe (4–5), news reports can again be accused of deception. By further writing that the media uses children as emotional propaganda (5–6), he implies that the images of suffering children are solely used as a tool to promote an agenda, rather than represent tragic events. This is similar to what was shown in Goodman and Narang's

(2019) analysis of a debate about child refugees, where the plight of these children was both challenged as untrue and used to argue against supporting child refugees. Here this claim about the use of sympathetic child refugees is used to imply that the media selectively uses the images that promote their cause in order to sell more newspapers.

The discussion forums in both the BBC and Dagbladet depict various arguments used to portray the media as manipulative and as spreading propaganda. Both examples function to present the media as misrepresenting the information to portray the refugees in a more victimised manner: "Kevin" refers to "sugar coating" the situation (BBC) and "Daniel" refers to the "blurring" of different categories of migrants (Dagbladet). A second strategy that can be found used in the forums in both countries was the criticism of the media for using what is presented as emotional rhetoric in order to (presumably) gain sympathy for the refugees from the audience. The commenter James claims that the BBC uses "poor refugee" rhetoric, and "Daniel" (on the Dagbladet forum) criticises a generalised "media" for using "emotional propaganda" by claiming that the media uses "big teary children's eyes" which echoes James' reference to "poor refugee rhetoric" attributed to the BBC. Differing explanations are given for this, with "Daniel" implying that this is to sell more newspapers. A contrasting element between the British and Norwegian discussion forums can be detected through the usage of the word propaganda. The commenters of the British news site BBC implied on several occasions that the news source was presenting untrue information, but it was never termed propaganda by any of the British commenters. In the Norwegian news site Dagbladet, however, this word was used on multiple occasions in order to describe how the media was deceiving its audience. This suggests that while it is difficult to directly compare the different countries' debates, a comparison of the different repertoires in different settings is possible.

Individuals with "Liberal" Views Are Portrayed as Naïve in Discussions

The following two extracts consist of a post supportive of refugees followed by the responses. In the first extract in The Independent, a supporter of refugees receives an adverse reaction from two other commenters with a more hostile opinion on the refugee situation, by accusing the supportive poster of being a "brain dead moron" and "bleeding heart" socialist.

Extract 9.3, The Independent, loslac, Angus 7777 and TheViking, 11 April 2016

loslac

1. You and your fascist buddies are the scum of this world. You mention their life isn't in
2. danger in Turkey? They actually are. Turkey has an incredibly oppressive government. These
3. people are not asking to live like king. They are forced to live in tents and barely have food to
4. feed their families. But you obviously won't believe that because you were born into the
5. fascist and corporatist society we live in today.
6. [four lines omitted]
7. YOU are the one corrupted by greed. YOU are the one who is rapidly destroying the world
8. with ILLEGAL wars. We need a revolution. We need a world with people that care for each
9. other. We need to build bridges not walls! #Antifa #Socialdemocracy

Angus7777

10. Apologist for western hating, non-integrating, homophobic, misogynistic, FGM practicing,
11. honour killing, Jew hating, moaning freeloading economic scum. Idiots like you are facilitating in
12. the human trafficking of illegal economic migrants and criminals. If they were genuine refugees
13. they would claim asylum in 1st safe country not marauding their way through Europe creating

14. filthy mess where they pass through on their benefit shopping. You should imprisoned for

15. encouraging this law breaking you brain dead moron. (↑13 ↓2)

Top of Form

Bottom of Form

TheViking

16. No one invited any of them to the UK, they are in a safe country in France, they are in a safe

17. ountry in Greece, and they have a tendency to live in their own filth, which is not nice, I am not

18. corrupted by greed, I am corrupted by democracy, and I have a right to say 'no thank

19. you, stay away' You do not have a clue about human beings do you, only your bleeding

20. hearts socialism. If ever they take over here, you and yours will be toast. (↑22 ↓1)

In the first comment, the author "loslac" is responding to a previous comment by "cansu", which included Islamophobic remarks such as "hijabi wearing coackroaches" [sic], by making an insulting accusation of racism (1 and 5). loslac builds an account where the refugees in questions are presented in need of humanitarian support that there are not getting. This builds a sympathetic portrayal of refugees and provides the warrant to support, rather than exclude them, from Europe. The post ends with a call to move towards a more supportive and collectivist world. Angus7777 responds to loslac with further Islamophobic comments (10–11) based on the supposed intolerance of Muslims, intolerance for which loslac is therefore accused of supporting. Notable here is that because of this support, loslac is deemed to be an idiot (11) and a brain dead moron (15). Angus7777's reference to "idiots like you" works to generalise all supporters of refugees as both stupid and of bringing about the alleged harm caused by refugees. Next TheViking continues the same line of argument through the dehumanisation of refugees. This poster direct responds to loslac's comments about being corrupted by greed and instead, reusing the original phrase, claims to be corrupted by democracy (18). The Viking then moves to account for loslac's supposed lack of understanding of people by way of "bleeding hearts socialism" (19–20).

Two features are common to both of these responses to loslac's post which was supportive of refugees. The first is the dehumanisation of refugees, brought about through the references to "scum" and "filth" who are therefore deemed unworthy of any support or sympathy as they are deemed to have brought about their own predicament (see Tileagă 2006). The second common feature is the attacking of Ioslac on the grounds of being stupid and left-wing and therefore unable to understand the "true" nature of these refugees. The reference to bleeding hearts socialism especially implies naivety on behalf of those who support refugees, and, in both cases, these supporters are deemed to be dangerous and in need of punishment, either in the form of imprisonment or being "toast".

The following extract, from a Norwegian news article, also contains similar criticisms being used against a more pro-refugee individual:

Extract 9.4, VG, 10 April 2016
Marianne
Synesikkesyndpå de! De fåroppføresegsom folk eller ta konsekvensene!

Chris
Du virkersom en trivelig person.

Lars
Chris André Winger Du virker til å være en naiv person

Chris
Ja, naivt å ikke syns det er greit å tåregasse barn.

Herregud så mange ignorante drittsekker vi tydeligvis har i dette landet. Skam dere.

Torbjørn

Chris André Winger Men det er helt greit å la egne barn delta når det kastes stein motpolitiet?
Jeg synes ikke en slik holdning er verdig for en lærer i den norske skolen!

Morten
Chris det er du som er naiv her og burde skamme deg, hadde du dratt med deg barna dine på den måten de gjør? Nei, de bruker barna sine for alt de er verdt. Makedonerne har enhver rett til å beskytte grensene sine, noe flere land burde gjøre.

Marianne
1 I don't feel pity for them ! They need to behave or suffer the consequences ! (↑125)

Chris
2 You seem like a nice person. (↑22)

Lars
3 Chris André Winger you seem like a naïve person. (↑123)

Chris
4 Yes, naïve to think it's not okay to teargas children.
5 Jesus how many ignorant assholes we clearly have in this country. Shame on you. (↑43)

Torbjørn
6 Chris but it's completely fine to let their own children participate when they throw rocks
7 against the police? I do not think these attitudes are worthy of a teacher in the Norwegian
8 school system! (↑100)

Morten
9 Chris it is you who are naïve here and you should be ashamed of yourself, would you pull your
10 children along the way they do? No, they're using their children for all they're worth. The
11 Macedonians have every right to protect their borders, something more countries should be
12 doing. (↑42)

9 Presenting Support for Refugees as Naivety: Responses... 249

This extract presents five different commenters, where one individual, Chris, presents a more liberal perspective when he criticises an earlier commenter for lacking pity towards refugees. The other five individuals, however, support the harsh treatment of the refugees at the Macedonian border and argue against Chris by terming him "naïve". The first commenter, Marianne, presents the situation as an ultimatum for the refugees, by claiming that the option is either "to behave or suffer the consequences" (1), which in turn justifies the actions taken against refugees who are presented as not "behaving" and therefore morally questionable. Thus, this commenter does that groundwork that allows her to claim that she "does not feel pity for them" (1). It is following this comment that Chris, ironically, terms the previous commenter as a "nice person" (2) and by doing so attempts to undermine Marianne's comment by questioning her personality and lack of compassion (see Nuolijärvi and Tiittula 2011 for more on the use of irony in debates).

At this point, the third commenter, Lars, joins the discussion and argues against Chris by copying the structure of his sentence (3) and replacing "nice person" with "naïve person" (3), which implies that Chris does not understand the implications of the current occurrences, while also functioning as an insult to Chris. Chris responds to Lars with further irony, by claiming that it is naïve to be against the use of teargas against children (4). This functions as a rejection of Lars' comment and challenges the terms of naivety. Further, Chris continues with an insult directed more widely to a significant amount of "ignorant assholes" (5) in Norway, which is targeted towards the other commenters, including Marianne and Lars. This general insult at a wider group may be related to the high number of "likes" that was given to the comments Chris is arguing against.

A fourth commenter, Torbjørn, makes an entry, joining in the argument against Chris by writing an ironic and loaded question regarding "allowing the children to participate in throwing rocks" (6–7), which indirectly suggests that Chris condones this type of behaviour due to his stance against using teargas on children and also adds to the criticism of refugees who are presented as criminal in nature (e.g. Leudar et al. 2008). By writing that "these attitudes are not worthy of a teacher" (7–8), the commenter makes a personal criticism of Chris, which implies that he is not suitable for his profession. As this comment section is linked to the commenters' private Facebook profiles, it is likely that Torbjørn derived this information by viewing Chris' personal profile.

The final comment in this extract, provided by Morten, is also targeted towards Chris. Morten uses the same arguments that have previously used towards Chris, by terming him "naïve" (9) in the face of the supposed "facts". This supposed naivety is used in a bid to undermine Chris' pro-refugee arguments as being unrealistic and not grounded in objective facts. Next, Morten uses a rhetorical question targeted towards Chris, where he asks whether he would "pull his children along the way they do" (9–10). Through this question, Morten creates a distinction between Chris and the refugees, where the refugees are placed in a negative light and Chris (and Norwegians in general) in a positive light.

Comparing the two discussion forums, commenters from both the UK and Norway provided personal insults (including those using the standard two-word formulation, such as "ignorant assholes" [5], identified by Stokoe and Edwards [2007]) directed towards the individual opposing the prejudicial majority; however, these were made alongside slightly differing arguments. The commenter "Angus7777" in The Independent categorised the opposing commenter as a "brain dead moron", and TheViking referred to "bleeding hearts socialism", which in turn functions as strong dismissal of the opposing commenter's opinion. This suggests that the category "socialist", when used by people opposed to this identity, comes with the category-tied assumption (Sacks 1972) of naivety, rather than (supposed) fact-driven rationality, possibly drawing on the idea that those on the political left are "traitors" against people in their own countries (Mols and Jetten 2016). In the Norwegian comment section, a supporter of refugees was presented as naïve and as someone not fit to be a school-teacher because of his views. Despite these differences, "naïve" works in much the same way as "idealistic"; in both cases supporters of refugees are presented as being unrealistic in response to the "facts".

Discussion

The discourse analysis identified several strategies that were similarly deployed in both the UK and Norway, which mainly functioned to argue against refugees' admittance to Europe and those who appear to support refugees. As found in previous studies, the comments directed towards refugees were overwhelmingly hostile (e.g. Bomberger 2004; Burke and Goodman 2012). However, a unique finding in this analysis is that it demonstrates hostility towards both supporters of refugees and news reports that contain arguably positive and/or sympathetic portrayals of refugees.

A key feature of the responses to arguably pro-refugee news articles is the rejection of the news sources as false. It was common to see comments stating that the media favoured refugees. This "deception" was attributed to intentional bias on the part of media, which was presented as designed to provide an unduly positive portrayal of refugee for propaganda reasons, or to increase newspaper sales. Any positive or sympathetic representation of refugees therefore comes to be presented as false, with only negative representations accepted as objective information. Thus, any news stories that did not suit these anti-refugee opinions were widely rejected as biased and untrue.

A second key finding consists of the portrayal of forum users who were positive towards refugees as "naïve lefties" or "politically correct". This finding is closely connected to the first finding of manipulative news, as the individuals defending refugees were presented as naïve for "believing" the news platforms and their information. Commenters who supported refugees were seen to be attacked for their support. The defenders of refugees were rarely seen to retaliate towards these accusations, however, which may be due to frequently appearing in minority. This means that support for refugees in these forums is already in the minority, and those who attempted to argue for refugees find themselves in a difficult situation, particularly having to deal with the suggestion that they are naïve and part of the "problem" of "politically correct", left-wing policies.

The atmosphere in all four discussion forums is overwhelmingly hostile towards refugees and their supporters. Noticeable similarities across both countries include the criticism of any news items that treat refugees sympathetically, which is achieved by criticising the source of the news as well as the content. In both countries individuals that support refugees are referred to as being naïve and are insulted because of their support for refugees. These similarities can be found despite the generally more positive portrayal of refugees in the Norwegian press (Parker et al. 2018). The analysis demonstrates that the readers do not simply digest the information they receive through media, but interact and challenge it to a wide extent, especially if it does not fit with a particular viewpoint. The phenomenon identified in this chapter involves criticism of the media on the grounds that it has an emotive, irrational, left-wing bias. It contains elements of a conspiracy theory (Byford 2014), mirroring that used by far-right leaders (Johnson and Goodman 2013). There are some similarities here with the strategy used by American president Donald Trump, of criticising mainstream media as providing biased and "fake news" suggesting that the strategies identified here resemble the "fake news" phenomenon. The term "fake news" has been used to discredit allegations of corruption, racially motivated policies and various claims that placed Trump in a disadvantageous position (Evans and Rothwell 2017). The rise of the term "fake news" has paved the way for "alternative facts", and consequently, it has also amplified and normalised the very same views observed in this study. Denying news that does not support one's viewpoint is a useful rhetorical strategy that allows people to continue to voice their opinion even in the face of opposing "facts" from news. This suggests that news sources do not have credibility as factual, which opens up alternative ways of arguing over what counts as fact. This use of language reinforces the notion that language has the ability to create structures of power (Augoustinos et al. 2006; Demasi 2019). Considering that the findings in the current study mostly derive from the time prior to the presidential election in America, it is evident that the notion of manipulative media was prevalent prior to the US election. Various individuals in the current study used words like "manipulative", "propaganda" and "lies" to describe objective information provided by the mainstream media, and the newly established term "fake news" seemingly verifies these individuals' perceptions, while also supporting further discrediting of objective news sources.

This study has provided a comprehensive understanding of how seemingly pro-refugee positions are strongly rejected in order to maintain prejudice towards Syrian refugees. While media representations of refugees have been shown to be overwhelmingly negative, there are nevertheless some examples of more positive representations. However, it is shown that these positive representations come to be criticised as false "propaganda" and individuals that support refugees come to be accused of being naïve and part of the wider "problem" of refugees.

References

Antaki, C., & Wetherell, M. (1999). Show concessions. *Discourse Studies, 1*(1), 7–27.

Augoustinos, M., Walker, I., & Donaghue, N. (2006). *Social cognition an integrated introduction*. London: Sage Publications.

BBC. (2016a). *Migrant Crisis: Greece brands Macedonian reaction 'deplorable'* [online] available from <http://www.bbc.com/news/world-europe-36009497> [26 July 2019]. The discussion forum is available from <https://www.facebook.com/pg/bbcnews/posts/?ref=page_internal>, through searching 'Macedonia' on the BBC's Facebook website.

BBC. (2016b). *Migrant crisis: Migration to Europe explained in seven charts* [online] available from <http://www.bbc.co.uk/news/world-europe-3413 1911> [26 July 2019]

BBC. (n.d.). *Moderation* [online] available from <https://www.bbc.co.uk/social/moderation> [10 September 2019]

Berry, M., Garcia-Blanco, I., & Moore, K. (2015). *Press coverage of the refugee and migrant crisis in the EU: A content analysis of five European countries* [online] available from <http://orca.cf.ac.uk/87078/1/UNHCR-%20 FINAL%20REPORT.pdf> [26 July 2019]

Bomberger, A. (2004). Ranting about race: Crushed eggshells in computer-mediated communication. *Computers and Composition, 21*, 197–216.

Burke, S., & Goodman, S. (2012). "Bring Back Hitler's Gas Chambers": Asylum seeking, Nazis and Facebook: A discursive analysis. *Discourse and Society, 23*(1), 19–33.

Byford, J. (2014). Beyond belief: The social psychology of conspiracy theories and the study of ideology. In C. Antaki & S. Condor (Eds.), *Rhetoric, ideology* and social psychology: Essays in Honour of Michael Billig. Explorations in social psychology (pp. 83–94). East Sussex: Routledge.

Crawley, H., McMahon, S., & Jones, K. (2016). Victims and Villains: Migrant voices in the British media. Coventry: Centre for trust, peace and social relations [online] available from <https://curve.coventry.ac.uk/open/file/3ff683bc-b508-40d6-86e5-422e955c5960/1/Victims%20and%20Villains_Digital.pdf> [26 July 2019]

Demasi, M. A. (2019). Facts as social action in political debates about the European Union. Political Psychology, 40, 3–20.

Edwards, D., & Potter, J. (1992). Discursive psychology. London: Sage Publications.

Ertesvåg, F. (2016). Bruktetåregass mot flyktning-opprør – minst 260 skadet [online] available from <http://www.vg.no/nyheter/utenriks/flyktningkrisen-i-europa/brukte-taaregass-mot-flyktning-opproer-minst-260-skadet/a/23656272/> [26 July 2019]

Evans, J., & Rothwell, J. (2017). Five times Donald Trump used 'fake news' to back up his most outrageous claims [online] available from <http://www.telegraph.co.uk/news/2017/03/17/five-times-donald-trump-used-fake-news-back-outrageous-claims/> [26 July 2019]

Goffman, E. (1981). Forms of talk. Pennsylvania: University of Pennsylvania Press.

Goodman, S., & Kirkwood, S. (2019). Political and media discourses about integrating refugees in the UK. European Journal of Social Psychology, 49(7), 1456–1470.

Goodman, S., & Narang, A. (2019). "Sad Day for the UK": The linking of debates about settling refugee children in the UK with Brexit. European Journal of Social Psychology, 49(6), 1161–1172.

Goodman, S., Sirriyeh, A., & McMahon, S. (2017). The evolving (re)categorisations of refugees throughout the 'refugee/migrant crisis. Journal of Community and Applied Social Psychology, 27(2), 105–114.

Goodman, S., & Speer, S. A. (2007). Category use in the construction of asylum seekers. Critical Discourse Studies, 4(2), 165–185.

Gray, R. (2017). Lies, Propaganda and fake news: A Challenge for our age [online] available from <http://www.bbc.com/future/story/20170301-lies-propaganda-and-fake-news-a-grand-challenge-of-our-age> [3 March 2017]

Hermstad, A. (2016). Løgnen om Velferdsstatens Endelikt [online] available from <http://www.dagbladet.no/kultur/lognen-om-velferdsstatens-endelikt/60675783> [26 July 2019]. The discussion forum is available from

<https://www.facebook.com/pg/dagbladet/posts/?ref=page_internal>, through searching 'løgnenomvelferdsstaten' on Dagbladet's Facebook website.

Jay, S., Batruch, A., Jetten, J., McGarty, C., & Muldoon, O. T. (2019). Economic inequality and the rise of far-right populism: A social psychological analysis. *Journal of Community and Applied Social Psychology, 29*, 418–428.

Johnson, A., & Goodman, S. (2013). Reversing racism and the elite conspiracy: Strategies used by the British national party leader in the justification of policy. *Discourse, Context and Media, 2*(3), 156–164.

Kirkwood, S. (2017). The humanisation of refugees: A discourse analysis of UK parliamentary debates on the European refugee 'crisis'. *Journal of Community & Applied Social Psychology, 27*, 115–1225.

Kirkwood, S., Goodman, S., McVittie, C., & McKinlay, A. (2016). *The language of asylum: Refugees and discourse.* Palgrave.

Leudar, I., Hayes, J., Nekvapil, J., & Turner Baker, J. (2008). Hostility themes in media, community and refugee narratives. *Discourse & Society, 19*, 187–221. https://doi.org/10.1177/0957926507085952

Meredith, J. (2016). Using conversation analysis and discursive psychology to analyse online data. In D. Silverman (Ed.), *Qualitative research* (pp. 261–276). Sage.

Mols, F., & Jetten, J. (2016). Explaining the appeal of populist right-wing parties in times of economic prosperity. *Political Psychology, 37*, 275–292. https://doi.org/10.1111/pops.12258

Nightingale, A., Quayle, M., & Muldoon, O. (2017). "It's just heart breaking": Doing inclusive political solidarity or ambivalent paternalism through sympathetic discourse within the "refugee crisis" debate. *Journal of Community and Applied Social Psychology, 27*, 137–146. https://doi.org/10.1002/casp.2303

Nordic Cooperation. (2020). *Facts about Norway* [online] Available from <https://www.norden.org/en/information/facts-about-norway> [20 June 2020].

Nuolijärvi, P., & Tiittula, L. (2011). Irony in political television debates. *Journal of Pragmatics, 43*(2), 572–587. https://doi.org/10.1016/j.pragma.2010.01.019

Office for National Statistics. (2016). *Internet access – households and individuals: 2016* [online] available from <https://www.ons.gov.uk/peoplepopulation-andcommunity/householdcharacteristics/homeinternetandsocialmedi-ausage/bulletins/internetaccesshouseholdsandindividuals/2016#activit ies-completed-on-the-internet> [26 July 2019]

Ostrand, N. (2015). The refugee crisis: A comparison of responses by Germany, Sweden, the United Kingdom, and the United States. *Journal on Migration and Human Security, 3*(3), 255–279.

Parker, S., Naper, A., & Goodman, S. (2018). How a photograph of a drowned refugee child turned a migrant crisis into a refugee crisis: A comparative discourse analysis. *For (E)Dialogue, 2*(1), 12–28. https://journals.le.ac.uk/ojs1/index.php/4edialog/article/view/601

Pomerantz, A. (1986). Extreme case formulations: A way of legitimizing claims. *Human Studies, 9*(3-4), 219–229. https://doi.org/10.1007/bf00148128

Population Matters. (2020). *Overpopulation in the UK* [online] Available from <https://populationmatters.org/the-facts/uk> [20 June 2020]

Potter, J. (1996). *Discourse analysis and constructionist approaches: Theoretical background.* Leicester: British Psychological Society.

Potter, J. (2004). Discourse analysis as a way of analysing naturally occurring talk. In D. Silverman (Ed.), *Qualitative analysis: issues of theory and method* (2nd ed., pp. 200–221). Sage.

Roberts, R. (2016). *The UK has taken just 18% of its 'fair share' of Syrian refugees, report shows* [online] available from <http://www.independent.co.uk/news/uk/home-news/syrian-refugees-uk-fair-share-report-a7478891.html> [26 July 2019]

Sacks, H. (1972). On the analyzability of stories by children. In J. J. Gumperz & D. Hymes (Eds.), *Directions in sociolinguistics: The ethnography of communication.* Rinehart & Winston.

Saeed, A. (2007). Media, racism and Islamophobia: The representation of Islam and Muslims in the media. *Sociology Compass, 1*, 1–20.

Salbi, Z. (2015). *Syrian refugees explain why Germany is top country in which to seek a new life* [online] available from <http://nytlive.nytimes.com/womenintheworld/2015/09/09/syrian-refugees-explain-why-germany-is-top-country-in-which-to-seek-a-new-life/> [26 July 2019]

Statistisk Sentralbyrå. (2015). *Norsk Mediebarometer* (2015) [online] available from <https://www.ssb.no/kultur-og-fritid/statistikker/medie/aar/2016-04-14> [3 March 2017]

Stokoe, E., & Edwards, D. (2007). 'Black this, black that': Racial insults and reported speech in neighbour complaints and police interrogations. *Discourse & Society, 18*(3), 337–372. https://doi.org/10.1177/0957926507075477

Thorseth, M. (2003). Applied ethics in internet research. *Programme for Applied Ethics Publication, 1*, 3–189.

Tileagă, C. (2006). Representing the 'other': A discursive analysis of prejudice and moral exclusion in talk about Romanies. *Journal of Community and Applied Social Psychology, 16*(1), 19–41. https://doi.org/10.1002/casp.846

Tileagă, C., & Stokoe, E. (2015). *Discursive psychology: Classic and contemporary issue*. Routledge.

UNHCR. (2016). *Syria emergency* [online] available from <http://www.unhcr.org/syria-emergency.html> [26 July 2019]

United Nations Office for the Coordination of Humanitarian Affairs (OHCR). (2019). *Syrian Arab Republic* [online] available from https://www.unocha.org/syria [24 July 2019]

van Dijk, T. (1995). Discourse semantics and ideology. *Discourse and Society, 6*(2), 243–289.

Wiggins, S. (2016). *Discursive psychology: Theory, method and applications*. Routledge.

Yeung, P. (2016). *Idomeni: Macedonian police fire tear gas and rubber bullets at refugees trying to break through Greek border* [online] available from <http://www.independent.co.uk/news/world/europe/idomeni-macedonia-police-tear-gas-refugee-border-greece-a6977141.html> [26 July 2019]

10

Consensual Politics and Pragmatism in Parliamentary Discourse on the 'Refugee Issue'

Lia Figgou and Dimitra Anagnostopoulou

Political Communication as Political Rhetoric

This chapter explores the rhetorical articulation and implications of appeals for consensus and pragmatism in parliamentary discourse on the 'refugee issue' in Greece. Using analytic concepts and tools informed by Rhetorical (Billig 1991) and Discursive Psychology (Edwards and Potter 1992), this study approaches parliamentary discourse as historically contingent and context-bound politically rhetoric and focuses on rhetorical aspects of political communication.

'Political rhetoric' is used to refer to the construction of persuasive, argumentative discourse in both institutional and everyday political contexts (Condor et al. 2013), and its study is, more often than not, linked to the promotion of democratic politics (Yack 2006). In social and political psychology, interest in rhetoric is particularly related to the work of

L. Figgou (✉) • D. Anagnostopoulou
Aristotle University of Thessaloniki, Thessaloniki, Greece
e-mail: figgou@psy.auth.gr

© The Author(s), under exclusive license to Springer Nature Switzerland AG 2020
M. A. Demasi et al. (eds.), *Political Communication*, Palgrave Studies in Discursive
Psychology, https://doi.org/10.1007/978-3-030-60223-9_10

259

Billig (1987, 1991) and his rhetorical psychology project. Aiming to highlight the argumentative nature of thinking and the thoughtful character of argumentation, Billig replaced the metaphor of the monolithic cognitive miser—fundamental in social cognition—with the metaphor of the orator who can think, argue and persuade others, drawing upon alternatives and dilemmas of ideological nature.

Billig made numerous references to ancient Greek rhetoric, while the dialectics of Ancient Greek Sophists as well as Aristotle's work on political rhetoric seem to have vitally influenced his work (Condor 2014). His critique of the social cognition model of thinking was grounded on the maxim of Protagoras that '*in every question, there are two sides to the argument, exactly opposite to each other*'. His appreciation of the spirit of contradiction was also widely predicated on the principles of Aristotle's *Rhetoric*. Aristotle defined political (deliberative) oratory as concerned with contingencies within human control. In other words, he constituted political argument as concerned with weighing up alternative (future) courses of action (Condor et al. 2013; Gleeson and Higgins 2008). According to his writings, the orator addresses important and timely topics (such as war, national defence, trade or legislation) in an attempt to assess what is harmful and beneficial and to persuade its audience about the most fruitful relationship between means and ends. Aristotle also distinguished political oratory from forensic (judicial) oratory, practised in the law courts, and from epideictic (ceremonial) oratory, concerned with the attribution of praise or censure.

The aforementioned Aristotle's description of the orator makes apparent that classical work on rhetoric was not confined to the political sphere (Condor et al. 2013). Similarly, Billig's rhetorical psychology project is not restricted to the analysis of political discourse. According to him, all discourse is rhetorical and indicative of dialogic thinking. In this chapter, though, we will focus on the rhetorical aspects of political communication and, in particular, on the rhetorical implications of appeals to consensus and pragmatism in a particular political context.

The Political Rhetoric of Pragmatism and Consensus

As Condor et al. (2013) maintained, although contradiction is the cornerstone of rhetoric, consensus is often a rhetorical objective or a resource used to orientate to important rhetorical ends. In fact in some rhetorical contexts, such as those classified as instances of *ceremonial oratory*, politicians' appeals to consensus and prioritization of unity instead of divisive rhetoric may be essential (Billig and Marinho 2017). Thus, it is not uncommon for scholars who are interested in the analysis of political rhetoric to focus on political 'consensus' as a rhetorical construction (e.g. Beasley 2001; Dickerson 1998; Weltman and Billig 2001; Kurz et al. 2010).

Existing research highlighted the tendency of political actors to strategically appeal for consensus, by claiming to put the national interest above their party interest. Dickerson (1998) analysed examples of politicians' televised discourse broadcast in the UK and the USA and documented the multiple functions of the repertoire of 'the national interest'. According to his account, in the local interactional context, the rhetorical construction of national interest was oriented to manage blame. At the ideological level, however, it served to construct an uncontested political reality and to refute alternatives. Similarly, Kurz et al. (2010), focusing on the ways in which the issue of climate change was rhetorically managed in political rhetoric, pointed out that 'national interest' was invoked by politicians from the major Australian political parties, in an attempt to warrant their policies on climate change. By claiming to put restrictions to climate change actions, in order to avoid jeopardizing 'national (economic) interest', politicians positioned themselves as being 'practical' and effective.

In the aforementioned analyses, politicians tended to argue that they—temporarily and strategically—put their party ideology aside, in order to serve the interest of the people. Other studies, however (Beasley 2001; Weltman 2004; Weltman and Billig 2001), focused on occasions of political communication in which political actors obscure or explicitly refuse ideological differences. Beasley (2001) explored how the USA's alleged ideological consensus has been invoked in presidential inaugurals in the

USA. According to her, inaugurals tend to de-ideologize political life, by constructing American people as a homogenous and unified group which shares a particular ideological vision. The author also maintained that this representation of ideological consensus needs an external 'enemy' and a specific type of opposition, in order to be meaningful and rhetorically effective. As she put it:

> It needs World Wars and Auschwitzes and Sarajevos and other examples of the kinds of un-American events that passionate tribalism can lead to. It needs hungry and tired immigrants, willing to face life-threatening conditions just to land on American shores. It needs constant, fresh evidence to support the country singer's proclamation, 'I'm proud to be an American, where at least I know I'm free.' (Beasley 2001, p. 181)

Attention to the ideological implications of the rhetoric of political consensus has also been paid by Weltman and Billig (2001) in an analysis of political interviews in Britain which documented a central contradiction. Specifically, although interviewees were affiliated with certain political parties, they argued against the parochialism of the left-right division and for the need to support consensual, non-ideologically divisive politics. According to Weltman and Billig (2001), the tendency of politicians to prioritize 'good' consensual governance and effectiveness vis-à-vis political controversy may serve to exclude radical politics and to discourage challenges to powerful vested interests.

The above-cited research indicates that appeals to consensus may be a useful rhetorical resource in different contexts of political communication. Some of these contexts, such as inaugural speeches, may be considered as 'epideictic' occasions, and therefore, the prioritization of national unity vis-à-vis divisive politics may be expected. Appeals to consensus, however, are also present in other contexts such as political interviews in which confrontation is also anticipated. This study aims at contributing to this literature by analysing appeals to pragmatism and consensus and their potential implications in a context deemed to be characteristic of political partisanship, a parliamentary debate. The debate is on the so-called refugee issue in Greece. Hence, by virtue of its topic, the study is also anchored in the rich tradition of social psychological analyses of political discourse on immigration and refugees.

Discursive Psychology and Political Rhetoric on Immigration and Refugees

Browsing through the literature of discursive social psychology during the past 30 years, we can find analyses of political rhetoric on immigration and refugee movements in various discursive (including media discourse, parliamentary debates, political speeches and interviews) and national contexts. A considerable number of studies conducted in the UK (Capdevila and Callaghan 2008; Goodman and Speer 2007; Kirkwood 2017), Greece, (Figgou 2015), the Netherlands (Rooyackers and Verkuyten 2012), Sweden (Sakki and Pettersson 2018), Ireland (Sambaraju et al. 2017) and Australia (Augoustinos and Every 2007; Hanson-Easey and Augoustinos 2010) documented the rhetorical organization and the argumentative resources used in discourse, in order to construct unfavourable categorizations of immigrants and refugees and to justify social exclusionary practices.

Common ground between the findings of the aforementioned studies constitutes the representation of contemporary discourse on immigration and refugees as flexible, subtle and even ambivalent. Being aware of the fact that their speeches are thoroughly monitored, political actors, according to the aforementioned research, prefer indirect ways to justify restrictive immigration policies and exclusion from (national) citizenship rights. Therefore, exclusionary political rhetoric is rich in racism denials and flexible categorical constructions and problematizes immigration, without direct references to ethno-culturalist and/or racial categorizations being needed.

According to Tileagă (2006, 2015), discursive social psychological studies on immigration and social exclusion have made clear that the rhetorical construction of inflexible boundaries between national in-groups and immigrants is not based on fortuitous criteria, but it is grounded on moral evaluations and judgments. Those who are constituted to enter 'our land' without permission are also portrayed to violate moral order. In the same vein, other authors (Condor 2000; Kirkwood 2019) maintained that the justification of immigration restriction policies in different discursive contexts is based on a self-representation which portrays the national in-group as morally superior in comparison to immigrant cultures. The glorification of the nation, as van Dijk (1992) put it, is grounded on its tradition of respecting democratic values and protecting human rights.

Other studies have emphasized the moral implications of categorical divisions (between good and bad, deserving and undeserving, lawful and unlawful immigrants and refugees) used in social exclusionary rhetoric. Lynn and Lea (2003) showed how a distinction between 'bogus' and 'genuine' asylum seekers is used to undermine the legitimacy of applications for asylum and the morality of people who have applied, positioning—at the same time—speakers as moral subjects concerned with (genuine) asylum seekers' safety and welfare (see also Goodman and Speer (2007) and Kirkwood et al. (2015)). Similarly, in his analysis of parliamentary speeches in the UK, Kirkwood (2017) indicated how politicians draw on the human qualities of both refugees and the national in-group, in order to manage issues of agency and responsibility regarding refugees' protection.

Issues of agency concerning the recent refugee movement to Europe are also frequently managed through the use of the category of 'crisis'. Research indicated that 'crisis' is flexibly constituted as either a crisis for Europe, a crisis for the nation or a crisis for the displaced people and shifts affect the construction of relevant social actors and the attribution of responsibility (Figgou 2020; Figgou et al. 2018; Goodman et al. 2017; Sakki and Pettersson 2018). Goodman et al. (2017) maintained that the terminology of the crisis in the UK media followed some milestone events, portraying the moving populations either as deserving solidarity or as a threat. Shifts in the representation of refugees coincided with shifts in the attribution of responsibility from national to EU policy. Constructions of the refugee issue as a 'crisis' were also flexibly used to manage issues of agency and accountability in the discourse of Prime Ministers of Sweden and Finland analysed by Sakki and Pettersson (2018). When the 'crisis' was distant, the discourse of sympathy and humanism was dominant, while when the number of newcomers was increased, the discourse of reasonableness prevailed. Finally, Figgou et al. (2018) also demonstrated the way in which members of the government in Greek parliamentary discourse used the rhetoric of 'crisis' and 'emergency', in order to manage accusations on the part of the opposition and to warrant restrictive immigration policies.

This study complements ways of constructing the 'refugee issue' discussed in Figgou et al. (2018), focusing on the tendency of political actors to appeal to consensus and pragmatic refugee policy in the context of Greece. Furthermore, it aims at contributing to the critical study of political discourse on the refugee issue by exploring particular aspects of political communication and its potential policy repercussions.

Method

Context and Material

Greece, by virtue of its location, has had a key role in the refugee movement from Syria, Afghanistan and Iraq. Although it is very difficult to make estimates, United Nations High Commissioner for Refugees (UNHCR) puts the number of those arriving by sea in Greece in 2015 at 258,365 people (UNHCR 2015). While most people intended to travel to Western European countries, their movement was impaired, due to the sealing of borders by key Balkan countries such as North Macedonia, Croatia and Slovenia. As a result of the above, Greece has turned from a short-term transit country to a long-term host country. By the end of 2016, about 47,400 refugees, asylum seekers and migrants were on mainland Greece while 15,384 were on the islands (Amnesty International 2017).

Although in the beginning EU approached the phenomenon as a 'humanitarian crisis' and facilitated the relocation of refugees within member states, by the common statement with Turkey, it clarified its will to refrain refugees from entering its borders. Preceding institutional practices of facilitating the entry to the rest of Europe gave way to increasingly strict policies of control, underpinning some already established discourses of security and risk (Figgou et al. 2011). Specifically, on 18 March 2016 in a joint statement, EU and Turkey stated that all 'irregular'[1] migrants arriving in Greece after 20 March 2016 would be returned to

---

[1] This is the term used in the official statement (European Commission 2016).

Turkey. Moreover, Turkey would take any necessary measures to prevent new sea or land routes for irregular migration opening from Turkey to the EU (European Commission 2016).

The implications of the EU and Turkey joint statement have constituted a matter of heated political debate in the Greek parliament. A few days after the statement, the plenary session of the Greek parliament included a discussion on the interpellation of 12 New Democracy (hereafter N.D, opposition party at that time) MPs regarding the implementation of the European Programme 'Actions for Immigration' on 21 March 2016. Furthermore, on 23 March 2016, the leader of N.D, Kyriakos Mitsotakis, requested a pre-agenda debate on security. His request was largely predicated upon what he called the *'dramatic situation concerning the refugee-migrant issue'* ('Parliamentary Debate on Security' 2016). Our analytic corpus consisted of the proceedings of the following parliamentary debates:

(a) The 94th plenary session of the Greek parliament, which included a discussion on the aforementioned interpellation
(b) The pre-agenda debate on the subject 'Citizens' Security' which was implemented on 20 April 2016

The proceedings are posted on the official website of the Greek Parliament (http://www.hellenicparliament.gr). The proceedings of the plenary session consist of 35 pages—numbered from 6940 to 6974. The proceedings of the pre-agenda debate on 'Citizens' Security' consist of 45 pages—numbered from 8763 to 8808. The material is transcribed mainly for content—although it may also include information on interruptions and applause.

The study focused on the discourse of the government and the major opposition party which dominated the debate. The coalition government consisted of two parties, Anexartiti Ellines (meaning Independent Greeks, hereafter AN.EL) and Synaspismos Rizospastikis Aristeras (meaning Coalition of the Radical Left, hereafter SY.RIZ.A) which itself constituted a coalition of left-wing and radical left parties turned to a unitary party in 2012 and won the elections in 2015 mainly by adopting an anti-austerity rhetoric. AN.EL is a conservative anti-austerity small party which was formed during the 'crisis' and which after the breakup of the coalition with SY.RIZ.A was shrunk and did not take part in the 2019 elections. The opposition party, the right-wing N.D, is one of the major parties in modern Greek politics. It was defeated by SY.RIZ.A in the September 2015 legislative election. In January 2016 Kyriakos Mitsotakis was elected as new party leader. Under his leadership N.D returned to power in the recent elections.

Analytic Procedure

Analysis used principles and concepts of Rhetorical (Billig 1991) and discursive sychology (Edwards and Potter 1992), aiming to explore the practical and local concerns related to political actors' plea for consensus and practical politics but also to capture the broader social and cultural resources that shape political rhetoric at a certain time and in a certain context.

Our initial analytic objective was to document potential regularities (in terms of content and form) in security-related discourse on the refugee issue. Considering (reading and re-reading) the original corpus, we identified that appeals to consensus/consensual politics were commonly used in the discourse of leading politicians. We selected from the original transcripts all of the relevant extracts and we put them in a separate file. During this process of recontextualization of speakers' accounts, an attempt was made to lose as little information as possible about their original context in the transcript, by segmenting the transcripts into fairly long stretches of talk.

At a second stage we focused on variability (within regularity) and we identified two main ways used by speakers to argue for a consensual refugee policy which were based on two rhetorical contradictions. The first was between national and party interest, while the second was between 'ideological' and practical politics. Analysis of extracts then proceeded to explore the ways in which dilemmas of stake or interest and fact construction were managed in the discourse of politicians. Finally, analysis attempted to situate participants' commonplace constructions to the broader argumentative ideological context (Billig 1987).

The extracts analysed below are typical of the common ways of accounting identified in the data with preference given to succinct exchanges.[2] Extracts have been translated from Greek to English by the first author.

Analysis

The first section includes extracts derived from the opposition discourse. Having requested the debate, the opposition sets the agenda and frames the issues. The second section includes extracts derived from the speeches of leading ministers of the government who, by virtue of their position, are entitled to respond to the opposition requests.

National Interest and Pragmatic Politics in the Discourse of the Opposition

Extract 10.1 is from the discussion on the interpellation of N.D regarding the implementation of the European Programme 'Actions for Immigration'. Stavros Kalafatis is one of the MPs who addressed the interpellation to the government. Immediately prior to his talk quoted below, Kalafatis accused SY.RIZ.A that while it was in power, the number of 'illegal immigrants' in Greece multiplied, giving rise to realistic fears about the security of the country, in particular, and of Europe, in general.

> Extract 10.1: 'Putting the national soccer team jersey on'
> 1. *It [the government] underestimated the interconnection between security and*
> 2. *immigration issues in Europe. There are statements by government officials*
> 3. *that admit this. You all know that some time ago these were taboo issues for*
> 4. *the party of SY.RIZ.A. If we talked about security issues, we would risk being*
> 5. *characterized in certain ways. The government is gradually becoming aware*
> 6. *that security issues and refugee and immigration issues are in fact*
> 7. *intertwined, something that has been indisputable in the civilized world and*

---

[2] In two cases in which lengthy digressions from the subject have occurred (to address issues concerned with the procedure), part of the exchange has been omitted. The omission is notated by the use of three dots in brackets.

8. *all over Europe. You tend, however, to discover it now, while you are in*
9. *government and you also discover the difficulties of being in government and*
10. *that criticism is cheap and easy when you are in opposition.*
11. *But we, the party of N.D, are here to offer support, and we put the*
12. *national soccer team jersey on when we are in international fora or in the*
13. *context of European institutions.*
    (S. Kalafatis, N.D MP)

Kalafatis accuses the government for underestimating the interconnection between security and immigration. According to Edwards and Potter (1992), blaming the government in this context evokes important accountability concerns on the part of the speaker. It is easy for the audience (both proximal and distant) to think that, as a member of the opposition, the speaker is oriented to serve the interests of his party. In order to manage the dilemma of stake and interest and to dodge potential face-threatening implications, Kalafatis has to manufacture the credibility of his claim. Towards this rhetorical end, he attempts to build a picture of unanimity and consensus by the use of a two-folded argument. Firstly, he argues that not only him but also government officials themselves admitted that the connection between immigration and security has been undervalued. Secondly, he maintains that the security-immigration link is indisputable in other contexts, namely, in the civilized world in general and in Europe in particular. The practices of Europe and those of the unspecified 'civilized'—a term which in Greek public discourse is commonly treated as interchangeable with the term 'Western' (cf. Bozatzis 2009; Figgou 2013)—world are constituted as the example upon which, according to the speaker, Greece's consensual politics should be modelled. Furthermore, the immigrants are implicitly constructed as coming from outside the civilized world.

According to other scholars of political rhetoric (e.g. Reicher and Hopkins 1996), political actors, even when they make appeals to consensus, are concerned to differentiate themselves from the out-group. Kalafatis constitutes the government's important differences from his own party by a double comparison. Firstly, it is a temporal comparison. The government has not always admitted this indisputable relation between immigration and security. It is something that it is gradually becoming aware of. In the past this relation was treated as a taboo issue and characterized in 'certain ways' (line 5) by whoever dared to discuss it. It is noteworthy that the exact terms used to characterize the supporters of the immigration-security link remain unsaid. Billig (1997, 1999) has pointed out the social-ideological significance of what remains unsaid and has revealed its multifaceted functions. By leaving the characterization unsaid, Kalafatis replaces a (probably offensive) political characterization with a vague and euphemistic term. By the same token, he seems to be oriented to emphasize the difference between the insightful stance of his own party and the narrow-minded attitude of the ruling party. There is, however, another comparison that differentiates N.D from the ruling party. The party of SY.RIZ.A, while it was in opposition, refused to show consensus and exerted criticism towards the government. N.D as opposition, on the other hand, tends to show consensus and to wear the 'Greek national soccer team jersey on', in order to represent Greece at an international forum. This metaphor (lines 11–13) reinforces the aim of the speaker to visualize his party's role as the only defender of national interest.

Extract 10.2 is from the beginning of the opposition leader's speech in the context of the pre-agenda debate on security that he himself requested. As it is expected he is concerned to account for his request and to construct it as disinterested, not oriented to serve his own and his party's interest.

Extract 10.2: Pragmatism versus ideological obsession
1. *Today's pre-agenda debate on security, ladies and gentlemen, is topical not*
2. *only because of the recent terrorist attacks in Brussels; not only because of the*
3. *increased feeling of insecurity on the part of the Greek citizens, due to the*
4. *way the government handled the refugee-migration problem. But it is topical,*
5. *Mr Tsipras, because in the whole world a debate has been advanced on how*
6. *organized societies approach the dilemma between freedom and security.*
7. *Today's debate has not been requested in order to scaremonger. Its aim is to*
8. *make everyone to take a responsible and thoughtful stance in front of today's*
9. *disappointing situation, but also in front of coming challenges [...] It annoys*
10. *you, because, unfortunately, over the past decades the debate on these issues*

10 Consensual Politics and Pragmatism in Parliamentary... 271

11. *has been dominated by the ideological hegemony of the left. They have not*
12. *been approached with pragmatism; they have been approached with the*
13. *ideological obsession of some left-wing groupings*

(K. Mitsotakis, N.D President)

According to Potter (1996), the management of the dilemma of stake and interest depends on the ways in which agency is constructed. In order to avoid appearing as someone who attempts to serve his own interest, Mitsotakis proceeds to ground his request for a debate on security and immigration on the problem's topicality and importance. He unfolds a three-part justification (lines 2–6). The three parts are formulated with categorical modality. First is the 'terrorist attacks' in Brussels. Second is the alleged feeling of insecurity on the part of Greek citizens, due to the way the government handled the refugee-migration problem. Third is the example of other 'organized societies' which are depicted to have started a debate on the 'dilemma between freedom and security'.

There are many interesting rhetorical features in the account of Mitsotakis. It is noteworthy, for example, that there is no explanation of how the terrorist attacks in Brussels may be related to security concerns in Greece or how immigration policy in Greece is related to the debate taking place around the world. These are treated as self-evident and they construct (by implication) an image of refugees as a 'threat' and a situation of 'moral panic' (Hier and Greenberg 2002). These constructions are rhetorically reinforced by the speaker's factual reporting of the feeling of insecurity on the part of Greek citizens, on whose behalf he allegedly requested the debate. It is also notable that while at the outset of his speech Mitsotakis addressed all the MPs, when referring to the initiation of the 'security vs. freedom' debate in other countries, he addressed the Prime Minister (Tsipras) personally. In this way he—as opposition leader and potential future prime minister—appears to follow the practices of 'organized societies' as opposed to the prime minister who is constructed as cut off from international practices and inefficient.

The relation between freedom and security in 'either-or' terms—which, according to other authors (Giroux 2018; Harmes 2012), constitutes a common trope in neoliberal nationalist discourse—is taken for granted. It is depicted as a common concern of the whole world and not as an ideological position. Similarly, Mitsotakis' decision to ally with the rest of the world is portrayed as a responsible and rational stance. The worldwide concern with security is juxtaposed to left-wing ideology and the way in which immigration issues have been approached through its lens. Ideology in general and left ideology in particular is depicted as the adversary of pragmatism (cf. Lemert 2015). Furthermore, the speaker constructs the status of left ideology in two potentially contradictory ways. Its representatives are given the status of 'groupings' (line 13). Their ideological position, though, despite being devalued as 'obsession', is represented as 'hegemonic' (line 11).

Ideology and Political Realism in Governmental Discourse

Extract 10.3 features Ioannis Mouzalas, the Deputy Minister of Interior and responsible to respond to opposition MP's question on governmental immigration policy, in the context of the 94th plenary session. From the beginning of his talk, Mouzalas constructs immigration as a 'national' issue which must be dealt with a 'national' policy. He explicitly defines national as 'consensual', above party divisions and disagreements. Also, in the beginning of his speech, he constructs the question of the opposition as 'expected criticism', aiming to disempower the government. Hence, he presents the other party as having a particular stake, while he positions himself as oriented exclusively to the national interest. In Extract 10.3, he refers specifically to the accusation of the opposition concerned with the way in which the government handled the issue of the Amygdaleza camp.[3]

> Extract 10.3: Ideology as a censure versus ideology as just another position
> 1. *You say "you closed the camp of Amygdaleza". "You fooled us on the issue*
> 2. *of Amygdaleza". I think that these are issues of an ideological nature on*

---

[3] It is a detention camp located in the north of Athens. When SY.RIZ.A was in the opposition, it recurrently criticized the governing party (N.D) for the wretched conditions prevailing in it. During spring of 2015 the SY.RIZ.A-led government began releasing migrants from Amygdaleza following two suicides at the camp. Nevertheless, in November 2016, the facilities of Amygdaleza were again used for the temporary hosting of families of refugees and migrants, as well as for the protective custody of unaccompanied minors.

10 Consensual Politics and Pragmatism in Parliamentary... 273

3. *which - and I do not put it as a censure - you just have another position. And*
4. *our stance on this issue is not characterized by ideological rigidity. Because I*
5. *am in a position to know that you know very well that we did not close the*
6. *camp of Amygdaleza. When we came to the government - I was not minister at*
7. *the time, but I visited Amygdaleza as a doctor- Amygdaleza was already*
8. *deserted for economic reasons – and although I may have blamed you at that*
9. *time, I now know that I was not right, now as a minister, I am aware of all the*
10. *difficulties concerned with money disbursement […] But I'm trying to imagine*
11. *the situation in France. There is no one, in the French parliament accusing*
12. *the French Minister "you did that and you did this in Calais or you did it this*
13. *way or that way"*
    (I. Mouzalas, Deputy Minister of Interior, in charge of immigration policy)

Mouzalas, by the use of active voicing (lines 1–2), vividly represents the opposition's accusations regarding the governmental policy on Amygdaleza in this talk. He then proceeds to undermine the accusations by constituting them as a matter of 'ideological difference' (lines 2–4). He is oriented, though, to manage the implications of framing the issue in terms of ideology by a disclaimer (Hewitt and Stokes 1975): he refuses that he uses the notion of ideology as a censure. Actually there are two notions of ideology on which the argumentative line unfolded by the deputy minister is grounded. According to the first (from which he distances himself and his party), ideology is synonymous with rigidity; it is against reason and, hence, it can be received as a censure. According to the second, ideology may constitute just another position. The word 'just' (line 3) does important rhetorical job here. By signifying a difference which is not important and unbridgeable, it opens the way for an appeal for consensus. In what follows Mouzalas is oriented to portray his rhetorical project as going beyond divisive arguments. Specifically, he adopts a *first I thought, then I realized* trope (Wooffitt 1992). When he visited Amygdaleza in the past, as a professional doctor, he could not recognize the reasons that lied behind the inability of the government of N.D. to change the situation. As a minister, though, he has appreciated the economic concerns (lines 7–10) and, hence, he has realized that he was not right to blame the previous government.

In the last part of Mouzalas' speech, an example from Western European politics and, particularly, from the French parliamentary practices is mobilized to support his appeal for consensus. According to this example, the opposition in France has not been critical of the government for its policy on the refugee camp of Calais, the situation in which is assumed to be similar to that of Amygdaleza. By the use of parallel, the speaker constructs consensus as an indication of a superior political culture which is again attributed to Europe (Andreouli et al. 2017).

The following extract is from the pre-agenda debate on security and in particular from the speech of Nikolaos Toskas, the Deputy Minister of Public Order and Citizen Protection. By virtue of his role, the speaker was responsible to account for the governmental policy on security. Prior to the exchange quoted below, Toskas criticized the security-immigration link constructed in the speech of N.D leader (Extract 10.2). He put forward that such a link which is dominant in the rhetoric of the extreme right has been rejected by international and EU institutions. In particular European policy on security has been treated as an example of progressiveness and good practice.

Extract 10.4: Political realism as common ground
1. *Either your consultants have old-fashioned perceptions or you do not want to*
2. *change politics, and you prefer to stick to the security concepts of the 1950s*
3. *and 1960s, that is, repression and demonstrating power, which of course*
4. *creates polarization and social unrest, power above the citizen and, of course,*
5. *ineffectiveness. Do you want us to talk on a political realism basis? Let's*
6. *leave humanism aside. Let's leave all the noble feelings aside. How did you*
7. *handle the issue in Igoumenitsa? Do you want us to take a look at the seven*
8. *years data, according to which there were four to six thousand immigrants [in*
9. *Igoumenitsa] and about two and a half thousand in Patras.[4] How were they*

---

[4] Patras and Igoumenitsa are ports located in Western and Southern Greece which have been transformed into informal centres of immigrants and refugees hoping to leave Greece and continue on to Northern Europe (through Italy).

10 Consensual Politics and Pragmatism in Parliamentary... 275

10. *dealt with? The police tended to go there, kicking them out, creating the*
11. *impression that something was done, and in an hour time they were back.*
   (*N. Toskas, Deputy Minister of Public Order and Citizen Protection*)

In contrast to the previous extract and Mouzalas' plea for consensus, Toskas in Extract 10.4 uses the rhetoric of difference, polarity and critique. He criticizes the opposition for the way in which it approaches the issue of security and constructs a negative representation of its policy on immigration and (by implication) a positive image of his handling of the issue (van Dijk 2006). Addressing the leader of the opposition personally, Toskas accuses him of using old-fashioned concepts and tools to approach issues of order and security, either by choice or because he is misinformed by his consultants. Repression, polarization, power abuse and ineffectiveness are considered to constitute these old-fashioned tools (lines 1–5). Amongst these, however, ineffectiveness is emphasized. According to other authors, practicality and effectiveness are principles deeply ingrained in the liberal intellectual tradition and tend to serve as 'virtue words' (Condor et al. 2013) or as 'rhetorically self-sufficient' arguments (Wetherell and Potter 1992, p. 177). Effectiveness, being counterposed to humanism, is constituted as a basis of agreement, as a common language between the two parties.

Having constructed political realism and effectiveness as indisputable criteria of policy assessment, Toskas proceeds to evaluate the immigration policy of N.D, while it was in power. He provides a vivid account of this policy, mobilizing typical tools of fact construction, such as numbers, as well as rhetorical questions, representing it as involving police violence and power abuse. Nevertheless, the ultimate criterion of his critique is effectiveness. The violent measures taken, in order to prevent the concentration of immigrants in two Greek ports, are depicted as ineffective, since migrants tend to return to their original positions and the 'problem' is not solved.

Conclusion

This chapter documented appeals to consensual politics, in parliamentary discourse on the 'refugee issue' in Greece. Analysis indicated that, in the context of debating the alleged connection between the refugee movement and security issues, leading Greek politicians of both the governing and the opposition party warranted their policy choices through recourse to pragmatism and realpolitik. Specifically, in one line of arguing, speakers used the language of unanimity and represented themselves (and their party) as putting the national above the party interest. According to another common way of arguing, political actors constituted political realism as an undisputable criterion of evaluating policy choices and portrayed their differences with their opponents as differences in effectiveness.

In their plea for consensus, politicians of both parties used examples from other European contexts and constructed their policy as being consistent with the rest of the 'civilized' world while portraying the policy of their opponents as outdated or idiosyncratic. Consensus was treated as an indication of a superior political culture which was attributed to Europe. This finding is in line with those of other studies, which maintained that both lay and media discourse in Greece represent 'Europe' as politically superior and institutionally efficient (Andreouli et al. 2017; Bozatzis 2009, 2014). Hence, by aspiring for Greece to act as other European societies do, politicians appear to draw on common stock of values of the Greek society.

Focusing on the local rhetorical context, analysis maintained that appeals to consensual, pragmatic politics were used as a stake inoculation strategy (Edwards and Potter 1992) and served to exonerate blame and warrant one's political choices and/or to downgrade the practices of their political opponents. Rhetorical psychology (Billig 1991) encourages us to also consider the potential (distant) social implications of particular rhetorical constructions and to pay attention to the broader historical ideological context which shapes argumentation. Within this line of thinking, it is noteworthy to point out to the potential social exclusionary implications of co-articulating appeals to (particular) national interest with pleas to (the alleged as universal) rationality and pragmatism in the context of discussing the refugee issue. This co-articulation, in other words, may serve to construct a representation of the security-refugee link in one way: refugees can pose a threat to national security.

Although it is difficult to claim the applicability of the current analysis to other contexts, it is worth pointing to some parallels with more global political debates. Other authors (Giroux 2018; Rancière 2015), for example, who have also pointed out the tendency of institutional and lay political actors to devalue divisive politics, express their concerns about the implications of this rhetoric in an era in which right-wing populism seems to be definitely back on the agenda (see also Figgou 2016; Stavrakakis et al. 2017). These authors point out that the rhetoric of consensual 'anti-ideological' politics in this context may in the end transfer to the representatives of the far right the privilege of ideological positioning, the privilege to claim that they are the only ones to defend ideological values.

Future research may further investigate the ways in which immigration and refugee policy issues are communicated in political contexts. The concepts and tools of rhetorical analysis are particularly significant for such an endeavour. Firstly, they turn our focus to the argumentative context and to the need to thoroughly explore the content and implications of arguments via their juxtaposition to (more or less explicit) counter-arguments. Secondly, they draw our attention to the multidimensional nature of political communication, highlighting the multiple voices involved in 'texts' and the multiple audiences that are simultaneously addressed. Last but not least, being approached through the lens of rhetoric, political communication is closely associated both with the historical milieu and with the social psychological processes of social influence and social display (Billig and Marinho 2019).

References

Amnesty International (2017). Amnesty International Annual Report 2016/2017. Retrieved from https://www.amnesty.org/en/latest/research/2017/02/amnesty-international-annual-report-201617/

Andreouli, E., Figgou, L., Kadianaki, I., Sapountzis, A., & Xenitidou, M. (2017). "Europe" in Greece: Lay constructions of Europe in the context of Greek immigration debates. *Journal of Community & Applied Social Psychology, 27*(2), 158–168.

Augoustinos, M., & Every, D. (2007). The language of "race" and prejudice: A discourse of denial, reason, and liberal-practical politics. *Journal of Language and Social Psychology, 26*(2), 123–141.

Beasley, V. (2001). The rhetoric of ideological consensus in the United States: American principles and American pose in presidential inaugurals. *Communication Monographs, 68*(2), 169–183.

Billig, M. (1987). Arguing and thinking. A rhetorical approach to social psychology. Cambridge University Press.

Billig, M. (1988). Methodology and scholarship in understanding ideological explanation. In C. Antaki (Ed.), *Analysing everyday explanation: A casebook of methods* (pp. 199–215). Sage.

Billig, M. (1991). *Ideology and opinions: Studies in rhetorical psychology*. Sage Publications.

Billig, M. (1997). The dialogic unconscious: Psychoanalysis, discursive psychology and the nature of repression. *British Journal of Social Psychology, 36*(2), 139–159.

Billig, M. (1999). Commodity fetishism and repression: Reflections on Marx, Freud and the psychology of consumer capitalism. *Theory and Psychology, 9*(3), 313–329.

Billig, M., & Marinho, C. (2017). *The politics and rhetoric of commemoration: How the Portuguese parliament celebrates the 1974 revolution*. Bloomsbury Publishing.

Billig, M., & Marinho, C. (2019). Literal and metaphorical silences in rhetoric: Examples from the celebration of the 1974 revolution in the Portuguese parliament. In A. J. Murray & K. Durrheim (Eds.), *Qualitative studies of silence: The unsaid as social action* (pp. 21–37). Cambridge University Press.

Bozatzis, N. (2009). Occidentalism and accountability: Constructing culture and cultural difference in majority Greek talk about the minority in Western Thrace. *Discourse & Society, 20*(4), 431–453.

10 Consensual Politics and Pragmatism in Parliamentary... 279

Bozatzis, N. (2014). Banal occidentalism. In C. Antaki & S. Condor (Eds.), *Rhetoric, ideology and social psychology: Essays in Honour of Michael Billig* (pp. 122–136). Routledge.

Capdevila, R., & Callaghan, J. E. (2008). 'It's not racist. It's common sense'. A critical analysis of political discourse around asylum and immigration in the UK. *Journal of Community and Applied Social Psychology, 18*(1), 1–16.

Condor, S. (2000). Pride and prejudice: Identity management in English people's talk about this country. *Discourse & Society, 11*(2), 175–205.

Condor, S. (2014). Small words, large circles and the spirit of contradiction: Celebrating Michael Billig's contribution to the social sciences. In C. Antaki & S. Condor (Eds.), *Rhetoric, ideology and social psychology: essays in honour of Michael Billig* (pp. 1–16). Routledge.

Condor, S., Tileagă, C., & Billig, M. (2013). Political rhetoric. In L. Huddy, D. O. Sears, & J. S. Levy (Eds.), *The Oxford handbook of political psychology* (pp. 262–300). Oxford University Press.

Dickerson, P. (1998). 'I did it for the nation': Repertoires of intent in televised political discourse. *British Journal of Social Psychology, 37*(4), 477–494.

Edwards, D., & Potter, J. (1992). Discursive psychology. London: Sage Publications.

European Commission. (2016, March 19). *Factsheet on the EU-Turkey Statement*. [Press release] Retrieved from http://europa.eu/rapid/press-release_MEMO-16-963_el.htm

Figgou, L. (2013). Essentialism, historical construction, and social influence: Representations of Pomakness in majority talk in Western Thrace (Greece). *British Journal of Social Psychology, 52*(4), 686–702.

Figgou, L. (2015). Constructions of 'illegal' immigration and entitlement to citizenship: Debating an Immigration Law in Greece. *Journal of Community & Applied Social Psychology, 26*(2), 150–163.

Figgou, L. (2016). Everyday politics and the extreme right: Lay explanations of the electoral performance of the neo-Nazi political party 'Golden Dawn' in Greece. In C. Howarth & E. Andreouli (Eds.), *The social psychology of everyday politics* (pp. 206–221). Routledge.

Figgou, L. (2020). Agency and accountability in (un)employment-related discourse in the Era of "Crisis". *Journal of Language and Social Psychology., 39*(2), 200–218.

Figgou, L., Sapountzis, A., Bozatzis, N., Gardikiotis, A., & Pantazis, P. (2011). Constructing the stereotype of immigrants' criminality: Accounts of fear and risk in talk about immigration to Greece. *Journal of Community & Applied Social Psychology, 21*(2), 164–177.

Figgou, L., Sourvinou, M., & Anagnostopoulou, D. (2018). Constructing the "Refugee Crisis" in Greece: A critical discursive social psychological analysis. In *Discourse, peace, and conflict* (pp. 205–222). Cham: Springer.

Giroux, H. A. (2018). *Terror of neoliberalism: Authoritarianism and the eclipse of democracy.* Routledge.

Gleeson, J. T., & Higgins, R. C. (Eds.). (2008). *Rediscovering rhetoric: Law, language, and the practice of persuasion.* Federation Press.

Goodman, S., & Speer, S. A. (2007). Category use in the construction of asylum seekers. *Critical Discourse Studies, 4*(2), 165–185.

Goodman, S., Sirriyeh, A., & McMahon, S. (2017). The evolving (re) categorisations of refugees throughout the "refugee/migrant crisis". *Journal of Community & Applied Social Psychology, 27*(2), 105–114.

Hanson-Easey, S., & Augoustinos, M. (2010). Out of Africa: Accounting for refugee policy and the language of causal attribution. *Discourse & Society, 21*(3), 295–323.

Harmes, A. (2012). The rise of neoliberal nationalism. *Review of International Political Economy, 19*(1), 59–86.

Hewitt, J. P., & Stokes, R. (1975). Disclaimers. *American Sociological Review, 40,* 1–11.

Hier, S. P., & Greenberg, J. L. (2002). Constructing a discursive crisis: Risk, problematization and illegal Chinese in Canada. *Ethnic and Racial Studies, 25*(3), 490–513.

Kirkwood, S., McKinlay, A., & McVittie, C. (2015). 'He's a cracking wee geezer from Pakistan': Lay accounts of refugee integration failure and success in Scotland. *Journal of Refugee Studies, 28*(1), 1–20.

Kirkwood, S. (2017). The humanisation of refugees: A discourse analysis of UK parliamentary debates on the European refugee 'crisis'. *Journal of Community & Applied Social Psychology, 27*(2), 115–125.

Kirkwood, S. (2019). History in the service of politics: Constructing narratives of history during the European Refugee "Crisis". *Political Psychology, 40*(2), 297–313.

Kurz, T., Augoustinos, M., & Crabb, S. (2010). Contesting the 'national interest' and maintaining 'our lifestyle': A discursive analysis of political rhetoric around climate change. *British Journal of Social Psychology, 49*(3), 601–625.

Lemert, C. C. (2015). The end of ideology, really! In C. C. Lemert (Ed.), *Sociology after the crisis* (pp. 91–121). Routledge.

Lynn, N., & Lea, S. (2003). A phantom menace and the new Apartheid': the social construction of asylum-seekers in the United Kingdom. *Discourse & Society, 14*(4), 425–452

Parliamentary debate on security was requested by K. Mitsotakis (2016, March 23). To Vima. Retrieved from http://www.tovima.gr/2016/03/23/politics/pro-imerisias-diataksis-syzitisi-gia-tin-asfaleia-zita-o-k-mitsotakis

Potter, J. (1996). *Representing reality: Discourse, rhetoric and social construction.* Sage Publications.

Rancière, J. (2015). *Dissensus: On politics and aesthetics.* Bloomsbury Publishing.

Reicher, S., & Hopkins, N. (1996). Self-category constructions in political rhetoric; an analysis of Thatcher's and Kinnock's speeches concerning the British miners' strike (1984–5). *European Journal of Social Psychology, 26*(3), 353–371.

Rooyackers, I. N., & Verkuyten, M. (2012). Mobilizing support for the extreme right: A discursive analysis of minority leadership. *British Journal of Social Psychology, 51*(1), 130–148.

Sakki, I., & Pettersson, K. (2018). Managing stake and accountability in Prime Ministers' accounts of the "refugee crisis": A longitudinal analysis. *Journal of Community & Applied Social Psychology, 28*(6), 406–429.

Sambaraju, R., McVittie, C., & Nolan, P. (2017). 'This is an EU crisis requiring an EU solution': Nation and transnational talk in negotiating warrants for further inclusion of refugees. *Journal of Community & Applied Social Psychology, 27*(2), 169–178.

Stavrakakis, Y., Katsambekis, G., Nikisianis, N., Kioupkiolis, A., & Siomos, T. (2017). Extreme right-wing populism in Europe: revisiting a reified association. *Critical Discourse Studies, 14*(4), 420–439.

Tileagă, C. (2006). Representing the 'Other': A discursive analysis of prejudice and moral exclusion in talk about Romanies. *Journal of Community & Applied Social Psychology, 16*(1), 19–41.

Tileagă, C. (2015). *The nature of prejudice: Society, discrimination and moral exclusion.* Routledge.

United Nations High Commissioner for Refugees. (2015). *Global report 2015.* Retrieved from http://www.unhcr.org/gr15/index.xml

Van Dijk, T. A. (1992). Discourse and the denial of racism. *Discourse & society, 3*(1), 87–118.

Van Dijk, T. A. (2006). Ideology and discourse analysis. *Journal of political ideologies, 11*(2), 115–140.

Weltman, D. (2004). Political identity and the Third Way: Some social-psychological implications of the current anti-ideological turn. *British Journal of Social Psychology, 43*(1), 83–98.

Weltman, D., & Billig, M. (2001). The political psychology of contemporary anti-politics: A discursive approach to the end-of-ideology era. *Political Psychology, 22*(2), 367–382.

Wetherell, M., & Potter, J. (1992). *Mapping the language of racism.* Harvester Wheatsheaf.

Wooffitt, R. (1992). *Telling tales of the unexpected: The organization of factual discourse.* Rowman & Littlefield.

Yack, B. (2006). Rhetoric and public reasoning: An Aristotelian understanding of political deliberation. *Political Theory, 34*(4), 417–438.

11

The Unsaid as Expressive and Repressive Political Communication: Examining Slippery Talk About Paid Domestic Labour in Post-apartheid South Africa

Amy Jo Murray

Introduction

Political communication and politics more generally are most often characterised by what is said: debates, parliament, press conferences, speeches, rallies, interviews, protests, accusations, counter-accusations, election campaigns, senate trials, "the voice of the people", sound bites on the Internet, social media posts and so forth. It is a realm in which we evaluate what is said by fact checking, noting who said what, and whether the statement offends, convinces, unites, oppresses, resists or a multitude of other reactions and implications. More recently, however, there has been a shift towards noticing the importance of silence and what is left out. This "turn to silence" (Murray and Durrheim 2019a) in discursive approaches to researching social life has permeated analyses of political communication specifically, providing an innovative approach to understanding the political nature of both the said and the unsaid (Huckin 2002; Schröter 2013; Ferguson 2003; Vieira et al. 2019).

A. J. Murray (✉)
University of KwaZulu-Natal, Pietermaritzburg, South Africa

© The Author(s), under exclusive license to Springer Nature Switzerland AG 2020   **283**
M. A. Demasi et al. (eds.), *Political Communication*, Palgrave Studies in Discursive Psychology, https://doi.org/10.1007/978-3-030-60223-9_11

This chapter explores white employer talk about paid domestic labour relationships to see how troubling topics are avoided, pushed aside or hinted at in discourse to produce subjects who are oriented to stereotypes rooted in South Africa's past. I begin by providing a brief overview of the importance of silence in political communication, focusing on aspects that make it such a challenging concept to analyse. It will be argued that while there are challenges to its study, its complexity constitutes both a feature and a flaw and its nuanced complexity is essential to its vitality (Murray and Durrheim 2019a). The unsaid will be viewed as necessarily and simultaneously expressive and repressive, as argued for in Michael Billig's (1997, 1999) scholarship on dialogic repression. The usefulness of expectation is emphasised in understanding what could (or should) have been said and yet is left unsaid in place of something else (Huckin 2002). The case of post-apartheid South Africa is examined, where talk can implicate both the speaker and the hearer as echoes of apartheid. This is especially significant within the context of paid domestic labour, which continues to mirror the racialised hierarchies and inequalities of the past.

Political Communication and the Unsaid

One of the key reasons why silence—particularly the unsaid—has not received equal attention as the said can be attributed to the importance of voice within political communication. In fact, the exercising of political voice is often equated to democracy itself. The withdrawal of voice from political engagement is viewed as a threat to legitimate democracy, especially when an entire portion of the population is silent (Vieira et al. 2019). However, it is increasingly being acknowledged that silence can meaningfully communicate and is not simply the opposite of speech (Ephratt 2011; Jaworski 1993). This leads to a more dynamic and nuanced appreciation of silence, as is insightfully stated by Ferguson (2003, p. 11):

> That [silence] has no necessary form, however, leads to an unexplored and unacknowledged capability: it can also enable and produce. Silence, in other words, can be constitutive. It can create identities and enable

communities. Once understood as freed from interpretive structures that necessarily condemn (or celebrate) it, the unlimited aspects of its multiplicitous functionality are freed for their creative and productive capacity.

The meaning, implications, forms and functions of silence have long been of interest to linguists and communication analysts (see Tannen and Saville-Troike 1985 and Jaworski 1997 for examples of early edited collections). While many of these works focused almost exclusively on audible silences, such as pauses, gaps, hesitations and so forth, there has been increasing attention paid to a different kind of silence: the unsaid. As Wetherell and Potter (1998, p. 385) note, "one of the features of considering variability in discourse is that it enables the researcher to make claims about both things which are said and those which are not said (sometimes not said with silence, sometimes without)". This type of silence is an absence of mention as speakers continue to talk about other topics (Huckin 2002; Jaworski 1993). In studying the unsaid, Billig (1997, p. 152) argues that "what is not said, but could easily have been, and, indeed, on occasions is almost said but then removed from the conversation, becomes of prime significance".

Michael Billig's (1997, 1999) innovative scholarship regarding dialogic repression has demonstrated how language is simultaneously repressive and expressive, leaving things that are toxic, taboo or troubling from entering discourse. With this understanding of the constitutive nature of silence in mind, what is left unsaid then becomes an achievement and a resource in political communication. It is an accomplishment as speakers discursively avoid a topic altogether or construct a topic with a more palatable gloss. Billig (1999, p. 54) argues that the unsaid can be considered as

> a form of changing the subject. It is a way of saying to oneself 'talk, or think, of this, not that'. One then becomes engrossed in 'this' topic, so 'that' topic becomes forgotten, as do the words one has said to oneself in order to produce the shift of topic.

Through seemingly innocuous routines of speaking, individuals can collaborate to collectively avoid troubling topics, issues, events, identities or themes. Even such small discursive events such as "yes but" or "well anyway" can be markers of a change in subject, changes that can amount to systematic avoidance when the same topics continue to be skirted around in conversation (Billig 1999). In this sense, language is both expressive and repressive. As speakers draw on strategies of avoidance, the unsaid becomes an absence that troubles what is said, threatening from the margins of the said, ready to spill into conversations that are routinely contained by conventions of politeness (Billig 1997, 1999).

Such routines can be seen in the use of euphemisms such as "the n-word" or "the k-word", where forms of politeness allow speakers to talk about racism without being implicated as racist. Speakers and hearers collaborate to keep the racial slur as an absence in conversation as a matter of moral import, even as they speak about the actions of "real racists". We can continue speaking while we skirt around things that are individually and collectively troubling. This is why Frosh (2019, p. 254) argues that "speaking can be a way of warding off the noisy murmurs from which everything develops". We must continue to speak about some things to keep others from being uttered.

Patterns of dialogic repression transcend individual ways of speaking to establish and maintain topics that eventually become unacknowledged and unspeakable. As Billig (1999, p. 100) argues, "by avoiding certain topics or lines of questioning, [speakers and hearers] can collaborate to keep disturbing thoughts from being uttered. The shared patterns may be common to a general culture or ideology". In this sense, the unsaid is also a form of social action (Murray and Durrheim 2019a). The unsaid can be used in discourse to maintain the status quo, to protect vested interests, to challenge voices of hegemony or to avoid awkwardness that has deep ideological roots. To use Durrheim and Murray's (2019) topographical metaphor, the unsaid is something we can draw on as a resource to steer conversation in familiar paths of discourse or to force discourse into uncomfortable areas where new paths must be worn.

This can include keeping a troubling collective past from rising to the surface of individual, collective and even national memory (Frosh 2019; Winter 2010); rhetorical and literal absences during official political speeches and debates to demonstrate political allegiances (Billig and Marinho 2019; Crenshaw 1997); or the repression of racial hierarchies among both elites and subalterns to maintain deep inequalities (Murray and Durrheim 2020; Sheriff 2000; Sue 2015). It is a resource to establish and maintain individual, collective and national memory, identity, agendas and ideology; a valuable political resource indeed.

Another example of the repressive and expressive functions of language is the case of humour (Billig 1999). Comedians and laypeople alike are able to side-step the conventions of politeness (with its necessary discursive restraint) to say what others cannot or will not. Jokes and humour provide a level of impunity from social sanction as the speaker says what others cannot and, instead of being offended or outraged, we laugh. Yet even this is a mark of the boundaries of the unsaid because such moments of speaking about what we individually and collectively repress show us how it is usually absent from the routines of our talk. It is a rare case where the troubling, toxic or taboo topics are openly expressed as opposed to being repressed. Yet there are some significant challenges to properly studying the unsaid, making it so difficult to pin down. It is talk where absences, implication, humour and "discursive tiptoeing" are central, finding its vitality in being slippery communication.

Slippery Communication

While there have been many attempts to create taxonomies of silence (see Ephratt 2011; Kurzon 2007, 2009), it unfortunately does not fit neatly into fixed definitions and categories, especially in the case of the unsaid. Because the unsaid is not marked by an absence of talk itself but rather an absence of *expected* talk, it is not measurable in the same way as an audible absence of speech. It is essentially a slippery form of communication (Murray and Durrheim 2019a). The more one tries to pin the unsaid down, analytically aiming for a clear meaning of an expression/repression, the more opportunities there are for that meaning to be vague, contested, evaded, reframed, skirted around or uncertain. As such, one can always be asked, "But how do you know there is something unsaid here?" This can potentially be seen as a "flaw" of the unsaid as the analyst must draw on expectations and interpretations as opposed to clear linguistic markers or hard-and-fast analytical definitions. It is a discourse that requires the analyst to "compensate with more attention to socio-political, cultural and rhetorical factors" (Huckin 2002, p. 353).

Properly understanding any particular instance of what is (not) said is largely a matter of interpretation. We must discursively sift through what is said and assess what is "hearable". In fact, one might only be aware of an absence after an interaction has concluded and one realises upon further reflection that something that could or should have been mentioned was left unsaid (Bischoping et al. 2001; Jaworski 1993). The issue of interpretation is often a source of a great deal of political controversy. One group interprets an utterance one way while another interprets it another, based on what was or was not mentioned, or perhaps stated more accurately, based on what each group assumes *should have* been mentioned.

This means that the very existence of an absence—let alone its meaning—can be contested or negotiated between any number of invested individuals or parties based on their expectations (Vieira et al. 2019). In fact, this is ironically one of the "features" of the unsaid. Because it is a slippery or ambiguous type of communication, alternate interpretations can be called upon when a speaker is invited to account for an utterance (Murray and Durrheim 2019a). As such, speakers can avoid being held to account for an absence and hearers can be left wondering if they heard properly.

The features and flaws that are attributed to the unsaid are largely determined by what the speaker, audience or analyst notices as missing, absent, avoided, denied or neglected, making expectations a useful consideration of silence, especially within political communication (Billig and Marinho 2019; Jaworski 1993; Schröter 2013). This notion leads Bilmes (1994, p. 82) to state that one must pay attention to "topics or points that the speaker or the author might have mentioned, things that he might have said, but didn't, and we note his silence". Using expectations and imagined possibilities—such as what could have or should have been said—can work as useful potential utterances with which to compare the said and the unsaid.

Because interpretation can be such a messy business, speakers and hearers (and indeed analysts) often look to intentionality as an answer. While intentionality can be a murky concept to wade into for hearers and analysts alike (Vieira et al. 2019), it is an important issue to consider. Billig and Marinho (2019, p. 34) eloquently lay out the task when they state that, when considering intentionality in the case of absences,

> it is likely that there is a combination of awareness and unawareness. This analytic judgement cannot be verified by accessing the minds of speakers and audience members. It depends upon closely examining what speakers and audience are doing to produce particular patterns of rhetorical presences and absences. The analyst needs to study carefully the rhetorical details and micro-details of delivery and response and also to interpret such details. Methodologically there can be no alternative to interpretation.

A close examination of the micro-details of talk-in-interaction is precisely what is needed for a robust analysis of the unsaid. The remainder of the chapter will attempt to provide such an analysis through a case study of paid domestic labour within post-apartheid South Africa. The case study will briefly review the context of post-apartheid South Africa and some of its troubling political and ideological implications for white South Africans, specifically those who are part of hierarchical and racialised relationships, such as domestic labour employers. The analysis will focus specifically on how speakers position themselves through repressive and expressive, slippery talk in relation to an archetypal apartheid figure: "the Madam".

Case Study: Domestic Labour Employers in Post-apartheid South Africa

During apartheid, South Africa was a place of grievous injustices, sociopolitical oppression and upheaval, segregation, marginalisation, silencing, violence and control, all organised along the lines of racialised hierarchies that privileged whites and made blacks invisible, at least in the white imagination. During the dismantling of formal, legalised apartheid, the country initially experienced a wave of hope as the Truth and Reconciliation Commission operated within discourses of healing and forgiveness between people (Statman 2000) and the inclusion of all creeds and colours was an explicit ideal of "the Rainbow Nation".

Yet some hallmarks of apartheid still remain in the current post-apartheid society, namely the socio-political divide between whites and the rest of the country. In an ever-changing social, economic and political landscape, whites have sought a level of control and security apart from contemporary South African government and its people through a series of inter-related migrations. Many whites have migrated from the business district of most urban centres, withdrawing their economic capital and their social engagement (Ballard 2004). They have avoided sub-urban integration by living in fortified properties with high walls, large dogs, electrified fences, cameras and private security services that keep out (often racialised) others. In many extreme cases, middle- to upper-class (largely but not exclusively) whites have retreated into gated communities, where their contact with (imagined, perceived and actual) municipal mismanagement, crime, insecurity and racialised others, such as poor blacks, can be kept to an absolute minimum (Ballard 2004; Lemanski 2004). This has led many theorists to label these racialised migratory avoidances as "the new apartheid" (Lemanski 2004, p. 101).

In short, a great deal of the intentions and optimism of the initial years of post-apartheid South Africa have not been realised. While the formalised system of apartheid is over, many of its legacies remain, casting a long shadow over present-day South Africa. Many of the structures, exclusions and stereotypes from the past still persist. This is summed up in criticism of white privilege and the need—articulated by Mngxitama—to "break the back of whiteness" (Mngxitama 2011, October 24). Apartheid is something that whites in particular find troubling because they are implicated in the violence and atrocities of the past through the privilege and benefits that they have inherited and continue to experience to their own advantage. Indeed, their moral position is tenuous because they continue to enjoy privilege that has been unjustly, even violently, gained. How, then, can such subjects exist, relate and speak in relation to the new order?

There has been some debate about whether or not whites should speak at all. In her philosophical essay entitled, "How Do I Live in This Strange Place?", Amanda Vice (2010) argues that whites in South Africa should

11 The Unsaid as Expressive and Repressive Political...   291

experience regret, guilt and shame as central to their identity, recommending that "reducing one's presence through silence and humility seems right" (p. 335). Vice (p. 335) goes on to state that for whites to live and speak appropriately in South Africa,

> one would live as quietly and decently as possible, refraining from airing one's view on the political situation in the public realm, realizing that it is not one's place to offer diagnoses and analyses [...] Whites have too long had influence and a public voice; now they should in humility step back from expressing their thoughts or managing others.

In his response to Vice's essay, Derek Hook (2011) suggests that silence and humility may not necessarily be as congruent as Vice assumes. Instead Hook asserts that silence can draw attention to itself and indeed be interpreted as an act of aggression. In this sense, according to Hook, silence can become and be interpreted as distance and superiority instead of humility or modesty. In a key section, Hook states that "silence needs to be understood in terms of *how others receive it, what it means to them*" (2011, p. 499, emphasis in the original). Based on the differing emphases and recommendations of these two articles, the same utterance may be deemed immoral by someone who agrees with Vice's perspective and deemed appropriate by one who takes up Hook's perspective. And one cannot forget the broad range of possibilities that exists between and around these two understandings of the meaning of talk and silence among whites.

The dilemma for white South Africans then lies in not only what to say but whether to speak at all because one cannot be certain how one's utterance will be received and interpreted. How will this be heard? How will it implicate me as a white South African? What should I say and what should I leave unsaid? This uncertainty is even greater in relation to intergroup contexts, especially if such contact mirrors our society's racialised and hierarchical past. Ironically, one of the most ongoing and intimate sites of contact between middle- to upper-class whites with black South Africans is within the paid domestic labour relationship (Durrheim et al. 2011), which has been described as "the last bastion of apartheid" (Fish 2006, p. 108). It is in discussing this relationship that speakers must be

Expressing and Repressing "the Madam"

Paid domestic labour across the globe is shaped by an entanglement of structural forces such as race, class, gender, citizenship, informal labour structures and the ongoing devalued nature of the work (Dickey 2000; Duffy 2007; Romero and Pérez 2016). In post-apartheid South Africa, it continues to be a deeply racialised institution which, despite specific legislation aimed to regulate this sector through Sectoral Determination 7 (RSA 2002), remains a site prone to exploitation, inequality and injustice. By and large, Jacklyn Cock's observations from the 1970s are still easily recognisable, namely that "this relationship is a microcosm of the exploitation and inequality on which the entire social order is based" (1980, p. 231).

In the South African context, stereotypes of employers abound, particularly the stereotype of "the Madam". It serves as an extreme crystallisation of stereotypes of whites more generally: racist, lazy, affluent, selfish, bossy, insular, controlling, abusive, exploiting, complacent, (passive) aggressive and invested in maintaining the racialised status quo. In the domestic labour context, this translates into employers who notoriously do not provide adequate leave or pay, are exploitative of workers, maintain distance and hierarchy and are (even subtly) physically, emotionally and verbally abusive. The apartheid-era notion of "the Madam" is one that still looms large for many white employers today. Talk and action that embodies such stereotypes can threaten to implicate one in a troubling past with which most South African whites avoid association (Durrheim et al. 2011).

Many middle- to upper-class white employers are in a troubling position of holding non-racist, liberal views while also being part of the incredibly hierarchical and racialised domestic labour relationship, expressing guilt and awareness of their privileged position (Archer 2011; Phyfer et al. 2020). Such employers often use ambiguous, unsaid and

11 The Unsaid as Expressive and Repressive Political... 293

implied communication to set out boundaries, as opposed to explicit communication that may be interpreted as overly "Madamish", bossy or controlling (Archer 2011). Acts of help and care are also common in domestic labour, allowing employers to simultaneously present themselves as generous while maintaining the racialised patriarchal foundations of the relationship from which they benefit (Durrheim et al. 2014). In fact, many employers have difficulty viewing themselves as employers at all, preferring to present their relationship as one that is primarily familial, as opposed to labour-based (Murray and Durrheim 2020). Such activities allow them to maintain the hierarchical nature of the relationship without fulfilling "the Madam" stereotype and its implications of racialised privilege and other troubling apartheid remnants.

Analysis and Discussion

To explore white's talk about the domestic labour relationship and its silences, Research Masters students under the author's supervision interviewed nine employers from the region of KwaZulu-Natal as part of their course requirements for 2019. The interviews were transcribed using a form of Jeffersonian Lite transcription, adapted from Silverman (2005, p. 376), to indicate basic elements of talk-in-interaction (see appendix for transcription conventions). The interview data were analysed using an ethnomethodological approach, as explained by Baker (2003), underpinned by Billig's (1997, 1999) theoretical framework of dialogical repression. The analysis aims to make the unsaid "intelligible" (Alasuutari 1995, p. 147) within the context of post-apartheid South African domestic labour and to suggest that the troubling figure of "the Madam" is one that is oriented to by speakers who are accountable, not only as employers but as whites more generally.

Because domestic labour continues to be highly racialised and hierarchical, it can be tricky for white employers to speak about the nature of their relationship without making its inequalities and racialised nature explicit. The notion of typicality is heard and treated as particularly toxic in a great deal of employer talk, possibly because "typical" is heard as "historically typical". In Extract 11.1, Pam works to ensure that neither she nor her domestic labour relationship is seen as a "typical".

Extract 11.1
1 Pam: That's <u>why</u> I've said you know from the outset that we
2   don't have the typical
3   (1.4)
4   "Madam and E:ve" relationship. We <u>don't</u>. Because:::
5   (1.2)
6   she's jus:t like I said before she's part of the
7   <u>family</u> and she just (.) she knows what she's going to
8   do and she just <u>does</u> it! And it's <u>veryveryveryv:ery</u>
9   seldom that I have to call her out about anything.
10 Int: You know put your foot down?
11 Pam: You know I don't I mean I just don't. I <u>don't</u>.

In this extract, we can see what the label "typical" (line 2) implies for this white employer. After a pause, Pam equates typicality with a "Madam and Eve relationship" (line 4). This is a comic strip that began in the mid-1990s in South Africa, caricaturing domestic labour through the sassy domestic worker, Eve, and her bossy, rich employer, Madam. It played on many stereotypes of domestic labour and wider racialised stereotypes, simultaneously satirising and reinforcing commonly understood tropes (Smith 1996). In dissociating from the label of "Madam and Eve", Pam distances herself from the apartheid past and its racialised and hierarchical foundations. Being "a Madam" is something to be avoided and denied, as can be seen in her emphatic denial in lines 4 and 11.

Instead, Pam draws on the familiar discourse of "part of the family" (lines 6–7). This is a common discourse in domestic labour, one that hides the hierarchy and boundaries of the relationship and presents it as one constituted primarily by equality, intimacy and loyalty (Lan 2003; Romero 1992). Their relationship is moved from the realm of stereotypical apartheid hierarchies to the non-racial family circle. However, all of this is achieved in short-hand, through the unsaid. The exact features of a "Madam and Eve" relationship are not spelt out nor does Pam explain specifically how her worker is like "part of the family". Foregrounding

11 The Unsaid as Expressive and Repressive Political... 295

their relationship as primarily familial gives a particular gloss to their interactions. Families work together for the common good of the household, each doing their part and accepting their role. This alternate construction then allows Pam's talk in lines 9 and 11 about "calling out" her employee to be heard in familial as opposed to employment terms, rhetorically flattening some of the inherent hierarchy and power in the relationship and putting everyone on more equitable footing.

It is interesting to consider some of the possibilities available to Pam in this moment. She could have drawn on eye-witness accounts of "Madam-like" behaviour among friends or family, past and present, to argue for the typicality or exceptionalism of her relationship. She could have drawn on the evolution of domestic labour from apartheid to present times through statistics. She could have gone into detail regarding the harsh realities of stereotypical domestic labour. Instead, the invocation of "Madam and Eve" provides a widely accepted caricature of typicality without fully unpacking the racialised inequalities of apartheid and post-apartheid domestic labour relationships. It sets up a strawman argument that allows Pam to present her relationship—and, by implication, her role therein—as standing in stark contrast to maid/madam relationships of the past. In this way, Pam is able to account for her relationship and her role not only as a fair domestic labour employer but also as a non-racist white in post-apartheid South Africa. By drawing on the resource of the unsaid, which negates any stereotypical connotations in her domestic labour relationship, Pam can quickly move on to focusing on the positive aspects of her relationship.

The notion of "the Madam" looms large in the talk-in-interaction of white employers. In Extract 11.2, Sue speaks about "scolding" (lines 1–8) her worker, something that can be heard as incredibly demeaning and patronising, an echo of the behaviour and attitudes of "the Madam".

Extract 11.2
1 Sue: So I can't remember the first time I scolded her to be
2   honest
3   (1.1)
4   but I know now::adays if I do if I do have to scold
5   her in anyway which I which is harder because she's

296   A. J. Murray

```
6       been with me for so long so so it's almost like
7       scolding your friend (.) so it makes it more
8          [difficult
9 Int:      [mmhhm
10 Sue: u:::m but I'll just kind of say to her she'll go
11        "o:kay" ((mimicking)) and she jokingly calls me ma'am
12       or madam
13 Int:  heheeehe
```

The "scolding" that Sue speaks of is set up very carefully through the honesty phrase "to be honest" (lines 1–2) (Edwards and Fasulo 2006). First, Sue speaks about the frequency, having difficulties in remembering when last such scolding took place (line 1). She also mentions "nowadays" (line 4), implying that it is not something that has happened recently, again emphasising that it is rare. This is especially so through the use of "if I do have to scold" (line 4) as opposed to the alternative utterance of "when I do have to scold". The "if" makes it a rare occasion, whereas "when" would imply a more frequent, regular event. Second, Sue speaks about the difficulty in scolding. She notes that scolding is not something that she wants to do but is obligated to do ("if I do have to scold": line 4). She presents their relationship as similar to that of a friendship, thereby negating the scolding as one that is occurring in a hierarchical relationship but rather among equals.

Finally, notice that the content of the scolding is completely absent, as presented in lines 10–11. This contrasts with expected retellings of scoldings by "the Madam" who would presumably outline details of the offence that is being scolded for. Here, Sue avoids going into such details by leaving out imagined content entirely. The hearer is only left with the worker's (humorous) reaction to the scolding. Sue's talk of scolding constructs such rare and obligatory situations as reluctantly arrived at rather than innate, personal prejudices or dispositions that Sue has (Edwards 2004), contrasting with "the Madam" who would frequently and eagerly scold and yell as part of her identity. Through all of these activities, Sue is able to achieve a distance from being implicated as a typical "Madam".

However, even with this work to manage the "scolding" talk, the idea of a white employer "scolding" a black employee cannot avoid being

11 The Unsaid as Expressive and Repressive Political... 297

heard as problematic in post-apartheid South Africa. Sue has some options available to her. She can defend her right as an employer to correct her worker. She can attempt to show how such feedback is useful to her worker in achieving her workload. She can even note how, in her employment situation, her boss also scolds her, thereby normalising such scolding. However, in all of these potential expectations, "scolding" is still heard as "a Madam's" activity. Instead of shying away from this, Sue brings the troubling identity of "the Madam" out into the light. She voices her worker's response to an imagined scolding with acceptance of the rebuke ("okay" line 11) and the worker calls her "ma'am or madam" (lines 11–12), something that is received as humorous through the interviewer's laughter. Sue's presentation of her worker's use of "ma'am or madam" as occurring "jokingly" (line 11) negates the toxicity of the implications of what Sue describes. It is a way of showing that, although the scolding can be heard as stereotypically "Madam-like", the worker is presented as not being offended, belittled or injured. This is a resource for Sue, allowing her to construct her scolding without being seen as threateningly "Madamish".

In this moment, Sue is accountable not only as a domestic labour employer but also as a white South African. By bringing "the Madam" explicitly into the presentation of their interactions as a harmless, mundane label, the scolding is transformed from being harsh and stereotypically racially loaded to being light and acceptable, even funny. "The Madam" is no longer a threatening, imposing, racist figure lurking in the unspeakable past, but rather a figure that can be mocked and belittled herself. As Billig (1999) demonstrates, humour is used to speak about what is usually unspeakable, topics and identities that are too troubling to bring into individual and collective discursive awareness. The joke is a strategy to express the troubling unsaid. Bringing "the Madam" into talk through a joke makes the unsaid speakable, yet also shows that this is something that is usually absent, threateningly so. Imagine the same story being told without the laughter and the word "jokingly". It has a totally different tone, one that too closely mirrors the era of "the Madam".

Conclusion

Although political communication is typically conceptualised through the lens of the present and the said, there is a great deal of value in paying attention to what is absent and unsaid as well. What goes unsaid has a constitutive nature, being both expressive and repressive (Billig 1999), allowing for the establishment and maintenance of identity work (Sue 2015), hierarchical relationships (Murray and Durrheim 2019b) and collective amnesia (De Kok 1998, in Hammond et al. 2007; Winter 2010), all of which have political implications.

This chapter has looked at some of the ways that the unsaid is both expressive and repressive (Billig 1999) in accomplishing important identity work in the context of the racialised and hierarchical relationship inherent in paid domestic labour. Being part of this relationship is tricky and troubling for all involved, especially because it continues to mirror the injustices of the apartheid era. White employers must be careful how they speak because of how the present context is troubled by the looming figure of "the Madam".

By speaking about their role as an employer in particular ways, contemporary white employers talk about themselves not only as an employer but also as an accountable white in post-apartheid South Africa. There is, I argue, a slippage between the identity "white" and "employer" within the discourse of paid domestic labour. Historically, the domestic labour relationship was one between a white employer and a black worker, making it a site loaded with racialised troubles. It was a maid/madam relationship. This socio-political, historical context makes current scenarios that mirror this past incredibly troubling. Slippery communication such as the unsaid can be employed as speakers do the tricky work of speaking and being heard within a continuingly racialised post-apartheid South Africa where there is an imperative for whites to "make themselves invisible and unheard" (Vice 2010, p. 335).

The white talk that has been examined here shows that, as Vice asserts, "the Madam" has social psychological implications for how we speak as political subjects. Talk avoiding "Madam-like" associations becomes so imperative that "the Madam" remains part of the discursive terrain of the said and unsaid within post-apartheid South Africa, continuing to trouble us from a past that is apparently not distant enough as to be spoken about without discomfort. To talk is, as Hook (2011) argues, morally loaded and, to be morally accountable in post-apartheid South Africa, even talk contains some things that are unsaid. For white South Africans, it is likely that talk about race and racialised identities will continue to be troubling. The decision lies in whether or not to speak (see Vice 2010; Hook 2011) and, if speaking occurs, how the talk will be heard (Hook 2011). The slippery talk of the unsaid, which has been conceptualised here as both expressive and repressive (Billig 1999), allows speakers to position themselves within the tricky and politically charged discursive terrain of talk about race and racialised relationships. This talk shows awareness that what they say does not occur in a contextual vacuum. Instead, as white domestic labour employers, their talk has the potential to be heard as "Madamish", a historical stereotype that must be avoided in order to be heard as acceptable within the post-apartheid social fabric.

References

Alasuutari, P. (1995). *Researching culture: Qualitative method and cultural studies.* Sage Publications.

Archer, S. (2011). 'Buying the maid Ricoffy': Domestic workers, employers and food. *South African Review of Sociology, 42*(2), 66–82.

Baker, C. D. (2003). Ethnomethodological analyses of interviews. In J. A. Hostein & J. F. Gubrium (Eds.), *Inside interviewing: New lenses, new concerns* (pp. 395–412). Sage Publications.

Ballard, R. (2004). Assimilation, emigration, semigration, and integration: 'White' peoples' strategies for finding a comfort zone. In N. Distiller & M. Steyn (Eds.), *Under construction: 'Race' and identity in South Africa today* (pp. 51–66). Heinemann.

Billig, M. (1997). The dialogic unconscious: Psychoanalysis, discursive psychology and the nature of repression. *British Journal of Social Psychology, 36*, 139–159.

Billig, M. (1999). *Freudian repression: Conversation creating the unconscious.* Cambridge University Press.

Billig, M., & Marinho, C. (2019). Literal and metaphorical silences in rhetoric: Examples from the celebration of the 1974 Revolution in the Portuguese Parliament. In A. J. Murray & K. Durrheim (Eds.), *Qualitative studies of silence: The unsaid as social action* (pp. 21–37). Cambridge University Press.

Bilmes, J. (1994). Constituting silence: Life in the world of total meaning. *Semiotica, 98*, 73–87.

Bischoping, K., Dodds, C., Jama, M., Johnson, C., Kalmin, A., & Reid, K. (2001). Talking about silence: Reflections on "race" in a university course on genocide. *Reflective Practice, 2*(2), 155–169.

Cock, J. (1980). *Maids and madams: A study in the politics of exploitation*. Ravan Press.

Crenshaw, C. (1997). Resisting whiteness' rhetorical silence. *Western Journal of Communication, 6*(3), 253–278.

Dickey, S. (2000). Permeable homes: Domestic service, household space and the vulnerability of class boundaries in urban India. *American Ethnologist, 27*(2), 462–489.

Duffy, M. (2007). Doing the dirty work: Gender, race, and reproductive labour in historical perspective. *Gender & Society, 21*(3), 313–336.

Durrheim, K., Jacobs, N., & Dixon, J. (2014). Explaining the paradoxical effects of intergroup contact: Paternalistic relations and system justification in domestic labour in South Africa. *International Journal of Intercultural Relations, 41*, 150–164.

Durrheim, K., Mtose, X., & Brown, L. (2011). *Race trouble: Race, identity and inequality in post-apartheid South Africa*. University of KwaZulu-Natal Press.

Durrheim, K., & Murray, A. J. (2019). Conclusion: Topographies of the said and unsaid. In A. J. Murray & K. Durrheim (Eds.), *Qualitative studies of silence: The unsaid as social action* (pp. 270–292). Cambridge University Press.

Edwards, D. (2004). Analysing racist discourse: The discursive psychology of mind-world relationships. In H. Van den Berg, H. Houtcoup, & M. Wetherell (Eds.), *Analysing interviews on racial issues* (pp. 31–48). Cambridge University Press.

Edwards, D., & Fasulo, A. (2006). "To be honest": Sequential uses of honesty phrases in talk-in-interaction. *Research on Language and Social Interaction, 39*(4), 343–376. https://doi.org/10.1207/s15327973rlsi3904_1

Ephratt, M. (2011). Linguistic, paralinguistic and extralinguistic speech and silence. *Journal of Pragmatics, 43*, 2286–2307.

Ferguson, K. (2003). Silence: A politics. *Contemporary Political Theory, 2*(1), 49–65.

Fish, J. (2006). Engendering democracy: Domestic labour and coalition-building in South Africa. *Journal of Southern African Studies, 32*, 107–127.

Frosh, S. (2019). The unsaid and the unheard: Acknowledgement, accountability, and recognition in the face of silence. In A. J. Murray & K. Durrheim (Eds.), *Qualitative studies of silence: The unsaid as social action* (pp. 254–269). Cambridge University Press.

Hammond, T., Arnold, P. J., & Clayton, B. M. (2007). Recounting a difficult past: A South African accounting firm's 'experiences in transformation'. *Accounting History, 12*(3), 253–281.

Hook, D. (2011). White privilege, psychoanalytic ethics, and the limitations of political silence. *South African Journal of Philosophy, 30*(4), 503–518.

Huckin, T. (2002). Textual silence and the discourse of homelessness. *Discourse and Society, 13*(3), 347–372.

Jaworski, A. (1993). *Power of silence: Social and pragmatic perspectives*. Newbury Park, CA: Sage Publications.

Jaworski, A. (Ed.). (1997). *Silence: Interdisciplinary perspectives*. Mouton de Gruyter.

Kurzon, D. (2007). Towards a typology of silence. *Journal of Pragmatics, 39*, 1673–1688.

Kurzon, D. (2009). Thematic silence as metaphor. In K. Turner & B. Fraser (Eds.), *Language in life, and a life in language: Jacob Mey – A Festschrift* (pp. 255–263). Emerald Group Publishing Limited.

Lan, P.-C. (2003). Negotiating social boundaries and private zones: The micropolitics of employing migrant domestic workers. *Social Problems, 50*(4), 525–549.

Lemanski, C. (2004). A new apartheid? The spatial implications of fear of crime in Cape Town, South Africa. *Environment and Urbanization, 16*(2), 101–111.

Mmngxitama, A. (2011, October 24). End to whiteness a black issue. *Mail & Guardian*. Retrieved June 10, 2020, from https://mg.co.za/article/2011-10-24-end-to-whiteness-a-black-issue/

Murray, A. J., & Durrheim, K. (2019a). Introduction: A turn to silence. In A. J. Murray & K. Durrheim (Eds.), *Qualitative Studies of Silence: The Unsaid as social action* (pp. 1–20). Cambridge University Press.

Murray, A. J., & Durrheim, K. (2019b). "There was much that went unspoken": Maintaining racial hierarchies in South African paid domestic labour through the unsaid. *Ethnic and Racial Studies, 42*(15), 2623–2640.

Murray, A. J., & Durrheim, K. (2020). Maintaining the status quo through repressed silences: The case of paid domestic labour in post-apartheid South Africa. *Sociology.* https://doi.org/10.1177/0038038520943103

Phyfer, J., Durrheim, K., & Murray, A. J. (2020). Buttressing whiteness by confessing guilt and rejecting racism: A study of white-talk about paid domestic labour. *South African Review of Sociology.* https://doi.org/10.1080/2152858 6.2020.1741442

Romero, M. (1992). *Maid in the USA.* Routledge.

Romero, M., & Pérez, N. (2016). Conceptualizing the foundation of inequalities in care work. *American Behavioral Scientist, 60*(2), 172–188.

RSA. (2002). *Basic Conditions of Employment Act (Act 75 of 1997): Sectoral Determination 7: Domestic Workers Sector.* Pretoria: Government Printer.

Schröter, M. (2013). *Silence and concealment in political discourse.* John Benjamins.

Sheriff, R. E. (2000). Exposing silence as cultural censorship: A Brazilian case. *American Anthropologist, 102*(1), 114–132.

Silverman, D. (2005). *Doing qualitative research.* Sage Publications.

Smith, G. (1996). Madam and Eve: A caricature of black women's subjectivity? *Agenda, 31,* 33–39.

Statman, J. M. (2000). Performing the truth: The social-psychological context of TRC narratives. *South Africa Journal of Psychology, 30,* 23–32.

Sue, C. A. (2015). Hegemony and silence: Confronting state-sponsored silences in the field. *Journal of Contemporary Ethnography, 44,* 113–140.

Tannen, D., & Saville-Troike, M. (Eds.). (1985). *Perspectives on silence.* Ablex Publishing Corporation.

Vice, S. (2010). How do I live in this strange place? *Journal of Social Philosophy, 41*(3), 323–342.

Vieira, M. B., Jung, T., Gray, S. W. D., & Rollo, T. (2019). The nature of silence and its democratic possibilities. *Contemporary Political Theory.* https://doi.org/10.1057/s41296-019-00330-2

Wetherell, M., & Potter, J. (1998). Discourse and social psychology: Silencing binaries. *Theory & Psychology, 8*(3), 377–388.

Winter, J. (2010). Thinking about silence. In E. Ben-Ze'ev, R. Ginio, & J. Winter (Eds.), *Shadows of war: A social history of silence in the twentieth century* (pp. 3–31). Cambridge: Cambridge University Press.

Index[1]

A

Action networks, 9
Age of information, 2, 7–10
Ambiguity, 15, 16, 82, 98, 101, 105,
   107–108, 116, 119, 121,
   122, 126, 136–139,
   160, 216
Anagnostopoulou, D., 19
Anderson, B., 115, 116
Andreouli, E., 13, 15, 16, 69–76,
   79–81, 83, 274, 276
Augoustinos, M., 11–13, 36, 37, 39,
   41, 45, 50, 54, 70,
   206–208, 212, 214, 223,
   234, 252, 263
Austerity policies, 69

B

Banal nationalism, 77, 116, 136, 184
   and 'hot' nationalism, 77
Bennett, W. L., 3, 4, 7, 9, 22, 81
Billig, M., 3n1, 11, 12, 16, 20, 36,
   49, 55, 57, 67, 68, 70, 73,
   77, 78, 91, 92, 96, 97, 102,
   106, 107, 115–117, 124,
   130, 133, 136–139,
   158–160, 163, 175, 181,
   182, 184, 194, 195,
   206–210, 214, 216n7, 220,
   221, 223, 224, 259–262,
   267, 270, 276, 277,
   284–289, 293, 297–299
Blumler, J. G., 1, 4, 8, 20

---

[1] Note: Page numbers followed by 'n' refer to notes.

© The Author(s), under exclusive license to Springer Nature Switzerland AG 2020
M. A. Demasi et al. (eds.), *Political Communication*, Palgrave Studies in Discursive
Psychology, https://doi.org/10.1007/978-3-030-60223-9

304 Index

Brexit, 1, 14–16, 63–83, 115–141
  remain *vs.* Leave, 63–65, 71–76,
    79, 81, 82
Burke, S., 12, 17–19, 74, 97, 119,
    176, 180, 182, 209, 214,
    217, 235, 236, 251

Carr, P., 15, 16, 91, 95, 96, 103,
    107, 108, 219
Cartoons, 2, 16, 115–141
Castells, M., 5, 7, 8
Categorisation, 18, 66, 67, 118,
    175, 207, 215, 222,
    240, 263
  us-them, 67
Class, 65–67, 65n2, 90, 92, 94,
    98–101, 105, 107, 108, 292
  distinction, 99
Collective action, 3, 149–170
Commonplaces, 12, 67, 70, 74, 83,
    116, 182, 267
Common-sense
  dilemmatic nature of, 69
  political nature of, 69
  thinking, 68
  'witcraft,' 68
Communication
  democratisation of, 8
  flows of, 8
Condor, S., 13, 38, 39, 45, 50, 56,
    58, 70, 75, 98, 107, 117,
    119, 120, 125, 138, 160,
    175, 205, 206, 218, 223,
    259–261, 263, 275
Connective action, 9, 22
Culture wars, 66, 67, 72

Demasi, M.A., 12, 18, 45, 55, 97,
    180, 252
Dialogical context, 42
Dialogical networks, 39, 45, 58
Dialogic repression, 19,
    270, 283–299
Discourse
  recipient designed nature of, 152
  as social action, 10
Discursive psychology, 1–23
  critical agenda of, 13
  and critical discourse studies
    (CDS), 2, 5, 6, 13, 120
  critical discursive psychology
    (CDP), 17, 176, 177, 181,
    182, 185, 196
  and multimodal critical discourse
    analysis (MCDA), 16,
    120, 138
Dixon, J., 35, 70
Domestic labour, 19, 20, 283–299
  See also Entertainment, domestic
    staff in
Durrheim, K., 39, 73, 75, 206, 207,
    210, 216, 216n7, 283, 284,
    286–288, 291–293, 298

Economic inequality, 14, 16, 90–98,
    101, 105, 106, 108, 116,
    120, 159, 163, 169, 284,
    287, 292, 293, 295
Edelman, M., 6, 11, 22, 64, 66, 82,
    90, 92, 93, 104
Edley, N., 90, 95, 176, 177,
    181, 182

Index

Edwards, D., 8, 10–13, 50, 54, 81, 95–97, 99, 138, 152, 154, 157–159, 163, 167, 169, 181, 206, 210, 216–218, 216n6, 220–222, 235, 250, 259, 267, 269, 276, 296
Electronic age, 9
Emotion words, 159
Entertainment
  domestic staff in, 105, 106
  as a form of political communication, 90, 91, 104, 108, 109
  poverty porn, 99
  super-rich programming (*see* Entertainment, wealth porn)
  wealth porn, 91, 93, 97, 104–106, 108
Entman, R. M., 7
Extreme case formulations, 157, 161, 162, 215, 217, 218, 241

Fake news, 19, 252
Farage, Nigel, 40, 42–45, 47, 48, 50–52, 54, 56, 58, 66, 67, 119
Far-right politics, 179n1, 218
  populist, 179n1
Figgou, L., 19, 38, 39, 69, 75, 80, 263–265, 269, 277
Finns Party, 176–178, 179n1, 185, 189, 193–195
Framing device, 128

Gaze, 17, 130, 134, 136, 183, 184, 193
Gibson, S., 13, 14, 39, 41, 46, 57, 69, 95, 105, 107, 119, 125
Goffman, E., 38, 39, 47, 58, 152, 182, 191, 218, 241
Goodman, S., 12, 17–19, 36–39, 41, 46, 57, 58, 74, 75, 95, 96, 108, 117–120, 169, 207, 209, 214, 217, 219, 234–236, 241, 243, 251, 252, 263, 264

Hall, S., 69
Halliday, M., 127
Hook, D., 35, 184, 291, 299
Humour
  as critique, 106
  disciplinary, 16, 137, 138
  joke, 287
  rebellious, 16, 137, 138
  ridicule, 102, 105, 106, 108
  satire (*see* Cartoons)
Huxtable, S., 90, 92

Identity
  and group identification, 150–151, 169
  management, 74
Ideological dilemmas, 15, 70, 73, 83, 136
Immigration, *see* Refugees
Inequality, *see* Economic inequality

306 Index

Internet, 4, 5, 22, 118, 176, 180, 235, 283
  promise of, 5

K

Kavanagh, D., 1, 20, 40
Kilby, L., 13, 16, 120, 122, 126, 134
Kinnvall, K., 83
Kress, G., 10, 102, 120, 123–133, 135, 177, 183–185, 193

L

Language
  constructive and constitutive, 20
    (*see also* Discourse)
  as medium for action, 11
Lennon, H. W., 13, 16, 122, 134
Leudar, I., 39, 45, 58, 220, 241, 249

M

Machin, D., 120, 126, 136, 137
Macmillan, K., 8, 12, 99, 139
Marinho, C., 68, 175, 261, 277, 286, 288, 289
Marková, I., 68
Mass communication
  effects (*see* Media, effects)
  vs. mediated communication, 8
Media
  effects, 4, 7
  use of the, 5
Mediated communication, 2, 8, 9, 12–14, 22, 182
Mediation, *see* Mediated communication

Mihelj, S., 5, 8, 90, 92
Mobilisation, 4, 17, 149–150, 152, 154, 159, 168, 170, 180
Multimodal communication
  cartoons, 115–141
  colour, 183, 184, 190, 192, 193
  composition, 183, 192
  multimodal discourse
    analysis, 115–141
  perspective
    objective, 135
    subjective, 135
  textual components of, 123, 128–130, 133–135
Multimodal discourse
  cartoons, 115–141
Murray, A. J., 13, 19, 20, 82, 283, 284, 286–288, 292, 293, 298

N

National identity, 13, 16, 115–117, 124, 137, 139, 184
  Britishness, 117
Nationalism
  banal, 77, 116, 124, 136
  and patriotism, 77
Nationhood, 8, 67, 77, 115–118, 123–125, 128, 130, 133, 134, 136–139, 208
Naturalistic data, 212, 237
Nekvapil, J., 39, 45, 58
Neoliberal individualism
  individual responsibility, 91
  protestant work ethic (PWE), 92
  self-improvement, 90

Neoliberalism, 91–92, 104–108
Nesbitt-Larking, P., 83
News/press reporting, 8–9, 241

Online discourse, 19, 152, 209
Osborne, George, 69

Pettersson, K., 13, 17, 176–181,
  179n1, 184, 185, 190–192,
  194, 197, 263, 264
Polarisation, 65, 67, 72, 76, 275
Political, 1–17, 3n1, 19, 22, 23,
  39–42, 45, 46, 55, 58,
  63–67, 69–71, 74, 76, 78,
  80–83, 89–91, 98,
  105–106, 115–141, 150,
  151, 153, 156, 160, 166,
  169, 175–198, 218, 238,
  250, 259–263, 265–267,
  269, 270, 272–277, 283,
  284, 286–291, 298
  commitment, 40, 169
Political communication
  blogging, 176
  content and form of, 7, 15, 90,
    91, 104, 105, 108, 109
  context of
    ideological, 122
    interactional, 14
  discursive psychology of, 89–109,
    119 (see Discursive
    psychology)
  in entertainment media, 16

online, 17, 180, 197
  psychology of (see Political
    communication, political
    psychology)
  third age of, 1
  traditions of theory and
    research in, 3
Political correctness, 179
Political mobilisation, 3
  online, 17, 180
Political psychology, 2–4,
  3n1, 83, 259
Political rhetoric, 3n1, 6,
  12, 66, 106, 119, 160,
  175, 259–265,
  267, 269
  and consensus, 259–262, 269
Potter, J., 11, 12, 36, 38, 50,
  54, 95–97, 138, 152,
  154, 155, 157–159, 164,
  165, 167, 181, 182, 191,
  192, 206, 208, 212, 214,
  216, 216n6, 217, 221,
  222, 235, 237, 259, 267,
  269, 271, 275, 276,
  285, 293
Prejudice
  challenge of, 57, 207, 220
  and dehumanisation, 207,
    212, 216
  hostile expressions of, 208–210
  ideological aspects of, 73
  the liberal norm against, 74
  and rationalisation, 207, 212, 220
  as social practice, 73
  and veiled threats, 219
Public engagement, 17

308 Index

R

Racism
  accusations of, 14, 36–38, 40, 41, 43, 45, 46, 48, 51, 53–57, 74, 246
    legitimacy of, 56
  dialogical approach to, 14
  discursive approaches to, 14
  and discursive deracialisation, 45
  idelogical dimensions of, 37
  new, 37, 45
  as social accomplishment, 38, 50, 56
Recontextualisation, 6, 136, 267
Refugees
  representations of, 18, 235–237, 239–244, 251, 253, 264
  as social threat, 19
  Syrian refugee 'crisis,' 1, 17, 18, 237
Rhetorical analysis, *see* Rhetorical psychology
Rhetorical psychology, 17, 72, 177, 182, 196, 277
  and dialogicality, 68
  and thematic analysis, 71
Rhetorical questions, 101, 157, 191, 195, 250, 275
Rhetorics, 9, 13, 63–83, 90, 116, 123, 126, 182–185, 194, 210, 240, 241, 244, 259–262, 264, 266, 274, 275, 277
  visual, 182, 183
Riggs, D. W., 37

S

Sakki, I., 13, 17, 176, 178–181, 184, 185, 190–192, 194, 197, 263, 264
Script formulations, 157, 162
Segerberg, A., 9
Silence, 19, 194, 283–285, 287, 288, 291, 293
  See also Dialogic repression
Sneijder, P., 17, 149, 152, 157, 165, 167, 168
Social movements, 4, 17, 149–170
Social practice, 2, 8, 10–13, 17, 20, 73, 136, 152
  domains of, 7–10
South Africa
  apartheid/new apartheid, 18, 284, 289, 290
  Truth and Reconciliation Commission, 289
Stake inoculation, 167, 276
Stokoe, E., 11–13, 21, 39, 95, 104, 105, 178, 181, 221, 235, 250

T

Tileagă, C., 3n1, 6, 9–13, 20–22, 35, 55, 58, 73, 120, 158, 159, 175, 178, 181, 197, 206, 208, 212, 214, 215, 218, 222, 223, 235, 247, 263
Topoi, *see* Common-places
Tropes, 12, 16, 18, 46, 57, 67, 119, 123–139, 224, 271, 273, 294
  synecdoche, 126

Trump, Donald, 1, 67, 252
Truth, 38, 123, 124, 190, 191, 194
  in discourse, 12
2015 UK General Election, 14, 40

U

United Kingdom Independence
    Party (UKIP), 14, 40–45,
    41n1, 47, 47n2, 51–58, 71
Unsaid, *see* Dialogic repression
Us/them, 66, 67, 76n4, 82n5
  antagonistic, 179

V

van Dijk, T. A., 6, 36, 37, 120, 207,
    215, 219, 234, 264, 275
van Leeuwen, T., 120, 123–133, 135,
    136, 177, 183–185, 193

W

Weltman, D., 261, 262
Wetherell, M., 12, 36, 38, 57, 95, 138,
    157, 164, 176, 177, 181,
    182, 206, 208, 243, 275, 285
Whitehead, K. A., 12, 39

Printed in the United States
By Bookmasters